Grow a Greener
Data Center

Douglas Alger

Cisco Press

800 East 96th Street

Indianapolis, IN 46240

Grow a Greener Data Center

Douglas Alger

Published by:
Cisco Press
800 East 96th Street
Indianapolis, IN 46240 USA

Printed in the United States of America

First Printing August 2009

Library of Congress Cataloging-in-Publication Data

Alger, Douglas.

 Grow a greener data center / Douglas Alger.

  p. cm.

 ISBN 978-1-58705-813-4 (pbk.)

 1. Data processing service centers--Energy conservation. 2. Electric power systems--Energy conservation. 3. Virtual computer systems. 4. Green technology. I. Title.

 TH6057.I53A44 2010

 725'.23--dc22

                                                    2009026628

 ISBN-13: 978-1-58705-813-4

 ISBN-10: 1-58705-813-8

Warning and Disclaimer

Trademark Acknowledgments

Corporate and Government Sales

The publisher offers excellent discounts on this book when ordered in quantity for bulk purchases or special sales, which may include electronic versions and/or custom covers and content particular to your business, training goals, marketing focus, and branding interests. For more information, please contact: **U.S. Corporate and Government Sales**   1-800-382-3419   corpsales@pearsontechgroup.com

For sales outside the United States please contact: **International Sales**   international@pearsoned.com

Feedback Information

At Cisco Press, our goal is to create in-depth technical books of the highest quality and value. Each book is crafted with care and precision, undergoing rigorous development that involves the unique expertise of members from the professional technical community.

Readers' feedback is a natural continuation of this process. If you have any comments regarding how we could improve the quality of this book, or otherwise alter it to better suit your needs, you can contact us through e-mail at feedback@ciscopress.com. Please make sure to include the book title and ISBN in your message.

We greatly appreciate your assistance.

Publisher: Paul Boger

Associate Publisher: Dave Dusthimer

Executive Editor: Mary Beth Ray

Managing Editor: Patrick Kanouse

Senior Development Editor: Christopher Cleveland

Project Editor: Mandie Frank

Editorial Assistant: Vanessa Evans

Designer: Louisa Adair

Composition: Mark Shirar

Indexer: Ken Johnson

Business Operation Manager, Cisco Press: Anand Sundaram

Manager Global Certification: Erik Ullanderson

Copy Editor: Apostrophe Editing Services

Technical Editors: Robert Aldrich, Andy Broer, Jack Holt, Mike Lavazza, Mike Matthews

Proofreader: Kelly Maish

Americas Headquarters	Asia Pacific Headquarters	Europe Headquarters
Cisco Systems, Inc.	Cisco Systems (USA) Pte. Ltd.	Cisco Systems International BV
San Jose, CA	Singapore	Amsterdam, The Netherlands

Cisco has more than 200 offices worldwide. Addresses, phone numbers, and fax numbers are listed on the Cisco Website at **www.cisco.com/go/offices**.

About the Author

Douglas Alger is the IT Architect for Physical Infrastructure for Cisco. He develops architecture roadmaps, solutions, and policies for the physical infrastructure of the company's Data Centers and other critical facilities around the world.

Doug has more than 20 years of varied professional experience including more than 12 years in Data Center physical design, Data Center operations, IT project management, construction project management, and IT infrastructure management. He has participated in more than 80 major Data Center projects, from all-new construction to substantially retrofitting existing facilities, and is the author of *Build the Best Data Center Facility for Your Business*.

Doug is a popular speaker, with more than 250 corporate customer engagements and dozens of presentations at various Data Center industry conferences. Prior to joining Cisco, Doug was a writer and editor in the News & Publications office of Syracuse University and, before that, a full-time stringer for the *Los Angeles Times*. He has a bachelor's degree in journalism from San Jose State University.

About the Contributing Author

Koen Denecker, CCIE No. 14407, is an IT Solutions Architect at Cisco Systems International. He is responsible for the IT Global Data Center strategy and the end-to-end IT Data Center architecture, including virtualization. Prior responsibilities over his eight years at Cisco include architecture roles in storage, application networking services, security, and advanced networking technologies. He frequently spends time with large customers on various IT architecture topics, including Data Center strategy. His network certifications include CCIE Routing and Switching, and CCIE Security.

Prior to joining Cisco, he worked as a Research Assistant at Ghent University, Belgium. He holds a PhD in computer science and a master's degree in physical engineering. He is author or coauthor of more than 50 scientific publications in international journals and conference proceedings. He was the contributing author for the Consolidation, Virtualization, and Automation material in Chapter 9 of this book.

About the Technical Reviewers

Robert Aldrich, Energy Solutions architect, has ten years in facilities design, deployment, and management experience. Rob has designed IP-enabled power and cooling systems for more than 20 enterprise class Data Centers in North America and the Asia Pacific region. His current role at Cisco involves working with Cisco IT and product engineering teams to drive the green agenda at Cisco. Rob has developed the Cisco Efficiency Assurance Program as a step-by-step methodology for Cisco customers to adopt more efficient IT operations (http://www.cisco.com/go/efficiency).

Andy Broer is a senior manager on the Cisco Infrastructure Critical Environments (ICE) team. His current role is that of Data Center "energy czar" watching over capacity constraints for Cisco. Recently he was the IT physical design and build manager for his company's first standalone Tier III Data Center in Texas (http://www.cisco.com/web/about/ciscoitatwork/data_center/flash/rcdn_dc_tour/index.html). Prior to that he headed and managed the Data Center Infrastructure Team through Cisco's explosive growth via global acquisitions in which his team built more than 50 server environments around the world.

He is a board and founding member of AFCOM's northern California branch and a trustee for a high tech mutual fund (BFOCX). He is also a member of the Critical Facilities Roundtable and The Uptime Institute. He holds two degrees from San Jose State University: a B.A. in creative arts and an M.A. in interdisciplinary studies.

Jack Holt, RCDD and PMP, is currently working as the program manager for the Cable Management Office (CMO) at Cisco. He has been at Cisco a little over a year in the Global Client Services & Operations (GCS&O) unit, recently releasing the new Cisco Global Cabling Standards for layer one infrastructure. He is responsible for layer one infrastructure in the Americas, Europe, and Emerging Markets for Cisco. Jack holds numerous certifications and most recently has been engaged in the Stanford Advanced Program Management track and is working towards LEED AP certification. Jack has been working in the data and communications industry for more than 20 years with extensive experience that includes hospital and research environments. Jack enjoys spending his time with his wife Holly, and three children Christina, Addison, and Ryan.

Mike Lavazza is manager of operations and engineering for the Cisco Workplace Resources team. He is responsible for the building infrastructure system design, building automation systems and maintenance engineering at Cisco for more than 13 years. Mike is also responsible for Critical Environment design and operations and Energy Management programs.

Mike has been in the operations and engineering industry for more than 25 years, working as an Operations and Engineering Manager for 3Com, IBM, Hughes Aircraft Company, and John Deere. He holds a bachelor's of science in industrial/electrical engineering with emphasis in building systems and operations.

Mike Matthews is currently responsible for the implementation of a cloud-based computing service within the Network and Data Center Services group at Cisco. He has been at Cisco for more than nine years with primary responsibility in the area of delivering service oriented-based architecture and designs built on virtualization solutions. Mike has been working in the IT industry for more than 12 years starting with his time in the U.S. Air Force and currently holds an M.B.A. in technology management. Mike enjoys spending time with his wife Sandy, and two daughters Courtney and Emily.

Acknowledgments

Several people graciously gave of themselves to help make the content of this book better than it would otherwise be.

Chief among these contributors are my Cisco co-workers Koen Denecker, Rob Aldrich, Andy Broer, Jack Holt, Mike Lavazza, and Mike Matthews. Koen wrote Chapter 9, "Greening Your Data Center Through Consolidation, Virtualization, and Automation," with greater depth and expertise than I could have. Rob Aldrich and Andy Broer provided valuable feedback over the book's entire scope whereas topic-specific expertise came from Jack (data cabling), Mike L. (electrical and mechanical), and Mike M. (virtualization).

Special mention must additionally go to Glenn Hasbrouck, Andy Broer (again), Scott Smith, Jerry Green, and Daniel Cole, also from Cisco. Glenn reprised his role from my first book, creating the two Data Center line drawings used as illustrations in this book. Andy, Scott, and Jerry granted permission to publish photographs they had taken of various Data Center projects and infrastructure. Daniel graciously delved through several years' worth of archived e-mails to find a remembered image of unruly cabling that, thanks to his diligence, has been included in this publication.

Special thanks as well to Mary Beth Ray, Chris Cleveland, and their peers at Cisco Press who made this publication a reality. Mary Beth's guidance and support were invaluable as I worked through some unanticipated circumstances that threatened to delay the book's completion. Chris, meanwhile, kept me honest by not only coordinating the feedback from technical reviewers but also highlighting what content needed elaboration or clarification.

I am repeatedly impressed at how many people across the Data Center industry actively and enthusiastically share their knowledge, allowing all of us to learn and be better at what we do. I am particularly grateful to the following people and their respective companies that allowed me to interview them for this book and leverage their expertise:

Paul Brenner of the University of Notre Dame's Center for Research Computing, for discussing his project to warm an Indiana greenhouse with server exhaust.

Art Diem of the U.S. Environmental Protection Agency, concerning carbon dioxide emissions and baseload versus nonbaseload power.

Anand Ekbote and Stephen Blakemore of Emerson Network Power, who discussed proportional energy usage in a Data Center.

Mark Germagian of Opengate Data Systems, for sharing data from a computer modeling study of Data Center thermal runaway.

Timothy Happychuk of Quebecor Media, for talking about the *Winnipeg Sun*'s use of Data Center waste heat to warm its newsroom.

Shawn Massey of Camera Corner/Connecting Point, for discussing the fire-related loss and later rebuild of his company's Data Center.

Richard McCormack and Ted Viviani of Fujitsu, for sharing information about the fuel cell installation on their campus. Brigit Valencia of Eastwick Communications, for putting me in touch with them and obtaining images of the installation.

Aniruddha (Ani) Natekar of Cummins Power Generation, for information on generator emissions and pertinent national standards. Richard Kiley of Roberts Communications, for putting me in touch with Ani and securing valuable content on the topic.

Nick Parfitt of the Datacenter Research Group, for sharing (and answering my endless questions about) survey data collected at various DataCenter Dynamics conferences.

Kristine Raabe of Intel, for not only providing images of an isolated cooling chamber from an Intel Data Center but also going so far as to commission a photographer to shoot them for inclusion in this book.

Ralph Renne of Netapp, for providing details about the financial incentives the company received in conjunction with the green Data Center it built in Sunnyvale, California.

Sebastian Schreiber of Corning Cable Systems, for discussing the relative environmental impacts of manufacturing fiber and copper cabling. Michele Carter, Doug Coleman, and Andy Honeycutt, also of Corning Cable Systems, for discussing per-port energy consumption associated with fiber and copper media.

Martin Townsend of the Building Research Establishment (BRE), for discussing the development of Data Center-specific standards for the BREEAM environmental building assessment system.

Dedications

For Melynda and Bryan, who top all of my lists.

 **Pearson employed
a 100% green
production method
for the publication
of this book.**

**This book was produced with paper
made with 30% post-consumer recycled
fiber. Using this type of paper saves...**

4,261 lbs wood—
A total of 14 trees that supply enough oxygen for 7 people annually

6,222 gal water—
Enough water to take 362 eight-minute showers

4mln BTUs energy—
Enough energy to power an average American household for 17 days

1,292 lbs emissions—
Carbon sequestered by 15 tree seedlings grown for 10 years

378 lbs solid waste—
Trash thrown away by 82 people in a single day

Contents

Introduction

Interest in green—*demand* for green, really—has come to the Data Center and in many ways its arrival was inevitable.

No social value has gained more momentum among consumers, government officials, and businesses in recent years than that of being green. Evidence of green's popularity can be seen everywhere, be it in the growing consumer purchases of hybrid automobiles (sales are projected to soon top 1 million hybrid vehicles per year), the abundance of green claims featured in product advertising and labeling, and even the recent winners of the Nobel Peace Prize (awarded in 2007 to former U.S. Vice President Al Gore and the Intergovernmental Panel on Climate Change, for disseminating knowledge of man-made climate change).

Data Centers are a prime target for greening due largely to their incessant consumption of energy. At many individual companies, Data Center power bills are now large enough that they have come to the attention of their chief executive officers. As a group, Data Center power consumption has grown so dramatically as to trigger government action. Consider, for instance, efforts by the United States Environmental Protection Agency to create separate Data Center and server energy-efficiency standards and the European Commission's creation of a voluntary Data Center Code of Conduct in which participating companies pledge to minimize Data Center energy usage.

Data Centers are also no longer relegated to being the hidden nexus of a company's technological plumbing but, for many, are showpieces that reflect their business values. The Data Center of a major financial institution has multiple layers of redundant infrastructure consistent with its emphasis upon reliability, for instance, whereas a fast-growing technology company is likely to have a Data Center designed with agility in mind, possessing physical infrastructure that can be deployed quickly and reconfigured as needed.

What, then, could be a better way for a business to exhibit its social responsibility and consideration for the environment than having an intelligently designed, energy-efficient Data Center that provides ample company productivity while using as few natural resources as possible?

Motivation for Writing This Book

Data Centers have historically had a huge, negative impact upon their surrounding environment—consuming massive quantities of electric power and water, emitting pollutants through standby generator systems, and discarding materials detrimental to the environment in the form of UPS batteries and outdated computing hardware. Today, however, it is possible to design Data Centers that are more ecologically sensitive and more cost-effective to operate while providing superior reliability and availability.

This book was written to help show business executives, IT managers, and facilities personnel how to design and operate Data Centers in such a way as to be energy-efficient and less impactful upon the environment, leaving more resources to future generations.

Sources for This Book

This book incorporates varied source material, reflecting the array of technologies used within Data Centers and the broad range of topics that fall under the umbrella categories of green building practices and green technologies.

Content includes multiple case studies and real-world examples of green technologies implemented in operational Data Centers and data culled from dozens of white papers and case studies pertaining to efficiency topics—in both Data Centers and general office commercial buildings—including energy consumption, cooling optimization, environmental impact of cabling media, and more.

Additional material is summarized from several environmental building assessment systems and efficiency metrics prevalent in the Data Center industry.

Who Should Read This Book

Anyone concerned with the physical design, construction, or ongoing management of their company Data Centers; anyone interested in greatly reducing the energy consumption and operational expenses of either Data Centers or lab environments; or people whose business contains a computing environment and who desire to make their company greener can find useful and relevant information within this book.

The job roles involving those areas of responsibility can vary widely, yet commonly include chief financial officers, green czars, construction project managers, IT or Data Center directors, network engineers, system administrators, and facilities managers.

If your job interacts in some way with your company Data Center and includes hardware purchasing decisions for such environments, this book contains information that can help you do your job more effectively, reduce your company's environmental impact, and save your company money.

How This Book Is Organized

This book provides a step-by-step walkthrough of various Data Center-related strategies and technologies that can be implemented to make a Data Center greener.

Chapters 1 and 2 present the benefits of designing and operating a green Data Center and standards used to measure how green a facility is whereas Chapters 3 through 9 include the book's core content of how to make Data Center infrastructure, both physical components and hardware, greener. Chapter 10 addresses green strategies that go beyond the Data Center but are still relevant to companies with a server environment.

- **Chapter 1, "Going Green in the Data Center"**: This chapter defines green, discusses the drivers for companies to build greener Data Centers, and presents the benefits a given business can see from environmentally friendlier server environments. The chapter also outlines incentive programs that reward green efforts and recaps environmental activities that several major companies pursue today.

- **Chapter 2, "Measuring Green Data Centers"**: This chapter presents assessment systems used around the world to measure how green buildings are, formulas for calculating Data Center energy efficiency, and an overview for industry organizations pursuing the development of each. This chapter also offers guidance for putting Data Center metrics in the appropriate context to understand a facility's performance.

- **Chapter 3, "Green Design and Build Strategies"**: This chapter discusses methods for limiting the environmental impact that occurs during the construction of a Data Center through decisions concerning physical location, choice of building materials, landscaping choices, and jobsite construction practices.

- **Chapter 4, "Powering Your Way to a Greener Data Center"**: This chapter discusses how energy is used in Data Centers, traces the potential for power savings along the electrical delivery chain, and presents carbon emission factors for different regions of the world. The chapter additionally presents alternative energy options and offers design strategies, technology solutions, and operational methods for reducing Data Center energy usage.

- **Chapter 5, "Cooling Your Way to a Greener Data Center"**: This chapter discusses how Data Center temperature settings impact energy usage and offers design strategies, technology solutions, and operational methods for improving cooling efficiency.

- **Chapter 6, "Cabling Your Way to a Greener Data Center"**: This chapter compares the environmental impacts of cabling media and illustrates the benefits of streamlining both structured cabling and patch cord installations in a Data Center to improve airflow and reduce energy consumption.

- **Chapter 7, "Refrigerants and Fire Suppressants"**: This chapter discusses the fire suppression materials commonly employed in Data Centers, reviews government regulations concerning their usage, and suggests green approaches for deploying them.

- **Chapter 8, "Choosing Greener Gear"**: This chapter offers strategies for making a Data Center greener through IT hardware choices, outlines server energy-efficiency standards and metrics, and discusses both hardware utilization and how to reduce hardware power consumption.

- **Chapter 9, "Greening Your Data Center Through Consolidation, Virtualization, and Automation"**: This chapter explores the energy-saving opportunities you can realize by transforming the way IT infrastructure provides, allocates, and operates Data Center resources.

- **Chapter 10, "Greening Other Business Practices":** This chapter discusses additional green measures that a company with a Data Center can pursue to make their facility and operations greener.

- **Appendix, "Sources of Data Center Green Information":** This appendix lists the entities and organizations that are valuable sources of information on green standards or metrics, green best practices, and case studies that form the basis of effective strategies for green Data Center design.

- **Glossary:** The glossary defines key terms and concepts discussed throughout the book.

Using The Material in This Book

The chapters of this book are written in such a way that each can serve as a standalone reference for a particular Data Center technology or topic—if you are interested in optimizing the cooling infrastructure of a Data Center, you can find all relevant information in Chapter 5, "Cooling Your Way to a Greener Data Center," for example. Keep two overarching principles in mind, however, when reading the many green strategies that are presented. First, because Data Centers are complex, highly integrated environments—hardware technologies, physical infrastructure technologies, and IT services are all intertwined within a company's server environment—the green improvements that you make to these facilities are likely to have benefits that ripple throughout your entire business. Virtualizing a single server, for instance, eliminates the need for the physical server, frees up cabinet space, reduces energy consumption, lowers cooling demand, and lessens the quantity of patch cords that are used. Doing so also reduces provisioning time and creates a resource that can be flexibly allocated as needed to perform a variety of services.

Second, the most-effective method for greening a Data Center (or any building for that matter) is to implement green improvements that are synergistic, combining for greater effect. Using enclosed cabinets to isolate hot and cold airflow and improve cooling efficiency is beneficial on its own, for instance, but using enclosed cabinets *and* choosing hardware with optimal airflow *and* streamlining cable bundles *and* diverting server exhaust to warm other portions of the building can achieve efficiencies beyond the linear accumulation of their individual improvements.

Some of the tips offered in the chapters that follow are more or less suitable to your Data Center depending upon specific conditions such as its business function, geographic location, or whether it is a major hosting space or minor server room. Most, however, are intended to be universal in nature and can be applied at any Data Center that you want to make greener.

Chapter 1

Going Green in the Data Center

This chapter defines green, discusses the drivers for companies to build greener Data Centers, and presents the benefits a business can see from environmentally friendlier server environments. The chapter also outlines incentive programs that reward green efforts and recaps environmental activities that several major companies pursue today.

Defining Green

If you're reading this book, you're obviously interested in having the server environments that house your company's computing equipment be green. What exactly does the term *green* mean, though, as it relates to a Data Center Facility and Data Center operations?

Does a green Data Center mean a facility that was constructed using fewer natural resources? Does a green Data Center mean a hosting space that produces fewer pollutants? Does a green Data Center mean a room that consumes less energy? Conceivably the term means all those things and more.

No single definition has been adopted across the Data Center industry for what constitutes a green Data Center. There are, however, generally accepted concepts from the greater building industry that are relevant to consider.

The term *green building* is defined as designing a building so that it uses resources—energy, water, and materials—more efficiently and has less impact upon people and the environment. Substitute *Data Center* for *building* and you have

> **Green Data Center:** A computing environment that uses resources in a more efficient manner and has less impact upon people and the environment.

Another relevant building industry term is *sustainable development*, which is defined as development that uses natural resources in such a way as to meet people's needs indefinitely. Or as stated by the World Commission on Environmental Development that first coined the term in a 1987 report to the United Nations General Assembly, "meeting the needs of the present without compromising the ability of future generations to meet their own needs."

Truly sustainable commercial buildings are extremely rare. Although you likely won't achieve 100 percent sustainability for your Data Center Facility, it's useful to keep the ideals in mind as you make design and management decisions concerning the facility. Even achieving a Data Center that is mostly sustainable is a major step forward from past server room designs and can provide significant benefits to your company.

The Reasons to Go Green

A company that is sensitive to the environment and demonstrates that sensitivity through its actions shows admirable social consciousness. In the competitive marketplace that many businesses function in, however, the simple desire to "do the right thing" isn't enough to enact green practices. Going green must be evaluated for its impact upon the company, particularly the company's bottom line.

Going green with a Data Center requires even more scrutiny because of the critical role the facility serves in enabling the business to function. Relevant factors when considering a green Data Center include the following:

- **Trade-offs in functionality and availability:** Does a green Data Center have more or less capacity (that is, power, cooling, and connectivity) than other server environments? Are its physical infrastructure components more or less susceptible to downtime?

- **Cost implications:** Is a green Data Center more or less expensive to build than a facility that doesn't bother with environmental considerations? Is it more or less expensive to operate? Is there enough return on investment that retrofitting an existing facility to be greener is worthwhile?

- **Use of technologies uncommon to the Data Center industry:** What operational changes or new expertise does a green Data Center require?

- **Ancillary issues:** Data Centers aren't islands. They are a key piece of how a company functions. What issues outside of the hosting space are influenced by having a green Data Center?

With these issues in mind, then, what are the merits of designing a new Data Center to be green or retrofitting an existing one? The following sections answer this question.

Growing Power Demand, Shrinking Availability

Data Centers as a group consume a staggering amount of power and their appetite is growing. An August 2007 report by the United States Environmental Protection Agency estimates that U.S. Data Center power usage doubled in 6 years, consuming 61 billion kilowatt hours (kWh) of energy by 2006. The report additionally projects that, unless Data Centers make efficiency improvements to both facilities and IT (Information Technology) components, that power consumption will reach 100 billion kWh by 2011. The European Commission, meanwhile, in the written introduction to its Code of Conduct on Data Centers (discussed elsewhere in this chapter) estimates Western

European Data Center consumption at 56 billion kWh per year in 2007, reaching 104 billion kWh by 2020.

Figure 1.1 illustrates estimated and projected U.S. Data Center power consumption between 2000 and 2011, according to the U.S. Environmental Protection Agency. You can find a copy of the report, "Report to Congress on Server and Data Center Energy Efficiency," at the EPA website: http://www.energystar.gov/index.cfm?c=prod_development.server_efficiency_study.

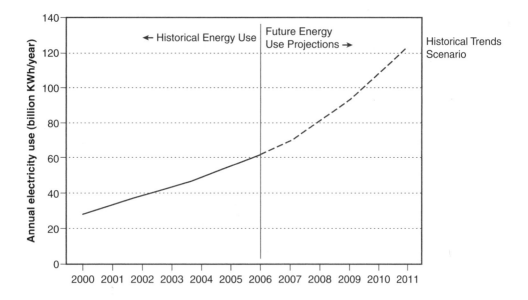

Figure 1.1   *Estimated U.S. Data Center Power Consumption Trend*

Such dramatic growth in consumption can be attributed in part to the overall proliferation of technology and Internet usage throughout society. More e-mails, instant messages, web searches, online financial transactions, and video downloads occur today than just a few years ago. More servers, networking gear, and storage devices are needed to facilitate that burgeoning Internet traffic—more in quantity, more in performance, and therefore more in power consumption.

Also, at many companies, Data Center power and cooling capacity are seen as unlimited resources, so few barriers exist to inhibit demand. If you allocate a budget each fiscal quarter to buy servers and there are no restrictions, why not buy the fastest machines with the most processing capability you can afford? Unfortunately, that top-end performance often translates to top-end power demand and heat production.

Another likely contributing factor is the shrinking form factor of Data Center equipment. Today's server models are physically smaller than yesterday's, allowing more of them to be placed in each Data Center cabinet than in years past. Even if a new machine consumes less energy than its predecessors, and not all do, the fact that you can install more equipment in the same physical space means that more overall power is consumed.

> **Note**   My personal lesson as to how small-profile servers can increase the demand for Data Center resources came in 2004 when one Cisco business unit chose to deploy a series of 1U-high boxes.
>
> The initial wave of what would ultimately include more than 200 machines was to be installed into a server row with 12 server cabinet locations. After filling a few 42U-high cabinets close to half-full with servers, the installers determined (thanks to amp-reading power strips) that the servers' cumulative electrical draw had already exceeded the standard power budget for an entire cabinet, despite taking up less than half the space.
>
> We also realized something else just by standing near the cabinets: The gear was hot. The older room's 60 watts per square foot (645.8 watts per square meter) of cooling simply wasn't up to the task of dissipating the heat generated by these higher-performing, tightly packed servers.
>
> Suddenly, interior cabinet space was no longer a true indicator of a Data Center's maximum capacity. Power and cooling was. (And is....)

Regardless of its cause, such steep growth in electrical demand among Data Centers can't continue indefinitely. There simply isn't an infinite number of real estate properties available that are—or can be—equipped with massive amounts of commercial power and well suited overall to house a Data Center. (Well suited means located away from environmental hazards, capable of accommodating sufficient floor space, close to a skilled work force, and so on.)

A modern Data Center of significant size, say 20,000 or 30,000 square feet (rounding down for convenience, 2,000 or 3,000 square meters) and designed with redundant standby electrical infrastructure can easily demand 20 megawatts (MW) of commercial power capacity. More massive installations, if built to house the same equipment density across its larger floor space, need power on a proportional scale. Therefore, a Data Center 10 times as large can conceivably need 10 times the power. As an example, published reports describe a Microsoft Data Center of 500,000 square feet (46,452 square meters) in Northlake, Illinois, having 198 MW of electrical capacity and Data Center space for Digital Realty Trust in Ashburn, Virginia, totaling 432,000 square feet (40,134 square meters)—distributed among three buildings—and having 225 MW of electrical capacity.

Properties readily possessing access to such large supplies of electricity are rare today and will be even less common tomorrow. At some level, everyone in a given region is fishing from the same proverbial pond. Your prospective Data Center competes for power resources with every other new home, office building, and major Data Center in your area. Whoever builds in the area first, or pays the utility company to reserve the capacity, gets it.

Greening your Data Center, which includes improving the electrical efficiency of both the building and the computing equipment it houses, enables you to get more out of the power capacity of a given property. When executed during the planning phase of a Data Center project, a green design can reduce the power needs of the facility and perhaps even enable it to be built in a location that otherwise could not sustain it. If greening is done to an existing Data Center, the improvements can slow or stop rising electrical demand from outstripping available capacity.

If you don't build such efficiencies into your Data Center, thereby lowering how much power it consumes, there might come a day when there simply isn't enough commercial power available locally to run the Data Center at full electrical load.

Figure 1.2 shows U.S. Data Center power consumption trends predicted by the U.S. Environmental Protection Agency, assuming various energy-efficiency measures are implemented. The strategies, which range from IT improvements—such as server and storage consolidation—to facilities improvements—such as airflow optimization and implementing high-efficiency electrical components—are all presented within later chapters of this book.

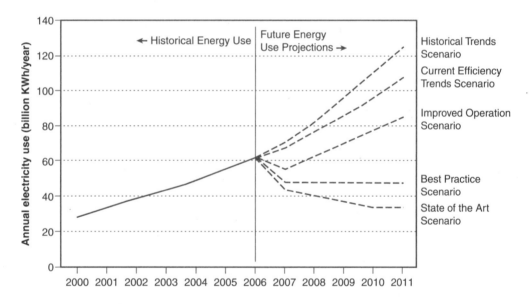

Figure 1.2   *Estimated U.S. Data Center Power Consumption Trend, With Green Measures*

Monetary Benefits

If you have ever built or maintained a Data Center, you know they're expensive. Companies routinely pay more per square foot (meter) to construct hosting areas than any other type of floor space in their buildings due to Data Centers' extensive physical infrastructure. Add to that the expense of the equipment you must purchase to make the room functional—servers, networking gear, and storage devices—and even a space with a small physical footprint can cost hundreds of thousands of dollars.

Over the lifetime of a Data Center, those initial construction and deployment costs are ultimately dwarfed by the room's operational expenses, led first and foremost by its power bills. The 61 billion kWh of annual energy that the EPA estimated for U.S. Data Centers in 2000 carried a price tag of $4.5 billion per year, for example; the 100 billion kWh estimated for 2011 will carry a cost of $7.4 billion.

Applying green materials and practices to a Data Center typically involves an increase in capital expenses—the initial cost for physical construction or deploying components—and then a decrease in operational costs. Because the capital cost is a one-time expenditure whereas the operational savings continue for years, most Data Center green improvements ultimately provide significant cost savings over time.

How significant? A cost-benefit analysis of 33 green building projects concluded that a 2 percent increase in upfront costs typically results in 20 percent savings over the life of the building—a tenfold return. The financial benefits included lower energy, waste disposal and water costs, lower environmental and emissions costs, lower operations and maintenance costs, and savings from improved employee productivity and health.

The study, *The Costs and Financial Benefits of Green Buildings*, was developed by clean energy industry consulting firm Capital E for California's Sustainable Building Task Force and reviewed 25 office buildings and 8 school buildings completed, or scheduled for completion, between 1995 and 2004.

"The findings of this report point to a clear conclusion: Building green is cost-effective and makes financial sense today," wrote the study's authors.

Table 1.1 shows the cost premiums and savings that green buildings incur compared to conventional construction, according to the study.

The data in Table 1.1 came from green building projects, not green Data Center projects, so costs and savings will differ for a server environment. For instance, because most employees typically spend only part of their work day in a Data Center, the productivity and health benefits are likely to be diminished.

Alternately, because Data Centers involve drawing much more power than other building spaces, green improvements can easily achieve much more than $5.79 per square foot ($62.32 per square meter) in energy savings over 20 years.

A study conducted by Lawrence Berkeley National Laboratories for the American Council for an Energy-Efficient Economy determined that Data Center energy costs are typically 15 times those of typical office buildings. The 2006 study, *Best Practices for Data Centers: Lessons Learned from Benchmarking 22 Data Centers*, reviewed 22 Data Center buildings and found some server environments were as much as 40 times as energy-intensive. Apply those multiples to the energy-savings figures in Table 1.1, and you have potential savings of $86.85 per square foot ($934.85 per square meter) in an average Data Center and of $231.60 per square foot ($2492.94 per square meter) in the most power-hungry rooms.

Table 1.1   *Financial Benefits of Green Buildings*

Category	20-Year Net Present Value (per Square Foot)	20-Year Net Present Value (per Square Meter)
Energy Savings	$5.79	$62.32
Emissions Savings	$1.18	$12.70
Water Savings	$0.51	$5.49
Water Savings (Construction Only)—1 Year	$0.03	$0.32
Operations and Maintenance Savings	$8.47	$91.17
Productivity and Health Benefits	$36.89 to $55.33	$397.08 to $595.57
Subtotal	$52.87 to $71.31	$569.09 to $767.58
Average Extra Cost of Green Building	($4.00)	($43.06)
Total 20-Year Net Benefit	$48.87 to $67.31	$526.04 to $724.52

If you develop a business justification about why to pursue green initiatives at your company, you undoubtedly need to quantify your return on investment. In simple terms, if the business expends resources on an initiative, typically in the form of money or staff time, how long will it take for that expenditure to be repaid as a result of the changes?

Even if you never performed a formal ROI analysis in your job role, you have probably done the mental exercise instinctively as a private consumer. For instance, if you consider buying a compact florescent lightbulb for your home, you likely thought, "If I have to pay x more for a fluorescent lightbulb than I do for a standard one, but the fluorescent bulb saves me y on my electric bill every month, that'll pay for itself in z months."

There are more variables when considering green improvements for a server environment, but the basic approach is the same: What's the upfront cost and how quickly can you recoup it?

Say, for example, you decide to cover the notched openings in the floor tiles of your Data Center's raised floor, to improve the static pressure in the room and thereby increase the efficiency of the air conditioning system. (Sealing unwanted openings across the Data Center prevents chilled air from leaking out and not fully reaching the equipment it is supposed to cool.)

If the Data Center has 100 cabinet locations with tile openings and you spend $50 per cover (there are many cover types on the market, from foam rubber to bristle brushes), that's $5,000 in upfront costs. Assuming the subsequent improvement to the Data Center's airflow reduces the power draw of the cooling system enough to save $200 worth of energy each month, you earn back the price of the caps in approximately 2 years ($200 × 25 months = $5000).

Changing any of the variables alters how long it takes for the improvement to pay for itself. The data points to consider in this case include the following:

- **The cost of the improvement:** In this example, the $50 price tag for the tile covers. More expensive covers obviously take more time to pay for; less expensive covers less time. Because your support staff will spend time installing the covers, you could conceivably factor in a labor cost as well. (You probably wouldn't in this particular case, because the work is negligible enough to be absorbed into the staff's regular workload.)

- **The baseline operational costs:** In this instance, the monthly electrical bill for the Data Center, which includes the cost of powering the cooling system before the tile covers are installed. Note that this actually includes two elements—how much energy is consumed and the local cost of electricity. This becomes relevant if you consider making an improvement in multiple Data Centers located in different cities that are, therefore, subject to different electric utility rates.

- **The projected impact of the operational improvement:** How much energy do you save by improving static pressure in the Data Center, and therefore how much lower will the electric bill be? The more dramatic the improvement, obviously the faster you recoup your initial expense. Accurately gauging the savings provided by some green improvements can be challenging. Installing a more efficient PDU can be relatively straightforward to measure, for instance, whereas other improvements such as floor tile covers can be less exact. Be prepared to estimate savings and take measurements after they are installed.

A more comprehensive analysis can also cover other impacts of making the improvement. For instance, the improved airflow might lower the overall temperature of the Data Center, which is generally better for servers and provides a greater safety margin if an air handler malfunctions.

A NetApp Data Center in Sunnyvale, California, illustrates the financial benefits that come with a green Data Center. The facility, opened at NetApp headquarters in 2008, in building space previously used for manufacturing, includes a variety of energy-efficient design elements that save the company more than $1 million per year compared to the operational costs of a conventional server environment.

The Data Center is 14,500 square feet (1,347 square meters) in size and involves an additional 5,500 square feet (511 square meters) of surrounding building space for air handlers that cool the hosting area. The 720-rack Data Center has 5.76 MW of electrical capacity for IT hardware and 7 MW overall. About 20 percent of the Data Center floor space is supported by standby electrical infrastructure; the remainder is not.

Energy-efficient measures including air economizers, a variable chiller plant, energy-efficient transformers, and rotary uninterruptible power supply (UPS) systems save more than 11.1 million kWh in annual energy usage, thereby conserving more than 6.7 million pounds (3039 metric tons) in carbon dioxide emissions and saving more than $1 million in operational costs per year, according to Ralph Renne, NetApp director of site operations.

Table 1.2 shows the annual energy, carbon, and costs savings of the facility over a conventional Data Center, broken out among three main categories of green improvements.

Each of the energy-efficient measures implemented by NetApp are explained in detail in Chapter 4, "Powering Your Way to a Greener Data Center," and Chapter 5, "Cooling Your Way to a Greener Data Center."

Table 1.2 *Annual Savings from a NetApp Green Data Center*

Green Element	Energy Savings (kWh)	Carbon Savings (lbs./Mtons)	Cost Savings
Mechanical systems	8,964,977	5,468,636 (2,481)	$813,940
Rotary UPS systems	1,446,834	882,569 (400)	$146,252
High-efficiency transformers	707,925	431,834 (196)	$71,560
Total	11,119,736	6,783,039 (3,077)	$1,031,752

Capacity Gains

Because the essence of a green Data Center is to use resources more efficiently, it follows that a green facility gets more out of those resources than a room that hasn't been designed in that manner. To put it another way, if one car is more fuel-efficient than another, it can go farther on the same amount of gas.

Many Data Centers, especially those built more than a few years ago, have power and cooling constraints that significantly limit to what extent a company can fill its server cabinets with gear. Making those server environments greener can stretch its power and cooling resources further, opening up valuable hosting capacity that was previously unusable.

Achieving such capacity gains could conceivably enable your company to defer construction of a Data Center—along with the capital and operational expenses that come with it.

Note   Imagine if you can make enough efficiency improvements to your existing Data Centers to actually take some of your server environments offline altogether. I can't think of a more dramatic example of a company making its Data Center portfolio greener.

Increasing Regulation

Even if your company doesn't see a driving need to make your server environments greener, it's likely that your government does—or soon will. Government officials worldwide are paying increasing attention to environmental concerns, from energy consumption rates to dependency upon oil to global warming.

Although no mandates specifically call out Data Center restrictions, the tremendous environmental impact of these rooms make them a prime target to place limits on to meet various environmental pledges. A green Data Center is much more likely to be compliant with current and future environmental regulations than a conventional Data Center.

Recent Government Green Commitments

China published a National Climate Change Program in 2007 that set goals to improve its energy efficiency by 20 percent in 2010 (compared to 2005 levels) and to raise the proportion of renewable energy to 10 percent of its primary energy supply by 2010. The country previously passed the Renewable Energy Law that targeted increases in the use of various renewable energies by 2010 and 2020 and committed to investing $180 billion in renewable energy during that time. If the targets are met, renewable energy will account for approximately 16 percent of the country's energy consumption in 2020.

India introduced the Energy Conservation Building Code in 2007 that is expected to reduce power consumption in commercial buildings 25 percent to 40 percent by way of minimum efficiency standards for external walls, roofs, glass structures, lighting, heating, ventilation, and air-conditioning systems. The codes are to be mandatory for commercial structures with an electrical load of at least 500 kW—a power budget easily exceeded by even medium-sized Data Centers.

Japan's Ministry of Economy, Trade, and Industry announced a New National Energy Strategy in 2006 that includes the goal to improve energy consumption efficiency at least 30 percent by 2030.

Sweden's Minister for Sustainable Development made headlines in 2005 by announcing a goal to eliminate the country's dependence upon fossil fuels by 2020. To achieve the goal, the government is increasing research on alternative fuels, expanding a quota system introduced in 2003 requiring all electricity customers to buy an increasing percentage of renewable energy, and offering tax breaks for homes and vehicles that use renewable fuels.

The United Kingdom has announced goals to reduce greenhouse gas emissions by at least 80 percent by 2050 (compared to 1990 levels) and is driving to that goal in part through its Carbon Reduction Commitment (CRC). The CRC is a mandatory carbon emissions trading scheme that, effective 2010, requires organizations that consume at least 6,000 MWh per year in electricity to buy carbon credits. For the first 3 years of the program, costs are £12—about $18—for each metric ton of CO_2. By 2013, carbon allowances will instead be auctioned, and the total number of them will be capped, ultimately forcing reductions in carbon emissions.

In the United States, a growing number of state governments have adopted renewable portfolio standards, which call for a certain portion of utility power to come from renewable sources. Twenty-four states and the District of Columbia have mandatory requirements, and four others have declared nonbinding goals. Their popularity appears to be growing, because half of the standards have been developed since 2004.

The portfolio standard programs vary widely, differing over details such as minimum thresholds of renewable energy, whether energy efficiency should figure into usage calculations, and deadlines to meet the standards. The inability to agree upon one common approach is why no federal renewable portfolio standards exist.

Note   When considering, from a green perspective, where to build a Data Center, it is useful to know what regional standards are in place for power content and emissions. The higher percentage of energy powering your facility that is renewable, obviously the greener the Data Center is to begin with. Chapter 4 discusses electrical mixes in greater detail.

The EPA report on U.S. Data Center power consumption, mentioned previously, was actually initiated by 2006 federal law (Public Law 109–431) "to study and promote the use of energy-efficient computer servers in the United States." When formally presented to Congress in 2007, there was some anticipation within the Data Center industry that U.S. legislators would respond by setting restrictions on Data Center energy usage. Although none have been introduced as of this writing, the EPA is continuing its focus on Data Centers by developing energy rating standards for servers and Data Centers. Chapter 4 and Chapter 8, "Choosing Greener Gear," provide additional details on those efforts.

More than nine out of ten Data Center owners and operators still expect some manner of increased regulation according to the Datacenter Research Group that conducts market surveys among attendees of the DatacenterDynamics conference series. Surveys of 540 attendees, conducted in 2008, reveal that only 7.8 percent believe increased regulation won't happen. (Interestingly, opinions differ over the effect of increased regulation and compliance—26 percent predict negative impact on their organization, 25.8 percent predict positive impact, and the remaining 40 percent anticipate neutral impact.) The surveys were conducted at DataCenterDynamics conferences in Chicago, Dallas, Miami, New York, San Francisco, Seattle, and Washington, D.C.

Multicountry Green Commitments

Several countries have meanwhile collectively pledged to be greener.

The European Commission has called for reducing energy usage across the 27 countries of the European Union at least 20 percent by 2020, cutting carbon dioxide emissions from primary energy sources 20 percent by 2020 and 50 percent by 2050, a 10 percent use of bio-fuels by 2020, and the development of a European Strategic Energy Technology plan to foster advances in renewable energy, energy conservation, nuclear power, clean coal, and carbon capture.

The commission has also stated a desire to establish an international agreement for all developed nations to cut energy usage 30 percent by 2020. (All energy reduction goals are in comparison to 1990 levels.)

Note   Carbon dioxide is one of several so-called greenhouse gases that trap heat from the sun and warm the Earth. If present in high enough quantities, such gases are believed to contribute to a rise in global temperatures that, in turn, cause environmental problems. Chapter 2, "Measuring Green Data Centers," discusses greenhouse gases and carbon dioxide emissions in greater detail.

Minimum standards for building energy performance have also begun to be applied with European Union member states, in accordance with the EU Energy Performance Building Directive. The directive, which was passed in 2002 and came into effect in 2006, established a common methodology for calculating building energy performance.

European Union countries are Austria, Belgium, Bulgaria, Cyprus, Czech Republic, Denmark, Estonia, Finland, France, Germany, Greece, Hungary, Ireland, Italy, Latvia, Lithuania, Luxembourg, Malta, Netherlands, Poland, Portugal, Romania, Slovakia, Slovenia, Spain, Sweden, and the United Kingdom.

As of this writing, the European Commission is also continuing a series of studies of electronic equipment for the purpose of establishing new energy and environmental restrictions for those products. The effort is the latest stage of the European Union's Eco-design Directive for Energy Using Products. Issued in 2005 and generally adopted into law by EU countries in 2007, the directive requires prevalent electronic devices (200,000-plus units selling per year in the EU) to meet minimum power consumption guidelines and for manufacturers to determine the environmental impact of products over their complete lifecycle, from design and manufacture to use and disposal.

Specific energy performance minimums for various equipment will ultimately be set in the form of "implementing measures." The first wave of equipment that the European Commission has focused on includes boilers, water heaters, personal computers, copiers and other imaging equipment, televisions, batteries and external power supplies, office lighting, street lighting, air conditioning, commercial refrigerators and freezers, laundry driers, vacuum cleaners, set top boxes, and domestic lighting.

You can find information about European Commission green-related activities in multiple languages, at http://www.ec.europa.eu/climateaction.

The 21-member countries of the Asia-Pacific Economic Cooperation announced in 2007 the goal to reduce their cumulative energy intensity by at least 25 percent by 2030 (compared to 2005). APEC is a cooperative, multilateral economic forum dedicated to promoting trade and economic growth, and its member economies account for more than one-third of the world's population (2.6 billion people), more than 50 percent of the world's gross domestic product ($19.25 trillion), and more than 41 percent of the world's trade.

APEC's member economies are Australia, Brunei Darussalam, Canada, Chile, China, Hong Kong, Indonesia, Japan, Korea, Malaysia, Mexico, New Zealand, Papua New Guinea, Peru, Philippines, Russia, Singapore, Chinese Taipei, Thailand, the United States, and Vietnam.

Note Economically speaking, energy intensity is the ratio of energy consumption to economic or physical output—energy use per unit of gross domestic product. A country that has a lower energy intensity is considered more energy-efficient because it produces more items or services using fewer energy resources.

A country's energy intensity is ultimately influenced by several factors, including standard of living (and associated quantity of energy-using devices); the energy efficiency of buildings, appliances and vehicles; severity of climate (influencing energy usage for heating and cooling); and the prevalence of energy-consuming mechanisms such as mass transit or energy conservation programs.

At the Second East Asia Summit in early 2007, leaders of 16 countries signed the Cebu Declaration on East Asian Energy Security, pledging to create voluntary energy-efficiency targets for their respective nations and to work for "intensified energy efficiency and conservation programs" and expanded renewable energy systems.

Officials took a further step at the Third East Asia Summit at the end of 2007, signing the Singapore Declaration on Climate Change, Energy and the Environment, committing to "working toward achieving a significant reduction in energy intensity" and setting energy efficiency goals by 2009.

Summit participants include Australia, Brunei, Cambodia, China, Indonesia, India, Japan, Laos, Malaysia, Myanmar (Burma), New Zealand, Philippines, Singapore, South Korea, Thailand, and Vietnam.

Note In what might be an indication of binding requirements to come for the Data Center industry, the European Commission in 2008 published a voluntary Code of Conduct on Data Centres Energy Efficiency calling for Data Center owners and operators, hardware manufacturers, and service providers to adopt several practices aimed to improve Data Center energy efficiency.

Data Center operators who agree to participate in the Code of Conduct are expected to collect and report energy usage of their IT hardware and overall facility and follow dozens of identified best practices, ranging from decommissioning unused hardware to installing blanking panels within server cabinets to considering temperature and humidity ranges as a key factor when choosing new hardware, so the Data Center that houses them can ultimately be operated at warmer settings.

A copy of the Code of Conduct, and a companion document that offers more than 100 best practices for participants to potentially pursue, is available at http://www.tinyurl.com/84cjun.

Of all the multigovernment commitments to being green, perhaps the best known and most symbolic is the Kyoto Protocol. Adopted in 1997 under the United Nations Framework Convention on Climate Change and legally in effect by 2005, the agreement calls for participating industrialized nations to reduce greenhouse gas emissions by a cumulative 5.2 percent between 2008 and 2012 (compared to 1990 levels).

Reduction targets vary by nation including 8 percent for the European Union; 7 percent for the United States; 6 percent for Canada, Hungary, Japan, and Poland; and 5 percent for Croatia. New Zealand, Russia, and Ukraine are to remain flat, at 0 percent, whereas Australia is allowed an 8 percent increase and Iceland a 10 percent increase. If accomplished, the cumulative 5.2 percent reduction represents a 29 percent drop from the emission levels that were otherwise projected for 2010.

As of mid-2008, 181 countries and the European Union ratified the protocol. Of those, 36 countries and the EU are required to meet specific emission reduction targets. Those that fail to meet their 2012 targets are required to reach those reductions plus an additional 30 percent in a second time frame from 2013.

Note   It's relevant to note that there is some debate over the ultimate value and impact of the Kyoto Protocol.

Critics disagree with the protocol's provisions for emissions trading, for example, which allows a country that fails to meet its reduction targets to buy excess capacity from other nations. They also oppose allowing countries to deduct from their emission totals for carbon sinks, natural areas of forest, or other vegetation that absorb carbon dioxide.

Also the United States, which is one of the largest producers of greenhouse gases in the world, has indicated it will not ratify the agreement. U.S. officials expressed concern that implementing the protocol would damage the U.S. economy and that it does not require developing countries to commit to emissions reductions. (This includes China and India, which are major producers of greenhouse gas.)

Proponents say that the Kyoto Protocol is still a major accomplishment, being the first legally binding treaty to mandate greenhouse gas reductions and paving the way for greater measures in the future. Several conferences have already occurred to discuss what steps can or should be taken after the protocol's 2012 deadline passes.

Large-scale mandates to reduce carbon emissions and improve energy efficiency can be expected to grow in scope in the future, underscoring how important it is for Data Centers to be greener than ever.

Technology Advances

As time goes on, Data Center technologies and designs evolve and improve. This occurs with facilities infrastructure and, at a much faster pace, with IT equipment. Many advances bring green opportunities with them.

Some of these are incremental changes that occur over time, such as a new generation of servers that have more processing capability than what came before. Others are more dramatic, such as virtualization technology that facilitates greater utilization of equipment.

Still others are foundational changes that are introduced when a server environment is first designed and built, such as when Data Center designers began establishing distinct hot and cold aisles to reduce the mixing of hot and cold air in the hosting space, thereby increasing the efficiency of its cooling system.

Public Perception

The final reason to go green is, for any business that sells a product or service, arguably the most compelling—your customers want you to. Opinion surveys taken on a range of topics and in many different regions of the world show a notable preference among consumers to do business with companies that are good to the environment. Many people are even willing to pay a premium, if needed, to buy green goods and services.

A massive public opinion survey of 27,000 Europeans, conducted across the European Union in late 2007 and published in 2008, indicated that 75 percent are "ready to buy environmentally friendly products even if they cost a little bit more." The Eurobarometer, a series of surveys performed regularly for the European Commission since 1973, was conducted through face-to-face interviews in people's homes and showed a strong interest in buying green products.

Table 1.3 shows the percentages of Europeans ready to buy green products according to the 2008 Eurobarometer survey "Attitudes of European citizens towards the environment."

An array of smaller polls taken around the world in 2007 show similar sentiment. Among them:

- More than six in ten U.S. homeowners said they are willing to pay more for products made with renewable resources. Respondents indicated 65 percent are willing to pay at least $5 more on a $100 product, and 40 percent are willing to pay at least $10 more. The survey of 1,001 U.S. homeowners was sponsored by DuPont and Mohawk Industries and conducted by MarketTools (http://www2.dupont.com/Sorona/en_US).

- Seven in ten utility consumers in Europe, North America, and Asia Pacific said environmental impact influences what they buy, and three in four said that companies' reputations for environmental practices influenced who they buy from. The survey of 1,900 utility consumers involved households and small businesses in Australia, Germany, Japan, the Netherlands, the United Kingdom, and the United States. It was conducted by IBM Global Business Services (http://www.tinyurl.com/dbjhob).

- Twelve percent of U.S. consumers said they strongly favor paying more for consumer electronics if those items use less energy or come from an environmentally friendly company, and an additional 41 percent indicated they have concerns about environmental issues. The survey of 5,000 U.S. consumers, "In Search of Green Technology Consumers," was conducted by Forrester Research, Inc. (http://www.tinyurl.com/dbadrl).

Table 1.3 *European Attitudes Toward Environmentally Friendly Purchases*

European Union Members	Ready to Buy Green
Denmark	86%
Sweden	88%
Austria	81%
Slovakia	69%
Romania	63%
Spain	64%
Czech Republic	71%
Ireland	70%
Luxembourg	84%
United Kingdom	79%
Malta	81%
Hungary	72%
Netherlands	76%
France	77%
Germany	76%
Belgium	79%
Bulgaria	66%
Italy	72%
Finland	85%
Slovenia	80%
Latvia	79%
Poland	77%
Lithuania	72%
Estonia	84%
Portugal	75%
Greece	88%
Cyprus	91%
EU27	75%

Data compiled from the March, 2008 report, "Attitudes of European citizens towards the environment": http://www.ec.europa.eu/public_opinion/archives/ebs/ebs_295_en.pdf.

Although answers to a poll don't always equate to everyday action—people don't always act on their stated good intentions—extrapolating the survey results to the consumer market shows the massive potential audience interested in green products. The three groups listed previously—U.S. homeowners; utility consumers in Europe, North America, and Asia Pacific, and overall U.S. consumers—encompass hundreds of millions of people. If even a fraction of that audience bases its purchasing decisions upon how green a company is, who wouldn't want to be in a position to benefit from that?

Green + Whitewashing = Greenwashing

Public sentiment is powerful regarding green, not only in supporting green efforts but also in reacting harshly to misleading or inflated claims around green—a practice dubbed *greenwashing*. Several websites now exist entirely for the purpose of exposing such activities and for good reason, because an ample number of green claims made by product makers or service providers are apparently of questionable merit.

During late 2008 and early 2009, TerraChoice Environmental Marketing reviewed the green claims of thousands of consumer products and determined that the vast majority are vague or misleading in some way. For the study, researchers visited 40 stores in the United States, Canada, Australia, and the United Kingdom. They evaluated 4,705 consumer products from baby care and household cleaning items to electronic goods and office products and determined that, among 10,419 green claims made about them, all but 30 claims were flawed. (TerraChoice performed a similar study 2 years earlier to similar findings—a review of 1,753 claims by 1,018 products in six North American stores determined that only one claim was without flaws.)

The firm categorized the deceptions into what it calls "Seven Sins of Greenwashing." These include

- **Sin of the Hidden Trade-Off:** Suggesting a product is green based on one characteristic without addressing other environmental issues. For example, promoting paper products for its recycled content while ignoring manufacturing-related concerns such as air and water emissions or global warming.

- **Sin of No Proof:** Making an environmental claim without providing evidence. For instance, touting lamps or lightbulbs for energy efficiency yet offering no supporting documentation.

- **Sin of Vagueness:** Making an environmental claim that is so unspecific it is likely to be misunderstood. Terms such as "green" and "environmentally friendly," for example, reveal little about a product if not qualified with additional information.

Continues

Continued

- **Sin of Worshiping False Labels:** Using a mock green-certification image to imply that a product has been verified as green by a legitimate agency.

- **Sin of Irrelevance:** Touting a green characteristic of a product that, although factually correct, isn't relevant. The study found frequent claims about items being free of ozone-depleting chlorofluorocarbons, which were banned in 1987 by international treaty (the Montreal Protocol on Substances that Deplete the Ozone Layer) and therefore by default not typically present in products.

- **Sin of Lesser of Two Evils:** Identifying an item as green or organic when the entire class of product as a whole poses environmental concerns. For example, organic cigarettes, which might indeed be made in a more environmentally friendly way than other cigarettes but still pose health concerns.

- **Sin of Fibbing:** Making false environmental claims.

Needless to say, you don't want to participate in greenwashing or have your business get a reputation for doing so. Although the preceding "sins" are in reference to the packaging and marketing of consumer products, the same potential exists to make imprecise or inaccurate claims around how green a given Data Center is.

Chapter 2 covers industry standards for accurately representing how environmentally friendly your Data Center is.

If You Don't Own Your Data Centers

What if your company doesn't own the facilities that house your servers and networking equipment? Does it matter how green the facilities are? Do you still have any ability to make those server environments greener?

Yes it does and yes you do.

Keep in mind that you still have financial incentives to be green in a leased Data Center. Every amp of energy that you avoid using is extra capacity that's available for you to use for another piece of equipment. Some hosting facilities also charge premiums for power consumption above certain thresholds, so greater efficiency can save you money on your leasing costs.

First, although you can't dictate to the owners of the Data Centers you lease how to build or operate their server environment, you still control the servers that you purchase. Chapter 8 and Chapter 9, "Greening Your Data Center Through Consolidation, Virtualization, and Automation," discuss how to choose and deploy servers, networking devices, and storage systems for greater efficiency.

Second, you have choices as to where to host your equipment. If being green is important to your business culture, you can make a choice about which colocation Data Center to house your equipment in based upon how green the facility is. Some of the questions to ask when evaluating a space include the following:

- What percentage of the power feeding the Data Center is renewable?

- What technologies have been designed into the Data Center to improve the efficiency of its electrical and mechanical systems?

- How energy-efficient is the Data Center? (The Data Center metrics discussed in Chapter 2 are relevant to inquire about.)

- What is the carbon footprint of the facility?

- What are the emissions from the Data Center's standby generators?

- For any equipment that is provided by the hosting service, what sort of e-waste recycling do they do?

Nearly all of the Data Center design strategies presented throughout this book apply as easily to a colocation facility as to an owner-operated Data Center. Consider using the chapter summaries or table of contents as the basis of a checklist for evaluating how green a hosting space is.

A final question to ask yourself when reviewing colocation facilities is what sort of availability do you truly need for your Data Center, and therefore how much redundant physical infrastructure do you require? Redundant systems provide greater protection for your Data Center against outages but unfortunately are also less green. Electrical losses are repeated in every additional layer of redundancy, plus more resources are consumed in the manufacture of the additional equipment and infrastructure components.

Note   Green considerations are prevalent enough today that many colocation operators are ready and willing to discuss their green features. Here are a handful of hosting facilities that are actively promoting their green features:

- Data Center developer and operator 365 Main, based in San Francisco, California, and with facilities in six U.S. cities, announced in 2007 that all its future server environments would be built to meet the U.S. Green Building Council's Leadership in Energy and Environmental Design (LEED) standards. (LEED standards are explained in detail in Chapter 2.)

- Wholesale Data Center provider Digital Realty Trust, which has 74 hosting spaces totaling more than 13 million square feet (1.2 million square meters) in Europe and North America, announced in 2009 that all its future Data Centers would be built according to Building Research Establishment Environmental Assessment Method (BREEAM) standards. (BREEAM standards are also explained in detail in Chapter 2.)

continues

continued

- Coreix, a 6,000-square foot (557.4-square meter) hosting facility in London, England, advertises itself as the UK's first carbon neutral Data Center thanks to donations it makes to a conservation charity that preserves rainforests.

- Green House Data, a 10,000-square foot (929-square meter) colocation Data Center in Cheyenne, Wyoming, indicates that it is powered entirely through renewable wind and solar energy.

Resistance to Green

Despite the merits of green Data Centers, there is still hesitation among some business executives, facilities personnel, and IT managers about placing environmental factors among their top criteria when designing a new facility.

This hesitation is typically due to four factors:

- **Hesitation to stray from familiar practices:** Although Data Centers are often viewed as symbols of rapidly changing, leading-edge technology, their business-critical nature makes those who build and operate them understandably reluctant to deviate from what has worked in the past. Known technology and designs, even if inefficient in some regards, can be preferable to something unproven—or at least unproven to them.

- **A lack of company incentives around Data Center environmental considerations:** The success or failure of a Data Center project—and those who build or maintain it—isn't often linked to the room's environmental impact. As an unidentified Data Center manager was quoted in a 2008 Data Center Journal article, "No one ever got fired for using too much electricity, but people get fired all the time for Data Center outages."

- **Skepticism:** Over the years, not all Data Center technologies have provided the benefits they were touted to. Marketing hype has bred healthy skepticism.

- **The assumption that green Data Center solutions are too expensive:** Information about the costs and savings of green Data Center materials and technologies is not widely available, so many people assume the costs are high and not worth the investment. Because green-related savings typically accrue over the long term, the "too expensive" perception can be reinforced at companies that evaluate performance based upon short time frames. Many businesses conduct operational reviews, set budget allocations, and do financial reporting quarterly, for example, an approach that doesn't showcase operational savings that take years to accumulate. Any additional upfront capital expenses associated with greening—even if they would ultimately provide a large return on investment over time—become a prime target for anyone trying to trim project costs in the name of so-called "value engineering."

Misunderstood Costs of Green Buildings

The World Business Council for Sustainable Development commissioned a global survey of more than 1,400 people associated with the property industry and found that even it significantly overestimate the cost to make a building green.

The aggregate perception was that a 17 percent premium is needed to construct a building that meets the U.S. Green Building Council's minimum LEED certification level—more than triple the actual typical premium of less than 5 percent.

Researchers conducted 45 in-depth interviews with architects, journalists, academics, policy makers, financiers, and property investment firms and polled another 1,423 engineers, contractors, landlords, and corporate tenants using telephone questionnaires. The surveys were conducted in late 2006 and early 2007 and spanned eight countries. Results were published in the World Business Council for Sustainable Development's 2007 Energy Efficiency in Buildings report.

Table 1.4 shows the extra costs that respondents assumed a green building would occur.

Much of the overestimation of costs can likely be attributed to a lack of direct experience that most people, including those polled in the survey, have with green building projects.

Table 1.5 shows the portion of survey respondents who had worked directly on a green building project.

How, then, do you overcome such resistance? If none of the aforementioned drivers are enough to push green considerations into your Data Center designs and operational practices, consider some of the incentive programs that many utility companies and government agencies offer.

Table 1.4   *Estimates of Cost Premium for a Green Building Project*

Country of Respondents	Perceived Cost Premium for Green Building
Brazil	22%
China	28%
France	12%
Germany	17%
India	11%
Japan	16%
Spain	19%
United States	16%
Overall	17%

Table 1.5   *Involvement of Property Professionals with Sustainable Buildings*

Country of Respondents	Direct Involvement with Green Building
Brazil	9%
China	10%
France	8%
Germany	45%
India	5%
Japan	3%
Spain	9%
United States	16%
Overall	13%

Green Incentive Programs

Several public agencies have realized the societal benefits of Data Centers and commercial buildings in general becoming greener and now offer financial inducements to encourage businesses to upgrade existing rooms or build efficient spaces from scratch. Such programs typically focus on reducing energy consumption and can help offset the upfront costs of making green capital improvements.

Utility Companies

Commercial power providers might not be an obvious source of incentives for reducing energy usage—they're in the business of selling power, after all—but many offer rebates and strategies for improving power efficiency. That's because conserving energy ultimately benefits utility companies, relieving demand on major power grids during peak times (typically during hot summer days and cold winter mornings) and lessening wholesale electric prices.

California-based Pacific Gas and Electric Co. (PG&E), for instance, offers rebates for businesses that consolidate older servers, paying 9 cents per kWh plus $100 per kW of demand reduction—up to 50 percent of the total cost of the project. The utility company offers similar rebates for upgrading disk storage equipment.

According to PG&E representatives, the design and construction of any commercial facility that significantly exceeds the state's energy efficiency standards (Title 24, Part 6 of the California Code of Regulations: California's Energy Efficiency Standards for Residential and Nonresidential Buildings) has the potential to qualify for financial incentives.

PG&E is also one of four utility companies (Sacramento Municipal Utility District, San Diego Gas and Electric, and Southern California Edison Co. are the others) that, under the auspices of the California Public Utilities Commission, administer a program promoting energy-efficient building and process design and construction.

Known as *Savings by Design*, the program offers

- Technical design assistance to analyze and design more energy-efficient buildings and process systems

- Owner incentives of up to $500,000 per project to help offset the investment in energy-efficient building and design, subject to project incremental costs

- Design team initiatives of up to $50,000 per project to reward designers who meet ambitious energy-efficiency goals

- Design tools and resources for architects and engineers to support energy-efficient design efforts

Each of these offerings can notably defray the capital costs associated with making green improvements, either at the hardware or building level. Contact the commercial power provider where your Data Center is located to determine what program it offers to promote energy efficiency. Many utility company incentive programs require its involvement at the start of a project, so be sure to contact them at the outset.

Note   There are countless energy providers worldwide, so it is impractical to list all of them and the specific incentive programs they offer. I chose to focus on Pacific Gas and Electric and its programs for three reasons:

- PG&E is a strong green proponent, through its own direct actions and by fostering green activities among its customers. From 2006 through 2008, the company lead nearly $1 billion in enhanced energy-efficiency programs, the largest gas and electric energy-efficiency effort of its kind by a U.S. utility company.

- The utility company's coverage area spans the Silicon Valley, which has a large concentration of companies with Data Centers. All told, PG&E provides natural gas and electric service to approximately 15 million people across a 70,000-square mile (181,299-square kilometer) service area in northern and central California.

- Dozens of other utility companies are thinking of offering rebate programs modeled after PG&E's. PG&E founded the IT Energy Efficiency Coalition in 2007 to facilitate the creation of uniform incentive programs, and more than 24 utilities from the United States and Canada now participate. If the programs are implemented as proposed, a company with Data Centers in multiple locations can consolidate servers in each of them and count on receiving similar rebates.

For an idea of the monies available for green Data Center construction, recall the NetApp Data Center in Sunnyvale, California, mentioned previously in this chapter. That project, which achieved more than 11.1 million kWh in annual energy savings and more than 6.7 million pounds (3,039 metric tons) of carbon dioxide savings per year, received the largest monetary incentive for energy-efficient new construction ever awarded by PG&E, totaling $1,427,477. The sizable rebate, together with the project's $1 million in annual energy-related savings, allowed NetApp to recoup the extra capital costs of the Data Center's green elements in less than 2 years.

Government Programs

National and local governments worldwide offer financial incentives, usually in the form of tax breaks, to encourage a range of green behaviors. Although many are focused on private consumer activities, such as buying hybrid automobiles and energy-efficient home appliances, businesses with Data Centers can usually tap into rewards offered for using renewable energy and for building more energy-efficient commercial buildings.

Hong Kong, for instance, announced in 2008 that it will offer a tax break to fully offset the capital costs of certain energy-efficient building installations and "environmental protection machinery"—typically equipment that produces renewable energy. A tax deduction equal to 20 percent of the capital expenditure is permitted for 5 consecutive years, beginning the year the installation occurs.

Japan's Energy Conservation Assistance Law meanwhile offers tax incentives and low interest loans to promote the use of energy conservation equipment and the investment into such technologies. A business can choose between a tax exemption equivalent to 7 percent of the equipment acquisition cost (to a maximum of 20 percent of its payable income or corporate tax) or a bonus of 30 percent depreciation of the equipment acquisition cost in the year it bought it.

Note   In addition to offering financial incentives for energy efficiency, Japan honors energy-efficient practices in an awards ceremony each year. Commendations are given in multiple categories, with an Energy Conservation Grand Prize going to the most deserving energy-efficient system or resource for the home, commercial, or automobile use.

Awards are presented by the Minister of Economy, Trade, and Industry, the director-general of the Agency of Natural Resources and Energy, and the president of the Energy Conservation Center, Japan.

The United Kingdom offers tax breaks known as *Enhanced Capital Allowances (ECA)* for the purchase of building plant and machinery that is energy-efficient or conserves water. (ECAs are also available for cars with low carbon dioxide emissions and hydrogen refueling infrastructure.) The program allows businesses to write off the entire first-year capital cost of the green technologies against their taxable profits.

Note Surprisingly, few UK businesses have taken advantage of the ECA tax incentives, apparently due to lack of awareness and the difficulty of the process to apply for them. Less than 1 in 20 companies have applied for the allowances according to a research study conducted by the University of the West of England's Bristol Business School.

The study, Environment and the Corporate Agenda, polled more than 100 finance directors from mostly small- and medium-sized businesses across the UK in 2007 to determine awareness of the tax breaks.

Less than 50 percent of the respondents were aware of the incentives, which were first introduced in 2001. Of those who were aware of the ECAs but did not apply for them, 13 percent said they were discouraged from applying because the process was too complex.

In the United States, federal tax credits for energy efficiency include a tax deduction of $1.80 per square foot ($19.38 per square meter) for cutting a new or pre-existing commercial building's heating, cooling, ventilation, water heating, and interior lighting energy costs by 50 percent. Partial deductions of up to $0.60 per square foot ($6.46 per square meter) are available for improvements to the building envelope, lighting, or heating and cooling systems that reduce energy costs by 25 percent to 50 percent. Both percentages are in comparison to the American Society of Heating, Refrigerating, and Air-Conditioning Engineers' energy-efficiency standard for commercial buildings (ASHRAE Standard 90.1-2001).

Check with both the local and national governments for the region where your Data Center is (or will be) located to learn about what green incentive programs are available. Specific departments that focus on construction or energy issues are a good place to start. A list of U.S.-based green building incentives, including grants, tax credits, and loans, is available on the website of the Environmental Protection Agency: http://www.epa.gov/greenbuilding/tools/funding.htm.

Another excellent source of information about renewable energy and energy-efficiency incentives available in the United States is the Database of State Incentives for Renewables and Efficiency at http://www.dsireusa.org. The website offers an interactive map of the country, allowing visitors to explore the incentives offered—per state—by national, state, utilities, and local agencies. The database is a joint effort of the North Carolina Solar Center and the Interstate Renewable Energy Council and funded by the U.S. Department of Energy.

Who Is Going Green

In addition to knowing the assortment of benefits that come with going green, both in the Data Center and beyond, it's telling to look at what successful companies have environmental considerations on their agendas.

Green from the Start

Companies that place environmental concerns among their top priorities—those businesses for which social responsibility is a leading part of their philosophy and identity—have been around for decades. Several such companies have thrived in the marketplace, demonstrating that it's possible to be both financially successful and environmentally considerate.

Greenest Company in the World

Perhaps the most obvious example of businesses that are both profitable and green are those with products that help other companies lessen their own consumption of resources.

Denmark's Vestas Wind Systems, the world's largest manufacturer of wind turbines, was named "Greenest Company in the World" in 2007, while earning €4.86 billion (about $7.5 billion) that year. The distinction was given by the British newspaper, *The Independent*, along with Ethical Investment Research Services, which evaluated nearly 3,000 companies for their environmental sustainability.

The eco-friendly nature of Vestas' product is obviously a key reason for the top rank. Its wind turbines are not only a source of renewable energy but also 80 percent recyclable. The units also generate enough energy within 8 months to offset what it takes to build, move, and disassemble them. To date, the company has installed more than 38,000 wind turbines, providing more than 60 million MWh a year in power to companies in more than 60 countries. Vestas also draws 68 percent of its own energy requirements from renewable sources.

The company projects even greater revenues in future years thanks to growing demand for wind power in the United States, China, and India. (More information about wind power as a source of energy for Data Centers is provided in Chapter 4.)

Most Socially Responsible

Making a commercial product that improves the environment isn't the only way to be green and profitable at the same time. Whole Foods Market earned $6.6 billion in revenue for 2007, just 1 year after cementing its reputation as the most socially responsible prominent company in the United States.

Whole Foods ranked number one in the category of social responsibility as part of the Annual Reputation Quotient (RQ) Survey conducted by Harris Interactive, which measures the reputations of the 60 most-visible companies in the United States. Whole Foods ranked number 12 overall, scoring 80 out of a possible 100 points. Other categories used to calculate the overall reputation rating are emotional appeal, financial performance, products and services, vision and leadership, and workplace environment.

The company's reputation for social consciousness has come from activities including store composting programs, selling the products of local growers, and contributions to community nonprofit organizations. Whole Foods has been recognized several times by the U.S. EPA for helping develop renewable energy capacity and in 2006 purchased renewable energy credits to fully offset the electricity used in all its stores, offices, and other facilities. Beginning in April 2008—on Earth Day—the company eliminated disposable plastic shopping bags from its stores in favor of reusable bags and those made of recycled paper.

For all the successes of such companies, however, for years there seemed to be a perception that they were unusual or unconventional—singular exceptions to the prevalent corporate mold that stresses bottom-line financial performance above social agendas. In recent years, though, growing numbers of conventional businesses have opted to adopt greener practices, undoubtedly for many of the same benefits of having greener Data Centers.

If you need any more convincing about the business value in going green, consider some of the activities that some major companies in the financial, technology, and retail markets are pursuing, as outlined in the following sections.

Note   Each of the companies highlighted here regularly place among *Fortune* magazine's Global 500, which annually ranks the world's largest corporations by revenue. Although it would be exaggerating to claim that their green efforts—or green Data Centers—fostered their financial successes, it's telling that these companies choose to go green. Large, successful corporations tend to be focused on doing things that make excellent business sense.

Financial Institutions

Banks are intrinsically conservative, and there are probably no companies more focused on the fiscal implications of various business practices. It's therefore probably safe to assume that any efforts on their parts to be greener can be taken as an implicit endorsement that doing so makes financial sense.

For instance, Bank of America Corp. in 2007 announced a $20 billion, 10-year initiative to promote environmentally sustainable business practices and low-carbon technologies. Ken Lewis, chairman and chief executive officer, cited the financial benefits of doing so in a 2008 speech to the North Carolina Emerging Issues Forum:

> "In my mind, this shift in the financial services industry is the ultimate example of doing well by doing good. Our $20 billion initiative isn't charity by any stretch. We expect an attractive risk-adjusted rate of return on this capital. Our initiative is an expression of our belief that the direction of the global economy is changing. And we are backing up that belief with cash."

A 2008 report on the climate change strategies of 40 of the world's largest banks indicated that a growing number of European, U.S., and Japanese banks are focusing on environmental issues, typically by providing greater financing for clean energy projects and climate-related equity research, and setting internal goals to reduce their own greenhouse gases. The report, "Corporate Governance and Climate Change: The Banking Sector," was commissioned by Ceres, a U.S.-based coalition of investors, environmental groups, and other public interest organizations.

Among the report's findings:

- The 40 banks have issued nearly 100 research reports on climate change and related investment and regulatory strategies—more than half of them in 2007. Twenty-three banks referenced climate change in their most-recent annual report to shareholders.

- Twenty-nine of the banks reported their financial support of alternative energy, with eight providing more than $12 billion of direct financing and investments in renewable energy and other clean energy projects.

- Twenty-two of the banks offer climate-related retail products, from preferred-rate green mortgages to climate-focused credit card programs and green car loans.

Citigroup achieved the highest rating among U.S. banks in the Ceres report, and HSBC Group earned the highest rating overall. Each company is pursuing several notable green efforts.

Citigroup

Citigroup announced in 2007 it would devote $50 billion over the next 10 years to green investments, alternative energy, and new technologies. The U.S.-based company has also pledged to reduce greenhouse gas emissions 10 percent by 2011 at its more than 14,000 facilities (compared to 2005).

One of its green projects is a 230,000-square foot (29,729-square meter) Data Center that it brought online in 2008, in Frankfurt, Germany. The facility, which supports Citigroup operations in Europe, the Middle East, and Africa, reportedly consumes only 30 percent of the power of a comparable conventional Data Center, avoids 23.5 million pounds (10,659 metric tons) of carbon dioxide emissions per year, and reduces water consumption for cooling by 13.2 million gallons (50 million liters) per year. It is the first Data Center to ever receive the U.S. Green Building Council's top LEED certification of platinum.

Citigroup was also one of 40 companies to participate in the pilot phase of the U.S. Green Building Council's Portfolio Program, which focuses on integrating green building and operational measures into a company's business practices. Through that program, 3 Citi branch offices were certified as green by 2008 and another 27, bearing the same features, were being reviewed and anticipated to be certified.

The company additionally purchases significant quantities of green power—more than 55 million kWh in 2008 and more than 36 million kWh in 2007.

Citigroup scored 59 points on the Ceres report. (The median score of the 40 banks was 42 out of a possible 100.)

HSBC Group

The London-based HSBC Group became the first major bank to become carbon neutral in 2005, offsetting all carbon dioxide emissions from its facilities and employee travel through a combination of energy reduction measures and the purchase of green electricity and carbon offsets. HSBC spent $11.4 million on carbon offsets, mitigating 4.14 billion pounds (1.88 million metric tons) of carbon dioxide from 2005 to 2007.

HSBC (named after its founding member, The Hong Kong and Shanghai Banking Corporation Limited) in 2007 established the HSBC Climate Partnership, investing $100 million with four environmental charities—The Climate Group, Earthwatch Institute, Smithsonian Tropic Research Institute, and the World Wildlife Fund—to counter the impact of climate change upon people, forests, water, and cities.

HSBC in 2008 also set reduction targets for energy (8 percent), water (11 percent), waste (10 percent), and carbon dioxide (6 percent) to be accomplished by senior executives by 2011 and began using software that automatically shut down computers at the end of the workday, powering down up to 300,000 systems.

HSBC scored 70 points on the Ceres report. The company also received the first-ever FT Sustainable Bank of the Year award in 2006. Created by London's *Financial Times* and the International Finance Corporation, the FT Sustainable Bank awards recognize banks for incorporating social, environmental, and corporate governance objectives into their operations.

Technology Companies

It's no surprise that high-tech companies are embracing green. The products they make are often ideal candidates for implementing efficiency improvements. A computer that consumes less energy, for instance, or a networking device that coordinates building environmental systems to work more efficiently, are model green products.

Note   Each of the technology companies cited in the following sections have authored multiple whitepapers about how to use their hardware and software offerings to be more energy-efficient and environmentally friendly in the Data Center.

Those strategies are not included in the company profiles here, which focus on what the businesses are doing to be greener themselves, but some are covered in Chapter 8, Chapter 9, and Chapter 10, "Greening Other Business Practices."

Cisco

Cisco announced in 2008 that it would reduce its greenhouse gas emissions by 25 percent by 2012 (compared to 2007), saving a projected 1.2 billion pounds (543,000 metric tons) of carbon dioxide. The reductions are to be accomplished through energy-efficient practices in its Data Centers and lab spaces such as server and storage virtualization, by using intelligent network architecture to reduce buildingwide energy usage and optimizing how building floor space is used, and by avoiding business travel through collaboration technologies.

The company has developed and piloted two software programs to improve energy efficiency within its facilities—the Automated Management Power System (AMPS) that powers down lab equipment when not in use and tMon, a web-based monitoring system that alerts when equipment has been left on. Use of the applications conserved 5.86 million kWh of energy in 2008.

Some of the company's internal green efforts include reducing water consumption (using reclaimed water at its California sites saves more than 81 million gallons [306.6 million liters] of water per year), recycling programs, and purchasing green power. The company bought 342 million kWh of green power for its 2008 fiscal year and a projected 484 million kWh for fiscal year 2009, for instance, and at the beginning of 2009 was ranked the seventh largest Fortune 500 purchaser of renewable energy in the United States by the U.S. Environmental Protection Agency.

The company also actively pursues opportunities to use networking technology to help others be greener. For instance, as part of the Clinton Global Initiative in 2006, Cisco allocated $15 million for the Connected Urban Development Program to streamline the flow of people and traffic in urban areas and reduce carbon emissions from cars, trains, buses, and other forms of transportation. The program was initially piloted in Amsterdam, the Netherlands; San Francisco, California; and Seoul, Korea and is now being introduced into several other cities around the world.

Cisco is additionally developing, in partnership with the United States government's National Aeronautics and Space Administration (NASA), an online global monitoring platform, called *Planetary Skin*, to track and analyze worldwide environmental conditions on a near real-time basis. Drawing upon data gathered by satellites and air-, land- and sea-based sensors, the platform is intended to help governments and businesses mitigate climate change and efficiently manage energy and natural resources. Planetary Skin's first pilot project, focusing on preventing the deforestation of tropical rainforests in Africa, Latin America, and Southeast Asia, began in 2009.

Hewlett-Packard Company

Fortune magazine named Hewlett-Packard Company one of its "10 Green Giants" in 2007, praising the hardware maker for its expansive e-waste recycling activities (HP equipment is fully recyclable and the company also accepts any brand of gear for recycling), ensuring that its major suppliers are environmentally sensitive and environmental accountability by way of its comprehensive Global Citizenship Report.

In addition to these efforts, HP has set several environmental reduction targets. By 2010, the company intends to reduce energy consumption and greenhouse gas emissions from its operations and products 25 percent (compared to 2005), reduce water consumption 5 percent (compared to 2007), and recover 2 billion pounds (7.26 million metric tons) of its products.

The company additionally purchased 61.4 million kWh of renewable energy and renewable energy credits in 2007, up from 11 million kWh in 2006.

HP opened a 70,000-square foot (6500-square meter) Data Center in Bangalore, India, in 2007, and anticipates saving 7,500 MWh of energy per year, compared to conventional server environments by automatically adjusting the room's air handlers, fans, and vents based on information from 7,500 sensors distributed throughout the room.

IBM

IBM in 2007 announced a $1 billion per-year initiative, Project Big Green, to increase Data Center energy efficiency, both as a service offering to customers and for its own more than 8 million square feet (743,224 square meters) of hosting space.

The U.S.-based company has also set goals to reduce carbon dioxide emissions associated with energy use 12 percent by 2012 (compared to 2005) through energy conservation, renewable energy, and the purchase of renewable energy certificates. The company purchased 453,000 MWh of renewable energy and renewable energy certificates in 2007—about 9 percent of its global electricity purchases that year. IBM estimates avoiding nearly 6.61 billion pounds (3 million metric tons) of carbon dioxide emissions from 1990 to 2006 through energy conservation efforts.

IBM also promotes programs to reduce employee commuting and estimates that nearly one-third of its 100,000 worldwide employees participates in its work-at-home or mobile employees program. IBM estimates that, in the United States, the work-at-home program saved 8 million gallons (30.3 million liters) of fuel and conserved 135.8 million pounds (61,600 metric tons) of carbon dioxide in 2006.

IBM was the first semiconductor manufacturer to voluntarily set reduction targets for perfluorocompound emissions, which are considered greenhouse gases. (Semiconductor manufacturers use PFCs for etching and cleaning.) In 1998, the company set a goal of a 40 percent emission reduction by 2002 (compared to 1995), which it met. From 2000 to 2005, it cut emissions more than 57 percent, from 1 million pounds (479 metric tons) to 450,000 pounds (204.1 metric tons).

IBM was also the first two-time recipient of the U.S. EPA's Climate Protection Award—first in 1998 and again in 2006.

Retailers

If financial institutions are typically conservative and technology companies are often bold, somewhere in the philosophical middle are retail companies.

Retailers are a key link in the chain through which people consume resources. Food, clothing, household goods, automobiles, and more are readily available for hundreds of millions of people to buy because of retail companies. The argument has been made that by providing products conveniently and inexpensively that major retailers foster the more rapid consumption of resources—the opposite of green. (Imagine if instead of buying an item through your local store that you had to make it yourself. You likely wouldn't consume it so quickly.)

As the middleman between supplier and consumer, though, retailers—especially major ones—are also in a position to influence the behaviors of both consumers and suppliers.

The Home Depot

The Home Depot Foundation in 2007 pledged to provide $400 million in grants in the next 10 years to nonprofit groups to develop 100,000 energy- and water-efficient affordable homes and for planting and preserving 3 million community trees.

The U.S.-based company also budgeted $50 million for internal energy-efficiency projects. With store lighting as its biggest source of energy consumption, the company in 2006 upgraded to more efficient lighting in approximately 600 stores and introduced strict lighting schedules. It also upgraded to more efficient air-conditioning systems in 200 stores. Other improvements have included the use of reflective roof membranes and shorter rooflines, and using low-watt bulbs in all lighting displays.

The Home Depot's largest green impact, though, has come through its influence on suppliers and customers. The company completes an estimated 1.3 billion customer transactions per year. Its Eco Options program highlights products that have less environmental impact than traditional ones, giving customers the ability to be greener in those transactions if they choose to. Eco Options products offer benefits in one or more of five categories:

- Sustainable forestry
- Energy efficiency
- Clean water
- Clean air
- Healthy home

Approximately 3,100 products received the Eco Options designation when the program began in 2007, and the quantity doubled by 2009.

Wal-Mart

Wal-Mart chief executive Lee Scott made news in 2005 when he announced during a speech to employees, *Twenty-First Century Leadership*, that the company's environmental goals were to be supplied 100 percent by renewable energy, to create zero waste, and to sell products that sustain natural resources and the environment.

Although no deadline was given to achieve those goals, the company specifically pledged to spend $500 million per year to double fuel efficiency in Wal-Mart's truck fleet by 2015, reduce greenhouse gases 20 percent by 2012, reduce energy use in Wal-Mart stores 30 percent, and reduce solid waste from U.S. stores by 25 percent by 2008.

In 2008, Wal-Mart met its 2007 Clinton Global Initiative pledge to sell only concentrated liquid laundry detergent in all its U.S. stores and Sam's Club. The change is projected to save more than 400 million gallons (1.51 billion liters) of water, more than 95 million pounds (43,091 metric tons) of plastic resin, and more than 125 million pounds (56,699 metric tons) of cardboard.

Wal-Mart in 2007 announced the start of a program in the United States that would show preference to suppliers who set goals and aggressively reduced their own greenhouse gas emissions. That same year, the company announced the purchase of solar energy to power 22 facilities, reducing greenhouse gas emissions by an estimated 14.3 million to 22 million pounds (6,500 to 10,000 metric tons) per year.

The company in 2006 installed supplemental diesel engines on all its trucks that make overnight trips. Turning off primary truck engines during breaks and using the auxiliary units to warm or cool the cabin and run the communication system is estimated to conserve 10 million gallons (37.9 million liters) of diesel fuel and save 220.5 million pounds (100,000 metric tons) of carbon dioxide.

Wal-Mart announced the goal to reduce packing materials 5 percent by 2013 and becoming "packaging neutral" by 2025. Just the 5 percent reduction is estimated to reduce millions of pounds of trash from reaching landfills and save 1.47 billion pounds (667,000 metric tons) of carbon dioxide.

Summary

A green Data Center is one that, compared to conventional server environments, uses resources more efficiently and has less impact upon people and the environment.

Several conditions today are driving companies to design and operate greener Data Centers:

- Although power consumption within conventional Data Centers is growing dramatically, there is a finite quantity of properties that can be provided with ample megawatts and are also otherwise suitable to house a server environment.

- Green Data Centers are less expensive to operate than others; any extra costs to implement green technologies or materials pay for themselves many times over during the life of the facility.

- The greater efficiencies of a green Data Center extends its power and cooling resources.

- A green Data Center can better meet the targets for reducing energy consumption and carbon dioxide emissions that are now appearing more and more frequently on the agendas of governments around the world.

- New Data Center technology advances naturally provide opportunities to be greener.

- Consumers generally prefer to do business with companies that have green practices, and the Data Center is a prominent forum in which to do so.

Although you can do more to green a Data Center that you own than one you lease, you can still reduce energy consumption at a colocation facility—lowering your bills and increasing your relative capacity—through your hardware choices and operational activities. You can also investigate how efficient and environmentally sensitive various hosting facilities are when you consider which of them to do business with.

Despite the benefits of green Data Centers, some people are hesitant to pursue green technologies because they are reluctant to adopt practices and technologies that they are unfamiliar with; they assume green solutions are too expensive; their company doesn't provide rewards for making a project or facility greener; and they are skeptical that green technologies can provide the benefits they claim.

Several public agencies offer financial incentives for constructing or retrofitting commercial buildings with green features. Many utility companies, in addition to being excellent sources of information for energy-saving strategies, offer rebates for capital projects or hardware purchases that improve energy consumption rates. Many governments meanwhile offer tax breaks for using renewable energy or constructing or upgrading buildings to be energy-efficient.

The business value of building greener facilities and adopting greener operational practices can be seen in the growing number of major corporations that are doing so. Industry leaders across multiple business sectors have adopted green measures including purchasing renewable energy, reducing greenhouse gas emissions, using automation systems to turn off power-consuming items such as lights and personal computers during nonbusiness hours, making charitable donations to environmental causes, and more.

Measuring Green Data Centers

This chapter presents assessment systems used around the world to measure green buildings, formulas for calculating Data Center energy efficiency, and an overview of industry organizations pursuing the development of each. This chapter also offers guidance for putting Data Center metrics in the appropriate context to understand a facility's performance.

Why Measure in the Data Center

There's an often-used management adage that says you can't manage what you don't measure, and it certainly applies to Data Centers.

You not only need to accurately gauge your Data Center's capacity and resources to operate the facility effectively, but you also need to know how quickly you consume those resources and what type and quantity of byproducts the Data Center produces to know how green it is. Taking measurements is also crucial to determine the impact of any green improvements that you make upon the server environment. Without such information you can't know whether those upgrades have been successful, and if so to what extent, how fast their return on investment is, or how to prioritize future Data Center upgrades.

The reason to measure Data Center efficiency might seem obvious, but many companies apparently don't see value in doing so. Surveys of more than 1,500 Data Center owners and operators at DatacenterDynamics conferences in 2008 indicate that fewer than one in three were using a Data Center efficiency metric and fewer than half definitely intended to use them in the future.

Just 461 (30.3 percent) of 1,523 respondents indicated they use a Data Center efficiency metric, according to the Datacenter Research Group that performed the studies, whereas the remaining 1,062 (69.7 percent) reported they did not. When the same group was asked whether they plan to employ efficiency metrics in the future, 642 (42.2 percent) indicated they did whereas 492 (32.3 percent) indicated they did not. The remaining 389 (25.5 percent) did not reply or else indicated that they did not know.

Table 2.1 summarizes the results, broken down by geographic theater. Interestingly, those in the United States appear to be using Data Center metrics most often yet those in Western Europe have the greatest intention to do so in the future.

Table 2.1   *Usage of Data Center Efficiency Metrics*

	United States	Western Europe	Emerging Markets	Total
Number of Respondents	540	792	191	1523
Use a Data Center efficiency metric	225 (41.7%)	177 (22.%)	59 (30.%)	461 (30.3%)
Don't use a Data Center efficiency metric	315 (58.3%)	615 (77.7%)	132 (69.3%)	1062 (69.7%)
Intend to use a Data Center efficiency metric in the future	196 (36.3%)	367 (46.3%)	79 (41.4%)	642 (42.2%)
Do not intend to use a Data Center efficiency metric in the future	190 (35.2%)	249 (31.4%)	53 (27.8%)	492 (32.3%)
Don't know/Did not reply	154 (28.5%)	176 (22.2%)	59 (30.9%)	389 (25.5%)

It's possible that the survey results in Table 2.1 show a greater adoption of Data Center metrics than is truly happening. All the survey participants were, as noted, attendees at Data Center conferences. Companies that commit money and staff time for employees to attend such events are actively seeking Data Center best practices for their facilities. How many more businesses, particularly those with makeshift server environments, aren't sending employees to such conferences and aren't focusing on the efficiency of their facility?

What to Measure in the Data Center

Knowing the importance of taking measurements in your Data Center, what elements are useful to measure to evaluate how green a room is and to quantify the impact of various upgrades? The sections that follow address this question.

Energy Usage

The single-most important resource for you to measure in your Data Center is energy. How much power the facility has and how much power is consumed by both IT equipment and supporting infrastructure such as cooling systems and lighting.

It's vital to measure energy for several reasons:

- **Power is a Data Center's most precious resource:** The small form factor and big energy demands of today's high performance servers mean most Data Centers will run out of power well before cabinet space or cooling. Even if you aren't interested in green considerations, measuring energy usage is critical to understand the true capacity of the room.

- **Power is the common element among disparate Data Center subsystems:** Air handlers, servers, and overhead lighting are all different infrastructure of a Data Center—so different that they're each installed and maintained by personnel that are trained in separate disciplines—yet they all need power to function. Measuring energy consumption creates a common standard by which you can tell how much they're each drawing upon your overall Data Center capacity.

- **Power consumption is the most expensive operational cost of a Data Center:** By measuring the specific energy usage of various Data Center components and applying the regional cost of electricity, you learn the true monthly expense of those components. This enables you to target which Data Center subsystems have the potential to save you the most energy and the most money through efficiency improvements.

- **Power consumption largely defines a Data Center's environmental impact:** The amount of power that a Data Center uses on a day-to-day basis determines how much irreplaceable fossil fuels it consumes and the quantity of carbon emissions it is responsible for.

Because of these four conditions, green Data Center improvements that conserve energy provide some of the largest benefits to your business. Measuring power in your Data Center is, therefore, also the best way to appraise that value and understand the real impact of those green improvements.

Carbon Footprint

Another benchmark of a Data Center's environmental impact is its carbon footprint—the amount of carbon dioxide produced as part of the ongoing operation of the facility.

Carbon dioxide is one of a handful of substances dubbed *greenhouse gases* that trap heat from the sun and warm the Earth. (Water vapor is the most common greenhouse gas, followed by carbon dioxide, methane, nitrous oxide, ozone, and chlorofluorocarbons.)

That warming effect is necessary to a certain degree. Without it, the Earth's mean surface temperature would be –2 degrees Fahrenheit (–19 degrees Celsius) rather than today's 57 degrees Fahrenheit (14 degrees Celsius), according to the Intergovernmental Panel on Climate Change document, "Climate Change 2007: The Physical Science Basis." Too much warming can cause environmental problems, though, changing weather patterns, causing sea levels to rise, and altering the habitats of various animals, plants, and, ultimately, people.

Many scientists and environmentalists today are concerned that human activity is causing such problems, prompting them and various government agencies worldwide to call for reductions in carbon dioxide emissions. Although carbon dioxide occurs naturally—people, animals, and plants all produce it; volcanoes and hot springs emit it as well—carbon is also a byproduct of burning fossil fuels.

More than 80 percent of greenhouse gas emissions in the United States, for example, are energy-related carbon dioxide—originating from the combustion of petroleum, coal, and natural gas—according to the U.S. Department of Energy's Energy Information Administration. (EIA reports of U.S. greenhouse gas emissions are available online for every year since 1996 at http://www.eia.doe.gov/oiaf/1605/ggrpt/index.html.)

The links from energy production to carbon dioxide to climate change mean that the less energy your Data Center uses, the smaller its impact upon the environment.

The other factor in a server environment's carbon footprint is the makeup of the electricity powering the facility. Several sources of energy are used to create electricity, and each generates a different amount of carbon dioxide. Turning coal into electricity produces more carbon dioxide than natural gas, for instance, so your Data Center will have a larger carbon footprint if your regional power company provides electricity derived from coal rather than natural gas. Cleaner energy sources, such as nuclear or hydroelectric power, create minimal amounts of carbon dioxide, so any Data Center powered by those sources, either directly or by way of a utility provider, will have an even smaller carbon footprint.

Carbon Offsets

One strategy for dealing with *carbon emissions* is to employ *carbon offsets*, measures that reduce carbon dioxide. In simple terms, you compensate for the amount of carbon that you (or in this case, your Data Center) generate by sponsoring a project that prevents an equal amount from being created.

Examples of carbon offsets include

- Providing a source of renewable energy, such as biofuels, hydroelectric, solar, or wind power

- Planting trees, which serve as natural carbon sinks

- Capturing and eliminating more potent greenhouse gases, such as methane produced by landfills or pollutants (that is, hydrofluorocarbons or perfluorocarbons) created during industrial processes

Although it's possible to directly introduce carbon-offsetting measures at your Data Center facility—building a wind farm on land that you own, for example—the more common approach is to pay an environmental organization to do the activity.

More information about renewable energy sources and regional electricity mixes is provided in Chapter 4, "Powering Your Way to a Greener Data Center."

Other Data Center Elements

Energy usage and carbon footprint are the features most commonly discussed and measured to determine how green a Data Center is; however, other elements warrant attention as well. Other green details to consider include the following:

- **Generator emissions:** Standby generators, used to keep a Data Center running when commercial power fails, consume fuel when in operation and can emit a range of pollutants including nitrogen oxides, hydrocarbons, carbon monoxide, carbon dioxide, and particulate matter. Knowing the consumption and emissions of your Data Center generators provide greater insight into the facility's environmental impact.

- **Heat waste:** Most strategies regarding Data Center temperatures focus on how to best remove hot server exhaust from the hosting environment yet pay little attention to the ultimate disposition of Data Center heat waste. If your Data Center cooling system is highly efficient and does a superb job of keeping equipment cool but raises temperatures outdoors, how green is it really? Hot building exhaust is blamed for increasing the severity of several undesirable environmental and health problems including air pollution, heat-related illnesses, deteriorated water quality, and increased energy consumption during summer evenings. The phenomenon known as *heat islands* is discussed further in Chapter 3, "Green Design and Build Strategies."

- **Water consumption:** Major Data Centers consume millions of gallons/liters of water per month through standard cooling processes as hot water is vaporized from a Data Center's cooling tower and has to be replaced. (Water used to replace what has evaporated is known as makeup water.) Although this consumption hasn't received the same level of attention from governments and the public in recent years as energy use and carbon emissions, removing such large amounts of water from local supplies is a tremendous environmental impact.

The more of these Data Center elements that you measure, the more opportunities to make your server environment greener that you uncover. Tips on reducing the impact of these features are provided in Chapter 4 and Chapter 5, "Cooling Your Way to a Greener Data Center."

Environmental Building Assessment Systems

The definition of a green Data Center as one that uses resources more efficiently and has less environmental impact is valid as far as it goes, but it comes with a lot of latitude. How much more efficient does a facility need to be before it can be considered green? How much less impact on the environment must it have than a conventional server environment? Five percent? Fifty percent? More?

In its *Seven Sins of Greenwashing* report mentioned in Chapter 1, "Going Green in the Data Center," TerraChoice Environmental Marketing rightly notes that the term *green* is essentially meaningless (and thereby committing its Sin of Vagueness) if not qualified in some manner.

Several environmental building assessment systems have been created in an attempt to quantify and qualify building performance. These assessment systems typically evaluate green features such as energy efficiency, carbon emissions, pollution, water consumption, building material selection, and more. In most assessment systems, a building or building project earns points for features within certain categories and achieves a rating level (for instance, bronze, silver, gold, or platinum) based on the cumulative score. Different assessment programs are popular in various regions of the world. As a group, they offer standards for a range of structures including commercial buildings, residences, schools, prisons, and more. Although these assessment systems were not specifically created to apply to server environments, many Data Center designers and builders look to them as a way to evaluate how green their new projects and existing facilities are. If you have a Data Center or Data Center project in a region where one of these programs is commonly used, consider following their guidelines. Even if your facility doesn't achieve formal certification, all of the building assessment systems generally provide good green principles to follow. Your project can only benefit from considering them.

Several municipalities offer incentives for construction projects that commit to earning a particular rating from whatever environmental building assessment system is prevalent in the area. Typical benefits can include

- Expedited permitting
- Free green building technical assistance
- Fee waivers
- Low interest loans
- Property tax credits

Other governments instead offer disincentives, financially penalizing projects that fail to obtain green building certification.

Note Assuming that building officials aren't requiring you to use a particular environmental building assessment system, there's nothing to stop you from ignoring what is most commonly used in the region in which your Data Center is in favor of another one, but I recommend at least reviewing the local assessment system first. Many of the rating programs reflect the green priorities that are most important in that region.

The building assessment system created and used in a country where droughts occur will stress (and be structured to award points for) water conservation more than a building assessment system developed for a region with ample water, for instance. Even if you don't seek to have your server environment certified under the local program, it's important to understand the value that is placed upon water as you approach your Data Center project.

Building Research Establishment Environmental Assessment Method (BREEAM)

The oldest and most widespread building assessment system is the Building Research Establishment Environmental Assessment Method (BREEAM). The system was created in 1990 by Building Research Establishment, a building research organization originally funded by the United Kingdom government. The organization has since been privatized and is now funded by the building industry.

Of all the building assessment systems, BREEAM has been the most influential. Not only have more than 110,000 buildings been BREEAM certified and more than 500,000 registered through the program, but several other assessment programs favored in various parts of the world also are based to a significant degree on the BREEAM system.

BREEAM is most commonly applied to office buildings and private residences, although standards also exist for schools, industrial buildings, retail facilities, health buildings, court buildings, and prisons. Other structures can also be rated using a customized BREEAM scoring system, known as BREEAM Bespoke.

BREAM assesses building performance according to nine categories:

- **Management:** Site commissioning, contractor issues, and overall policy management

- **Energy use:** Power consumption and carbon emissions, heating and cooling efficiencies and metering

- **Health and well being:** Elements that impact building user comfort and health, such as fresh air ventilation and controls for lighting and temperature

- **Pollution:** Air and water pollution

- **Transport:** Elements to reduce carbon emissions associated with transportation, from the use of local building materials (avoiding the need to ship supplies from far away) to the proximity to public transit to encourage employee usage

- **Land use:** Use of existing facilities rather than undeveloped land, or cleanup of previously contaminated property

- **Ecology:** Ecological conservation or creation of habitat

- **Materials:** Building materials

- **Water:** Water consumption and efficiencies

Buildings are rated on a scale of 1 to 100. Points are awarded for each category, and the total score determines whether a building is rated pass (25 percent), good (40 percent), very good (55 percent), excellent (70 percent), or outstanding (85 percent). The system is designed to measure the environmental impact of a building during its entire lifespan.

Notable amendments were made to BREEAM in 2008. These included changes to the environmental weightings within the system, new benchmarks for carbon dioxide emissions, the addition of minimum requirements for energy and water consumption, and the introduction of the "outstanding" rating level. Building designers can now also receive extra credits for implementing innovative technologies that have environmental benefits.

Also in 2008, a BREEAM certification was awarded for the first time to a Data Center project—a 107,640-square foot (10,000-square meter) Digital Realty Trust facility in suburban London built for financial firm HSBC. The Data Center earned a BREEAM rating of excellent thanks to green design elements ranging from high-efficiency chilled-water cooling and heat recovery systems to the use of solar panels and recycled building materials. More BREEAM certifications for Data Centers can be expected in the future. Having customized its rating criteria for the DRT project, BRE now has it as an ongoing offering under its BREEAM Bespoke category.

You can find more information about BREEAM at www.breeam.org.

Note   Most environmental building assessment systems have different rating criteria for existing facilities than for new construction and for various types of buildings—a commercial office building, a school, and a residential building are all likely evaluated according to different factors, for instance. Unless stated otherwise, the assessment system criteria referenced in this book are for new construction and are office building standards, which—lacking more Data Center-specific standards—are the ones typically considered for a Data Center build.

Green Globes

Green Globes, used in Canada and the United States, is one of the environmental building assessment systems that can be traced back to BREEAM. The Canadian Standards Association published BREEAM Canada for Existing Buildings in 1996, with several new elements and capabilities added since then, most notably the online assessment tool Green Globes for Existing Buildings in 2000.

Environmental impact is rated in seven categories:

- **Energy:** Performance, efficiency, demand reduction, energy efficient features, use of renewable energy, and transportation

- **Indoor environment:** Ventilation, lighting, thermal and acoustical comfort, and ventilation system

- **Site impact:** Ecological impact, development area, watershed features, and enhancement

- **Resources:** Low impact materials, reuse, demolition, durability, and recycling

- **Water:** Performance, conservation, and treatment

- **Emissions and effluents:** Air emissions (boilers), ozone depletion, water and sewer protection, and pollution controls

- **Project management:** Design process, environmental purchasing, and commissioning

Although 1,000 points are conceivably available in the Green Globes system, the actual maximum number that can be achieved vary by project.

A key difference between the Canadian and U.S. versions of Green Globes is in the rating levels used. Buildings in Canada are awarded up to five globes whereas those in the United States are awarded up to four. As shown by Table 2.2, the difference comes from the elimination of the bottom scoring category for U.S. projects.

Table 2.2 *Green Globes Ratings*

Percentage	Canada	United States
85 to 100	Five globes	Four globes
70 to 84	Four globes	Three globes
55 to 69	Three globes	Two globes
35 to 54	Two globes	One globe
15 to 34	One globe	—

In Canada, Green Globes for Existing Buildings is owned and operated by the Building Owners and Managers Association of Canada under the brand name Go Green, whereas other Green Globes products are owned and operated by ECD Energy and Environment Canada. In the United States, Green Globes is owned and operated by the Green Building Initiative.

More information about Green Globes is available for the Canadian version at www.greenglobes.com and for the U.S. version at http://www.thegbi.org/.

Haute Qualité Environmentale (HQE)

Green building standards are defined in France by the Haute Qualité Environmentale (High Environmental Quality) approach. *The Association pour la Haute Qualité Environmentale*, formed in 1996, defines 14 target areas for HQE under four themes:

- **Eco-construction:** Relationship between buildings and immediate surroundings, integrated choice of construction products and methods, and low-nuisance construction processes

- **Eco-management:** Energy management, water management, waste management, and maintenance

- **User comfort:** Humidity, acoustics, visual comfort, and odor control

- **User health:** Indoor air quality, water quality, and sanitary treatment

A formal certification program for HQE was developed in 2002 by Centre Scientifique et Technique du Bâtiment. Its three rankings include the following:

- Basic (pass)

- Performant (high performing)

- Très performant (very high performing)

The program applies to offices, schools, hotels, and commercial centers, and there are plans to expand it to other types of buildings in the future.

More information about HQE is available (in French) at http://www.assohqe.org/.

Hong Kong Building Environmental Assessment Method (HK-BEAM)

The Hong Kong Building Environmental Assessment Method was created in 1996 by the Real Estate Developers Association of Hong Kong, based largely upon BREEAM. Originally applied to just new and existing office buildings, HK-BEAM now addresses a wide range of structures including commercial buildings, residential developments, hotels, apartments, hospitals, and municipal buildings.

New building designs are evaluated according to 19 criteria in 5 categories, with a sixth category of bonus credits available for innovations that provide performance enhancements:

- **Site aspects:** Location and design of the building, emissions from the site, and site management

- **Materials aspects:** Selection of materials, efficient use of materials, and waste disposal and recycling

- **Energy use:** Annual energy use, energy-efficient systems and equipment, and energy management

- **Water use:** Water quality, water conservation, and effluent discharges

- **Indoor environmental quality:** Safety, hygiene, indoor air quality and ventilation, thermal comfort, lighting, acoustics and noise, and building amenities

- **Environmental innovations:** Innovative techniques and performance enhancements

HK-BEAM ratings include bronze (40 percent, above average), silver (55 percent, good), gold (65 percent, very good), and platinum (75 percent, excellent).

More than 150 premises, encompassing 70 million square feet (6.5 million square meters) of floor space, have been submitted for HK-BEAM assessment. That includes more than 36,000 residential units, making it the most widely used system of its kind—on a per capita basis—in the world. The program is currently owned and operated by the not-for-profit HK-BEAM Society.

You can find more information about HK-BEAM at http://www.hk-beam.org.hk.

Ecology, Energy Saving, Waste Reduction, and Health (EEWH)

Taiwan's system for assessing green buildings, developed in 1998 by the Ministry of the Interior's Architecture and Building Research Institute (ABRI), takes its name from its four overall focus areas of ecology, energy saving, waste reduction and health. EEWH rates structures according to nine categories:

- **Biodiversity:** Biological habitat, ecological network, plant diversity, and soil ecology

- **Greenery:** Carbon dioxide absorption factor

- **Soil water content:** Permeability

- **Energy conservation:** Air conditioning, building envelope, and lighting energy efficiency

- **Carbon dioxide emission reductions:** Building material selection and construction methods

- **Construction waste reduction:** Solid waste and particle pollution

- **Indoor environmental quality:** Building acoustic environments, lighting and ventilation environments, and building materials

- **Water conservation:** Water savings and recycling

- **Sewage and garbage:** Landscape design, sewer plumbing, and garbage containment sanitation

EEWH has five levels—certified, bronze, silver, gold, and diamond. To qualify as green, a project must at minimum pass the energy and water conservation indicators and any two of the remaining seven.

The Taiwainese government began offering a Green Building Promotion Program in 2001, subsidizing green remodeling projects and air-conditioning efficiency improvements and ultimately requiring that all new public buildings (receiving more than $1.5 million in government funding) achieve green building certification before being allowed to obtain a building license. The program concluded in 2007, by which time more than 1,400 buildings or building projects had been certified as green.

More information about EEWH is available (in Taiwanese and English) at http://www.cabc.org.tw/ or http://www.abri.gov.tw.

The SB Tool

If your company has sites in more than one country, you're probably thinking that it would be nice to have a universal assessment system rather than distinct methods for different parts of the world. The main challenge to this is that geographic regions often prioritize environmental issues and qualities differently from one another. This is typically due to local environmental conditions, abundance or scarcity of various natural resources, and even social values.

One solution is the Sustainable Building (SB) Tool, a generic framework for rating green buildings and projects created through the Sustainable Building Challenge. Originally known as the Green Building (GB) Tool, the SB Tool software enables users to incorporate as many as 125 rating criteria and to weight key parameters to reflect regional priorities.

The Sustainable Building Challenge (first called the Green Building Challenge) began in 1996 to highlight green building design techniques and enable regions to meaningfully compare green building data. More than 20 countries participate in the Sustainable Building Challenge conferences, which are usually held about every 3 years.

You can find more information about the SB Tool and Sustainable Building Challenge at www.iisbe.org.

Leadership in Energy and Environmental Design (LEED)

The Leadership in Energy and Environmental Design building rating system is in use in several countries around the world and, based upon the number of other assessment systems modeled upon it, is second only to BREEAM in terms of influence.

LEED debuted in the United States in 1998 after 4 years of development, and versions of it are now used in several countries including Canada, China, India, Korea, and Spain. More than 20,000 projects encompassing more than 5 billion square feet (464.5 million square meters) of building projects have been registered, seeking LEED certification.

LEED standards are overseen by the U.S. Green Building Council, with the LEED certification process administered by the Green Building Certification Institute. LEED certifications are applied to a variety of building types including offices, retail and service establishments, institutional buildings (such as libraries, schools, museums, and religious institutions), hotels, and homes.

Adjustments were made to the LEED system in 2009, changing the weighting of various project elements, expanding the scoring system, and introducing new bonus points.

Rating criteria fall into six categories:

- **Sustainable sites:** Site selection, building reuse, alternative transportation measures, protection or restoration of habitat, open space, storm-water design, heat island reduction, and light pollution reduction

- **Water efficiency:** Water use reduction, landscaping, and wastewater technologies

- **Energy and atmosphere:** Energy efficiency, renewable energy, commissioning, refrigerant management, measurement and verification, and green power

- **Materials and resources:** Building reuse, construction waste management, materials reuse, recycled content, regional materials, rapidly renewable materials, and certified wood

- **Indoor environmental quality:** Outdoor air delivery monitoring, ventilation, indoor air quality management planning, low-emitting materials, exposure to indoor pollutants, lighting, thermal comfort, and day lighting

- **Innovation and design:** Exceptional or innovative performance

LEED allows for a degree of customization based upon geography, awarding bonus points for projects that provide "regionally important benefit."

All together, projects can earn up to 110 points. Rating levels include certified (40 points), silver (50 points), gold (60 points), and platinum (80 points).

You can find more information about LEED at http://www.leedbuilding.org/ or http://www.usgbc.org.

LEED Certified Data Centers

Of all the environmental building assessment systems in the world, none has drawn more attention from the Data Center industry than LEED.

Mortgage provider Fannie Mae's Urbana Technology Center, a 247,000-square feet (22,947-square meter) facility in Urbana, Maryland, that includes both server environment and office space was the first Data Center to receive LEED certification. It earned the distinction in 2005 through an energy-efficient design, use of recycled materials and low emission paints and carpeting, sustainable landscaping elements, construction waste recycling, and other green features.

Per the U.S. Green Building Council, at the time of this book's publication, only five Data Centers have received LEED certification, while more than 32 Data Center projects are registered with the intention of becoming LEED-rated upon their completion. More Data Center projects will undoubtedly seek LEED status in the future. For instance, Cisco has five Data Center projects in various stages of planning and design as of this writing, and the charter documents of each project call for achieving LEED certification.

Most server environments that are LEED-rated or registered to become so are part of mixed-use facilities. That's because LEED—as with all general-purpose environmental building assessment systems—can be an awkward fit for standalone Data Centers, awarding points for features that are pertinent for office spaces but not server environments, while not addressing other Data Center characteristics that have major environmental impact.

Interest in having a LEED certification that better addresses Data Center issues is so high that a list of rating criteria has been submitted to the U.S. Green Building Council in hopes the organization will create a formal "LEED for Data Centers" standard, addressing new

continues

continued

Data Center construction. The California Energy Commission funded development of the criteria list by Lawrence Berkeley National Labs (LBNL), which in turn created it with input from Data Center industry groups including the 7 x 24 Exchange, the American Society of Heating, Refrigeration and Air Conditioning Engineers (ASHRAE), the Critical Facilities Round Table, The Green Grid, the Silicon Valley Leadership Group, and the Uptime Institute, and Data Center technology companies including Cisco, Emerson Network Power, Google, Hewlett-Packard, IBM, Intel, NetApp, Sun Microsystems, and Yahoo.

As proposed by LBNL and others, the Data Center rating criteria would eliminate traditional LEED credits for alternate transportation measures (bike racks and shower facilities), certain renewable building materials (such as sustainably certifiable wood), and indoor environmental quality measures (such as ventilation, thermal comfort, and daylighting). It would instead offer new credits for mitigating generator and cooling tower noise, reducing water usage, and measuring and reporting Data Center energy efficiency.

Although no specific timeline is in place, U.S. Green Building Council representatives say they do intend to establish specific credits for Data Center projects—perhaps as early as 2010. At press time, the USGBC is developing a working group to pursue the issue. LBNL has meanwhile begun development work on a second set of suggested environmental criteria for LEED that would pertain to existing Data Centers.

National Australian Built Environment Rating System (NABERS)

Although some building assessment systems evaluate efficiency based upon a project's proposed design, the National Australian Built Environment Rating System (NABERS) measures the operational performance of existing buildings.

Introduced in 2001 by the Australian government's Department of Environment and Heritage, NABERS is now managed by the Department of Energy Utilities Sustainability NSW Government.

NABERS evaluates the building's impact upon the broader environment, upon building occupants, and upon the surrounding area, based upon four categories:

- **Energy:** Energy efficiency, greenhouse gas emissions, and renewable energy usage
- **Water:** Water reuse and water consumption per person
- **Waste:** Waste reduction measures
- **Indoor environment:** Acoustic comfort, air quality, thermal comfort, and lighting

Additional NABERS categories that have either been used on a trial basis or are planned for later development include refrigerants, storm-water runoff and pollution, sewage, landscape diversity, transport, and occupant satisfaction.

Buildings are awarded one (poor), two (below average), three (above average), four (excellent), or five (exceptional) stars. A score of 2.5 is considered the median. Ratings are based on a building's performance data for the prior 12 months.

NABERS initially focused on office buildings, homes, and hotels but has since developed ratings for stores, schools, and hospitals. In 2008 NABERS also incorporated the

Australian Building Greenhouse Rating system, which focuses on greenhouse gas emissions and used a similar five-star rating scheme.

You can find more information about NABERS at www.nabers.com.au.

Comprehensive Assessment System for Building Environmental Efficiency (CASBEE)

The Japan Sustainable Building Consortium promotes green building design and upgrades through the use of the Comprehensive Assessment System for Building Environmental Efficiency (CASBEE), which it introduced in 2002.

CASBEE is predominantly used in Japan and other parts of Asia. Some local governments now require property owners to include a CASBEE assessment of their building, which the municipality uses to report on sustainable buildings. Some cities have additionally introduced localized versions of CASBEE, customized to reflect local environmental factors or priorities.

CASBEE focuses on four categories: energy efficiency, resource efficiency, local environment, and indoor environment. As part of a CASBEE assessment a building site receives two separate evaluations. One is the building's environmental quality and performance, which encompasses

- **Indoor environment:** Noise and acoustics, thermal comfort, lighting and illumination, and air quality

- **Quality of service:** Service ability, durability and reliability, flexibility, and adaptability

- **Outdoor environment on site:** Biological environment, townscape and landscape, and land characteristics and outdoor amenity

This rating (Q) addresses the conditions for those residing within the building property. The other is the building's environmental loading, which includes

- **Energy:** Building thermal load, natural energy utilization, efficiency in building service system, and efficient operation

- **Resources and materials:** Water resources, reduction of nonrenewable material use, and materials with low health risks

- **Off-site environment:** Global warming, local environment, and surrounding environment

This rating (L) evaluates the environmental impact of the site upon those outside its boundaries.

A building's energy-efficiency score (the BEE in CASBEE) is then calculated by dividing the building's environmental quality and performance (Q) by the building's environmental loadings (L):

$$\text{Building Environmental Efficiency (BEE)} = \frac{Q \text{ (Building environmental quality and performance)}}{L \text{ (Building environmental loadings)}}$$

Higher scores are achieved by having the most favorable conditions within the building site while having the least environmental impact upon those beyond the site. Buildings receive one of five classes, C (poor), B−, B+, A, and S (excellent).

You can find more information about CASBEE (in Japanese) at www.ibec.or.jp/CASBEE/ or (in English) at www.ibec.or.jp/CASBEE/english/index.htm.

Green Star

Green Star, launched in 2003 and overseen by the Green Building Council of Australia, is a second environmental building rating system used in that country. Where NABERS evaluates the operational performance of existing buildings, Green Star focuses on the design and management processes.

Green Star rating tools are available for several building types, including commercial offices, shopping centers, health-care facilities, multi-unit residential buildings, and schools. Nine criteria are used to rate projects:

- **Management:** Credits address the adoption of sustainable development principles from project conception through design, construction, commissioning, tuning, and operation.

- **Indoor environmental quality:** Credits target environmental impact along with occupant well-being and performance by addressing the air conditioning system, lighting, occupant comfort, and pollutants.

- **Energy:** Credits target reduction of greenhouse gas emissions from building operation by addressing energy demand reduction, use efficiency, and generation from alternative sources.

- **Transport:** Credits reward the reduction of demand for individual cars by both discouraging car commuting and encouraging use of alternative transportation.

- **Water:** Credits address reduction of potable water through efficient design of building services, water reuse, and substitution with other water sources (specifically rainwater).

- **Materials:** Credits target resource consumption through material selection, reuse initiatives, and efficient management practices.

- **Land use and ecology:** Credits address a project's impact on its immediate ecosystem by discouraging degradation and encouraging restoration of flora and fauna.

- **Emissions:** Credits address point source pollution from buildings and building services to the atmosphere, watercourse, and local ecosystems.

- **Innovation:** Green Star seeks to reward marketplace innovation that fosters the industry's transition to sustainable building.

Projects are awarded one through six stars, although the Green Building Council of Australia only certifies buildings that achieve four (best practice), five (Australian excellence), or six (world leadership) stars. Scoring thresholds are one star (10 points), two stars

(20 points), three stars (30 points), four stars (45 points), five stars (60 points), and six stars (75 points). The Green Star scoring of up to 100 points includes environmental weighting factors that differ among Australia's states and territories.

You can find more information about Green Star at http://www.gbcaus.org/au/green-star/.

Green Mark

Singapore's Building and Construction Authority initiated its Green Mark rating system in 2005 to evaluate the environmental impact and performance of new and existing buildings.

Rating criteria include

- **Energy efficiency:** Air conditioning, building envelope, lighting, ventilation, and use of renewable energy

- **Water efficiency:** Water-efficient fittings, water usage and leak detection, irrigation system, and water consumption of cooling tower

- **Environmental protection:** Sustainable construction, greenery, environmental management practice, public transport accessibility, and refrigerants

- **Indoor environmental quality:** Thermal comfort, noise level, indoor air pollutants, and high frequency ballasts

- **Environmental innovations:** Green features and innovations

Projects are scored on a 100-point scale, with four Green Mark ranking levels: certified (50 points), gold (75 points), gold-plus (85 points), and platinum (90 points).

As of 2007, all new public buildings and those undergoing major retrofitting in Singapore have been required to be Green Mark-certified. Singapore additionally offers financial incentives for building projects to be green-certified, setting aside approximately $13 million (20 million Singapore dollars) for 3 years under its Green Mark Incentive Scheme to provide cash incentives of up to 3 million Singapore dollars per building and 100,000 Singapore dollars for engineers and architects to achieve at least a Green Mark Gold rating.

You can find more information about Green Mark at http://www.bca.gov.sg or www.greenmark.sg.

Comprehensive Environmental Performance Assessment Scheme (CEPAS)

HK-BEAM isn't the only building assessment system in use in Hong Kong. The Hong Kong government's Building Department launched a new rating system in 2005, the Comprehensive Environmental Performance Assessment Scheme (CEPAS).

CEPAS evaluates building designs according to 34 criteria in eight categories:

- **Indoor environmental quality:** Health and hygiene, indoor air quality, noise and acoustic environment, and lighting environment

- **Building amenities:** Safety, management, controllability, serviceability, adaptability, and living quality

- **Resources use:** Energy consumption, energy efficiency, use of renewable energy, water conservation, timber use, material use, and building reuse

- **Loadings:** Pollution and waste management

- **Site amenities:** Landscape, cultural character, building economics, and security

- **Neighborhood amenities:** Provisions for the community, transportation, and sustainability economics

- **Site impacts:** Site environment, nature conservation, heritage conservation, and buildability

- **Neighborhood impacts:** Environmental impact assessment, environmental interactions, and impacts to communities

Ratings include unclassified, bronze, silver, gold, and platinum. Certifications are valid for 5 years.

You can find more information about CEPAS (in Chinese) at http://www.bd.gov.hk/chineseT/documents/index_CEPAS.html and (in English) at http://www.bd.gov.hk/english/documents/index_CEPAS.html.

German Sustainable Building Certificate

Germany began awarding green certifications to buildings in 2008, using criteria developed by the German Sustainability Council (the Deutsche Gesellschaft für Nachhaltiges Bauen or DGNB) and the German Federal Ministry of Transport, Building and Urban Affairs (the Bundesministerium für Verkehr, Bau und Stadtentwicklung or BMVBS)

Unlike other building assessment systems, the German Sustainable Building Certificate focuses not only on environmental impacts but also on economic performance, socio-cultural aspects, and functional aspects of buildings.

DGNB criteria fall into six categories:

- **Ecological quality:** Global warming potential, ozone depletion potential, photochemical ozone creation potential, acidification potential, eutrophication potential, risks to the regional environment, other impacts to the global environment, microclimate, nonrenewable primary energy demands, total primary energy demands and proportion of renewable primary energy, potable water consumption and sewage generation, and surface area usage

- **Economical quality:** Building-related lifecycle costs and value stability

- **Socio-cultural and functional quality:** Thermal comfort, indoor hygiene, acoustical comfort, visual comfort, influences by users, roof design, safety and risks of failure, barrier free accessibility, area efficiency, feasibility of conversion, accessibility, bicycle comfort, assurance of the quality of design and for urban development for competition, and art within architecture

- **Technical quality:** Fire protection, noise protection, energetic and moisture proofing quality of the building's shell, ease of cleaning and maintenance of the structure, and ease of deconstruction, recycling, and dismantling

- **Process quality:** Quality of the project's preparation, integral planning, optimization and complexity of the approach to planning, evidence of sustainability considerations during bid invitation and awarding, establishment of preconditions for optimized use and operation, construction site and phase, quality of executing companies and pre-qualifications, quality assurance of the construction activities, and systematic commissioning

- **Quality of the location:** Risks at the microlocation, circumstances at the microlocation, image and condition of the location and neighborhood, connection to transportation, vicinity to usage-specific facilities, and adjoining media, and infrastructure development

Certain criteria are weighted more heavily than others. Scores from the first five categories, from which a maximum of 855 points can be earned, determine a project's rating of bronze (50 percent), silver (65 percent), or gold (80 percent). Projects are alternatively given grades of 5.0 (20 percent), 4.0 (35 percent), 3.0 (50 percent), 2.0 (65 percent), 1.5 (80 percent), or 1.0 (95 percent). The certificate's sixth category, location, is listed separately from a project's rating, as a percentage of a total possible 130 points.

Certification was originally applied to only office and administrative buildings but has since been expanded to other types of construction.

You can find more information about DGNB (in German) at www.dgnb.de/.

Summary of Environmental Building Assessment Systems

Table 2.3 summarizes, in alphabetical order, green building assessment systems in use around the world.

Note While building assessment systems are valuable for setting green targets for building owners, designers, and construction personnel to aspire to, they are sometimes an awkward fit for Data Centers. Consider two of the LEED credits suggested for removal by LBNL and others in order to create a Data Center-specific certification, for instance, daylighting and alternative transportation. If a structure is a fully dedicated Data Center building, containing no general office space, the physical security needs of the server environment are going to preclude the presence of skylights or windows bringing outdoor light inside, thereby eliminating the chance of earning daylighting credits. Meanwhile, supporting alternate transportation by providing secure bike racks and shower and changing facilities is admirable, but it's not a very good indicator of whether a Data Center is green.

Although such mismatches don't make it impossible to achieve a green certification—as proven by the Data Centers that have secured LEED ratings—don't lose sight of your ultimate goal in the design of your green Data Center. Don't chase points in any assessment system by introducing design or operational elements that don't benefit your Data Center. Likewise, don't avoid useful measures just because they won't earn points.

Table 2.3   *Building Assessment System Criteria and Ratings*

System	BREEAM	CASBEE	CEPAS	EEWH	German Sustainable Building Certificate	Green Globes
Countries	UK, others	Japan	Hong Kong	Taiwan	Germany	Canada, U.S.
Year Introduced	1990	2002	2005	1998	2008	1996 (BREEAM Canada)
Criteria	Management Energy use Health and well-being Pollution Transport Land use Ecology Materials Water	Q (Environmental Quality) Indoor environment Quality of service On-site outdoor environment L (Environmental loading) Energy Resources and materials Off-site environment	Indoor environmental quality Building amenities Resources use Loadings Site amenities Neighborhood amenities Site impacts Neighborhood impacts	Biodiversity Greenery Soil water content Energy conservation Carbon emission reductions Construction waste reduction Indoor environmental quality Water conservation Sewage and garbage	Ecological quality Economical quality Social quality Technical quality Quality of the process Quality of the location	Energy Indoor environment Site impact Resources Water Emissions and effluents Project management
Ratings	Pass Good Very good Excellent Outstanding	C (poor) B B+ A S (excellent)	Unclassified Bronze Silver Gold Platinum	Certified Bronze Silver Gold Diamond	Bronze Silver Gold	One globe Two globes Three globes Four globes (U.S. maximum) Five globes (Canada maximum)

System	Green Mark	Green Star	HQE	HK-BEAM	LEED	NABERS
Countries	**Singapore**	**Australia**	**France**	**Hong Kong**	**U.S., others**	**Australia**
Year Introduced	2005	2003	1996	1996	1998	2001
Criteria	Energy efficiency Water efficiency Environmental protection Indoor environmental quality Environmental innovations	Management Indoor environmental quality Energy Transport Water Materials Land use and ecology Emissions Innovation	Relationship between buildings and immediate surroundings Integrated choice of construction products and methods Low-nuisance construction processes Energy management Water management Waste management and maintenance Humidity Acoustics Visual comfort Odor control Indoor air quality Water quality Sanitary treatment	Site aspects Materials aspects Energy aspects Water aspects Indoor environmental quality Environmental innovations	Sustainable sites Water efficiency Energy and atmosphere Materials and resources Indoor environmental quality Innovation and design process Regional bonus credits	Energy Water waste Indoor environment

continues

Table 2.3   *Building Assessment System Criteria and Ratings   (continued)*

System	Green Mark	Green Star	HQE	HK-BEAM	LEED	NABERS
Countries	**Singapore**	**Australia**	**France**	**Hong Kong**	**U.S., others**	**Australia**
Ratings	Certified Gold Gold-plus Platinum	One stars Two stars Three stars Four stars (best practice) Five stars (Australian excellence) Six stars (World leadership)	Base (basic) Performant (high performing) Très performant (very high performing)	Bronze Silver Gold Platinum	Certified Silver Gold Platinum	One star (poor) Two stars (good) Three stars (very good) Four stars (excellent) Five stars (exceptional)

Organizations Influencing Green Data Center Metrics

Although environmental building assessment systems don't typically focus upon server environments, a handful of organizations are actively developing or promoting Data Center-specific metrics to pinpoint how green these facilities are.

Keep an eye on their activities and published works to stay current on what metrics are prominent in the industry today or might be coming in the future. The sections that follow cover the most notable agencies and their influential green activities. A broader list of entities that are doing work relevant to the design and operation of a green Data Center is provided in the Appendix, "Sources of Data Center Green Information."

The European Commission

The European Union is ahead of most other regions of the world with its focus on energy efficiency, reducing greenhouse gas emissions, and other environmental concerns. As mentioned in Chapter 1, the European Commission has developed a voluntary Data Center Code of Conduct to promote Data Center energy efficiency, passed an EU Energy Performance Building Directive, adopted an Eco-design Directive for Energy Using Products, and set energy and carbon emission reduction goals for its member countries.

The Commission, which is the executive branch of the EU, has also formulated individual Codes of Conduct pertaining to the electrical efficiency of broadband equipment, digital television equipment, power supplies of electronic and electrical appliances, and UPS systems.

Additional environmental directives from the European Commission, whether in the form of legal mandates or voluntary programs, will undoubtedly follow in the future with some influencing the Data Center industry.

You can find more information about the European Commission's environmental legislation (in multiple languages) at http://ec.europa.eu/environment/index.htm.

The Green Grid

The Green Grid is a global consortium of companies focused upon Data Center energy efficiency. Launched in 2007, the group's more than 150 members include a broad range of Data Center hardware and software manufacturers. (Cisco is one of them.)

The group's stated goals and activities are

- Defining meaningful, user-centric models and metrics

- Developing standards, measurement methods, processes, and new technologies to improve performance against the defined metrics

- Promoting the adoption of energy-efficient standards processes, measurements, and technologies

The group has issued several whitepapers on Data Center energy efficiency metrics—including power usage effectiveness (PUE) and Data Center infrastructure efficiency (DCIE), detailed elsewhere in this chapter.

At press time, the Green Grid's board of directors includes Advanced Micro Devices (AMD), American Power Conversion (APC), Dell, EMC, Hewlett-Packard (HP), IBM, Intel, Microsoft, and Sun Microsystems.

You can find more information on the Green Grid (in English) at http://www.thegreengrid.org/home or (in Japanese) at http://www.thegreengrid.org/japanese/home.

Uptime Institute

The Uptime Institute is a prominent Data Center education and consulting organization best known for its widely adopted Data Center tier classification system. Launched in 1993, the organization's Site Uptime Network includes more than 100-member companies that share operational and design best practices based upon their real-world experience. (Cisco has been an Uptime participant since 2001, and an official member since 2003.)

Much like the Data Center industry as a whole, the Uptime Institute originally concentrated on Data Center availability, but in recent years has devoted attention to energy efficiency and environmental considerations. The organization regularly hosts seminars and has authored several whitepapers on green Data Center topics. In 2008, the Uptime

Institute also launched a Green Enterprise IT Awards program to recognize Data Center energy efficiencies by companies.

You can find more information about the Uptime Institute at http://www.uptimeinstitute.org/.

The U.S. Environmental Protection Agency

The U.S. Environmental Protection Agency has focused on environmental consideration and energy efficiency for decades and in recent years has turned attention to the Data Center industry. The EPA is currently in the midst of creating a series of energy-efficiency standards for Data Center facilities and the hardware housed within them under its Energy Star label.

The Energy Star program, begun in 1992 to highlight energy efficient products, was initially applied to computers and monitors and later expanded—involving participation from the U.S. Department of Energy and applying to office equipment, major appliances, lighting, home electronics, new homes, commercial and industrial buildings, and more.

At press time, the EPA is gathering data on energy use and operating characteristics from dozens of server environments, both standalone facilities and those in mixed-use buildings, to develop the Energy Star rating for Data Centers. More than 60 companies have shared information on approximately 120 Data Centers, including geographic location (to determine climate influences), function, assumed reliability (using the Uptime Institute's tier classification system), and a year's worth of data on IT power consumption and total facility energy usage.

The EPA rating methodology for Data Centers will be similar to that of its building program, scoring facilities on a 100-point scale and giving the Energy Star designation to those that achieve at least 75 points. A building's energy performance is compared to equivalent structures across the United States—not other facilities in the program—and each point represents a percentile of performance. The system is to be applicable for both Data Center-only and mixed-use buildings.

Note   Cisco contributed information from two of its Data Centers for the Energy Star program—a Tier II, 10,000-square foot (929-square meter) facility in Mountain View, California, and a Tier III, 30,000-square foot (2,787-square meter) facility in Richardson, Texas.

By 2008, the energy performance of more than 62,000 buildings were tracked by the Energy Star's online Portfolio Manager tool, and more than 4,000 had been awarded the Energy Star label, with those structures typically using 35 percent less energy than average buildings. The EPA intends to add a Data Center Infrastructure Rating to the Portfolio Manager tool by 2010. Chapter 8, "Choosing Greener Gear," provides details on the Energy Star standard for servers that was issued in 2009, and efforts to develop future standards for storage devices and networking hardware. You can find more information about all of the Data Center-related Energy Star programs at www.energystar.gov/datacenters.

Data Center Green Metrics

Data Center managers have long desired a way to accurately, yet simply, capture the efficiency of their server environments. In essence, how green the rooms are. Often compared to the miles-per-gallon ratings given to automobiles sold in the United States, Data Center efficiency metrics help both IT and Facilities personnel to better understand the performance of their server environment.

Data Center metrics are by and large still evolving. Even those that are the most widely used today are relatively young, introduced only a handful of years ago. New formulas continue to be developed and proposed every few years, most often by Data Center industry groups or technology consulting firms, whereas existing metrics are refined and clarified by their authors on an ongoing basis. The sections that follow outline metrics that capture key Data Center efficiency and environmental characteristics and are worthy candidates to consider using for your server environment.

Power Usage Effectiveness (PUE)

The Data Center metric enjoying the most widespread use these days is Power Usage Effectiveness (PUE), which gauges the electrical efficiency of a server environment by focusing on its electrical overhead.

Created by members of The Green Grid in 2006, PUE divides a facility's total power draw by the amount of power used solely by the Data Center's IT equipment:

$$\text{Power Usage Effectiveness (PUE)} = \frac{\text{Total Facility Power}}{\text{IT Equipment Power}}$$

IT equipment power includes that which is consumed by servers, networking devices, storage units, and peripheral items such as monitors or workstation machines—any equipment used to manage, process, store, or route data in the Data Center.

Total facility power includes that IT equipment plus all Data Center-related primary electrical systems (power distribution units, and electrical switching gear), standby power systems (uninterruptible power sources [UPS]), air-conditioning components (chillers, air handlers, water pumps, and cooling towers), and other infrastructure such as lighting and keyboard, video, and mouse (KVM) equipment.

The lower a Data Center's PUE, the more efficient it is considered to be. That's because a lower PUE indicates that a greater portion of the power going to a Data Center is used for its essential mission—processing and storing information. For example, a PUE of 1.5 means a Data Center needs half-again as much power to operate as is solely needed for the IT equipment whereas a PUE of 3.0 means a Data Center needs twice as much additional power for non-IT elements as it does for IT hardware.

A perfect (and in reality, unattainable) PUE score is 1.0, which represents a server environment in which all the power provided to it is used by IT equipment.

When calculated, PUE can be applied down to the level of a single machine. If a server draws 500 watts and the Data Center's PUE is 1.5, for instance, the room will draw 750 watts to power the machine. Put that same server in a Data Center with a PUE of 3.0, and the room will draw 1,500 watts to power it.

Opinions differ regarding what is a typical Data Center PUE rating. Various Data Center industry groups have suggested 2.0, 2.5, or even 3.0 are common ratings.

Although PUE is sometimes discussed as a static number for a Data Center, it actually varies over time—even during a span as brief as a few hours. Server loads change throughout the day. The rise and fall of external temperatures can also influence how hard a Data Center's cooling system must work—and therefore how much energy it consumes—to regulate the room's temperatures. The IT equipment power profile of a Data Center also changes over time as new devices replace older systems.

Sample PUE Calculations

The following are PUE measurements for two sample Data Centers:

Data Center A actively draws 7,500 kW of total power. Of that, 3,100 kW are consumed by its IT equipment. That facility has a PUE score of 2.4:

Total Facility Power = 7,500 kW

IT Equipment Power = 3,100 kW

7500 / 3100 = 2.4 PUE

Data Center B draws 12,250 kw of total power. Of that, 6,700 kw are consumed by its IT equipment. That facility has a PUE score of 1.8:

Total Facility Power = 12,250 kW

IT Equipment Power = 6,700 kW

12250 / 6700 = 1.8 PUE

Although Data Center B consumes more energy than Data Center A—12,250 kW compared to 7,500 kW—on a proportional basis more of its power goes to IT gear, so from that perspective it is considered more efficient.

Data Center Infrastructure Efficiency (DCIE)

A second metric regarding Data Center electrical efficiency is Data Center Infrastructure Efficiency (DCIE). DCIE is the reciprocal of PUE: The same values are used, but their positions in the formula are inverted. IT equipment power is divided by total facility power. (If you've already calculated PUE, you can also determine DCIE by dividing 1 by the PUE value.) DCIE is expressed as a percentage:

$$\text{Data Center Infrastructure Efficiency (DCIE)} = \frac{\text{IT Equipment Power}}{\text{Total Facility Power}}$$

Because DCIE and PUE involve the same data, they're just different ways to look at the same information. For example, a Data Center with a PUE of 1.5 has a DCIE of 66 percent (1 / 1.5 = 66 percent). PUE highlights that it takes half-again as much power to operate the Data Center as is needed by its IT equipment. DCIE illustrates that two-thirds (66 percent) of the Data Center power is consumed by the IT equipment.

Note   Data Center Infrastructure Efficiency was originally known as just Data Center Efficiency or DCE. The Green Grid, which advocates use of the metric and PUE, added the word infrastructure to clear up what it considered misunderstandings over the term Data Center Efficiency. The metric itself did not change.

Although PUE is more commonly used today, some people prefer DCIE because Data Centers with greater electrical efficiency achieve a higher score than less efficient facilities rather than scoring lower, as happens with PUE.

Sample DCIE Calculations

Continuing with the two sample Data Centers used to illustrate PUE, the following are their PUE and DCIE percentages:

As before, Data Center A draws 7,500 kW of total power. Of that, 3,100 kW are consumed by its IT equipment. That facility has a PUE score of 2.4 and a DCIE score of 41.33 percent:

Total Facility Power = 7,500 kW

IT Equipment Power = 3,100 kW

7500 / 3100 = 2.4 PUE

3100 / 7500 = 41.33 percent DCIE

As before, Data Center B draws 12,250 kw of total power. Of that, 6,700 kw are consumed by its IT equipment. That facility has a PUE score of 1.8 and a DCIE score of 54.69 percent:

Total Facility Power = 12,250 kW

IT Equipment Power = 6,700 kW

12250 / 6700 = 1.8 PUE

6700 / 12250 = 54.69 percent DCIE

One quirk of PUE and DCIE is that a Data Center's score can potentially suffer if you implement efficiency measures that reduce the power drawn by your IT equipment.

For instance, say that in Data Center A you consolidate servers by way of a significant virtualization project—discussed in Chapter 9, "Greening Your Data Center Through Consolidation, Virtualization, and Automation"—and in doing so you reduce your server power usage by 300 kW. That adjusts the IT equipment power load in Data Center A from 3,100 kW to 2,800 kW—a 9.7 percent reduction. If the building's facility infrastructure is closely aligned to the IT load and scales with it, it could conceivably see a similar 9.7-percent reduction in total facility power consumption, saving 726 kW and maintaining the Data Center's PUE and DCIE scores at 2.4. It's just as likely, though, that the facility infrastructure isn't in exact step with the IT demand, so the total facility power won't be reduced as much. Say that removal of 300 kW in IT equipment power equates to just 450 kW in total facility power load savings (a 6-percent gain rather than 9.7 percent), reducing it from 7,500 to 7,050 kW. This worsens its PUE from 2.4 to 2.5 and its DCIE from 41.33 percent to 39.72 percent. You've reduced power consumption by the IT equipment by nearly 10 percent (300 kW out of 3,100 kW), but your efficiency metrics look worse.

Tip   Just as you shouldn't chase points offered in an environmental building assessment system by adding design elements that don't truly make your Data Center greener, don't let a desire for impressive Data Center metrics deter you from optimizing the power consumption of your IT equipment. You want your Data Center to be as green and slim on energy usage as possible even if building assessment systems and power-efficiency formulas can't reflect it.

Assessment systems and metrics will undoubtedly be developed in the future that showcase those efficiencies. Until then, you can always document the energy you are saving around your IT equipment and include it as a footnote to your PUE and DCIE numbers.

Data Center Energy Profiler

As part of its Save Energy Now program, the U.S. Department of Energy offers an online tool to help assess Data Center energy efficiency. Known as the Data Center Energy Profiler (DC Pro), the application defines a server environment's energy usage based upon information provided by the user and offers design and operational tips for improving efficiency.

Users answer more than 80 questions about the design and operations of their Data Center ranging from physical size, geographic location, and level of redundant electrical infrastructure to details about server lifecycles, use of virtualization, and air-conditioning set points. The tool uses the data to calculate a DCIE score for the server environment and then suggests measures to improve the rating.

The Department of Energy hopes to have thousands of Data Centers assessed by DC Pro and—by following the tool's recommendations—for 1,500 facilities to improve their energy efficiency by an average 25 percent by 2011 and 200 to improve their energy efficiency by an average 50 percent.

DC Pro was developed with contributions from Lawrence Berkeley National Laboratory (LBNL), Ancis Inc., EYP Mission Critical, Rumsey Engineers, Taylor Engineering, and Project Performance Corporation.

You can find more information about the Data Center Energy Profiler at www.eere.energy.gov/datacenters.

Compute Power Efficiency (CPE)

Another approach to evaluating a Data Center's performance is to calculate its electrical overhead and then factor in the average CPU utilization of the servers it houses. Known as Compute Power Efficiency (CPE), this metric was first introduced in 2007:

$$\text{Compute Power Efficiency (CPE)} = \frac{\text{IT Equipment Utilization} \times \text{IT Equipment Power}}{\text{Total Facility Power}}$$

CPE builds off of PUE, so it's no surprise that it was also created by members of The Green Grid. In fact, if you know a Data Center's PUE score, you can divide the average IT equipment utilization by that score as another way to calculate its CPE. Because PUE scores are typically rounded off at one number past the decimal place, CPE and other metrics that incorporate PUE are more precise when you use the original IT equipment and total facility power figures rather than the PUE score itself.

Sample CPE Calculations

The following are the PUE, DCIE, and CPE metrics for the two sample Data Centers mentioned previously:

As before, Data Center A draws 7,500 kW of total power. Of that, 3,100 kW are consumed by its IT equipment. CPU utilization for the servers in that Data Center averages 10 percent. That facility has a PUE score of 2.4, a DCIE score of 41.33 percent, and a CPE score of 4.13 percent:

Total Facility Power = 7,500 kW

IT Equipment Power = 3,100 kW

IT Utilization = 10 percent

7500 / 3100 = 2.4 PUE

3100 / 7500 = 41.33 percent DCIE

10 percent × 3100 / 7500 = 4.13 percent CPE

As before, Data Center B draws 12,250 kw of total power. Of that, 6,700 kw are consumed by its IT equipment. CPU utilization for the servers in that Data Center averages 5 percent. That facility has a PUE score of 1.8, a DCIE score of 54.69 percent, and a CPE score of 2.73 percent:

Total Facility Power = 12,250 kW

IT Equipment Power = 6,700 kW

IT Utilization = 5 percent

12250 / 6700 = 1.8 PUE

6700 / 12250 = 54.69 percent DCIE

5 percent × 6700 / 12250 = 2.73 percent CPE

Technology Carbon Efficiency (TCE)

For another look at how green a Data Center is, multiply the room's electrical efficiency by the carbon emissions factor of the energy powering it. Called Technology Carbon Efficiency (TCE), this metric was introduced in 2007 by CS Technology.

As mentioned in the beginning of this chapter, a variety of energy sources are used to produce electricity and the exact electrical mix that comes from your regional power provider influences the carbon footprint of your Data Center. Combining that emissions factor with the server environment's power efficiency shows how many pounds of carbon dioxide are produced for every kilowatt hour of energy delivered to your IT equipment:

$$\text{Technology Carbon Efficiency (TCE)} = \frac{\text{Total Facility Power}}{\text{IT Equipment Power}} \times \text{Electricity Carbon Emission Rate}$$

As with PUE, the lower a TCE score a Data Center has, the better.

Besides effectively illustrating the relationship between energy use and carbon emissions at a given Data Center, TCE is also useful for showing how different facilities can have similar overall environmental impact. For instance, a server environment with a very efficient PUE rating, but whose electricity comes mostly from coal might have the same or even worse TCE than one with a mediocre (higher) PUE score yet powered by a hydroelectric source.

Sample TCE Calculations

The following are the PUE, DCIE, CPE, and TCE metrics for the two sample Data Centers:

Data Center A draws 7,500 kW of total power. Of that, 3,100 kW are consumed by its IT equipment. CPU utilization for the servers in that Data Center averages 10 percent. Say that Data Center is located in Silicon Valley, which has a carbon emissions rate of 0.71299 pounds of carbon dioxide per kWh of electricity produced.

That facility has a PUE score of 2.4, a DCIE score of 41.33 percent, a CPE score of 4.13 percent, and a TCE score of 1.725:

Total Facility Power = 7,500 kW

IT Equipment Power = 3,100 kW

IT Utilization = 10 percent

7500 / 3100 = 2.4 PUE

3100 / 7500 = 41.33 percent DCIE

10 percent × 3100 / 7500 = 4.13 percent CPE

7500 / 3100 × 0.71299 = 1.725 TCE

Data Center B draws 12,250 kw of total power. Of that, 6,700 kw are consumed by its IT equipment. CPU utilization for the servers in that Data Center averages 5 percent. Say that

---

Data Center is located in the central part of Texas, which has a carbon emissions rate of 1.32435 pounds of carbon dioxide per kWh of electricity produced.

That facility has a PUE score of 1.8, a DCIE score of 54.69 percent, a CPE score of 2.73 percent, and a TCE score of 2.421:

Total Facility Power = 12,250 kW

IT Equipment Power = 6,700 kW

IT Utilization = 5 percent

12250 / 6700 = 1.8 PUE

6700 / 12250 = 54.69 percent DCIE

5 percent × 6700 / 12250 = 2.73 percent CPE

12250 / 6700 × 1.32435 = 2.421 TCE

Although Data Center A has a much higher (worse) PUE than Data Center B, the mix of electricity powering that facility produces much less carbon, so its TCE is less (better).

Obviously, you can only calculate TCE if you know the carbon emissions rate of the power that is supplying your Data Center. Chapter 4 provides information about regional electricity mixes, including their carbon emission rates. (Carbon emission rates used in the sample TCE calculations are provided in Table 4.3 of Chapter 4, except shown in pounds per MWh rather than pounds per kWh. Silicon Valley is within the California-Mexico Power Area, abbreviated as CAMX in the table, and central Texas is within the region governed by the Electric Reliability Council of Texas, abbreviated as ERCT.)

Corporate Average Data Center Efficiency (CADE)

Looking for a way to measure Data Center performance in a way that encompasses both IT and Facilities technologies, management consulting firm McKinsey & Co. and the Uptime Institute introduced the Corporate Average Data Center Efficiency (CADE) metric in 2008.

CADE uses the same three factors as CPE and proposes a fourth aspect to be developed in the future:

- **Facility energy efficiency:** How much of the power the Data Center is drawing from the electric grid is being used by IT equipment

- **Facility asset utilization:** How much of the Data Center's maximum electrical capacity is in use

- **IT asset utilization:** The average CPU utilization of servers in the Data Center

- **IT energy efficiency:** This measurement hasn't been formulated yet, but is intended to capture how fully servers, networking equipment, and storage units use the power they are drawing to perform their functions

Combining the first two factors determines the efficiency of the facility; combining the second two determines the efficiency of the IT assets. Each factor is expressed as a percentage and then multiplied by the others:

Corporate Average Data Center Efficiency (CADE) = Facility Efficiency (FE) × Asset Efficiency (AE)

Facility Efficiency = Facility Energy Efficiency × Facility Utilization

Asset Efficiency = IT Energy Efficiency × IT Utilization

The greater proportion of a Data Center's power draw that is used by IT equipment and the closer a Data Center is to operating at its maximum electrical capacity and the higher CPU utilization of its servers, the higher (and better) its CADE score.

CADE's facility energy-efficiency component has the same quirk that PUE and DCIE do in that IT energy savings can potentially lower that portion of your score, but this is largely offset by its IT utilization component. Virtualization projects that lower the facility energy-efficiency score, for instance, in turn increase the IT utilization score.

When calculated, CADE scores are then rated on a tier system:

- Level one (0 percent to 5 percent)

- Level two (5 percent to 10 percent)

- Level three (10 percent to 20 percent)

- Level four (20 percent to 40 percent)

- Level five (greater than 40 percent)

During their initial presentation of the metric, McKinsey and Uptime predicted many Data Centers would receive level one or two CADE scores.

Sample CADE Calculations

Continuing with the two sample Data Centers used to illustrate the other metrics:

The following are the PUE, DCIE, CPE, TCE, and CADE metrics for the two sample Data Centers:

Data Center A draws 7,500 kW of total power. Of that, 3,100 kW are consumed by its IT equipment. CPU utilization for the servers in that Data Center averages 10 percent. Say that Data Center is located in Silicon Valley, which has a carbon emissions rate of 0.71299 pounds of carbon dioxide per kWh of electricity produced.

That facility has a PUE score of 2.4, a DCIE score of 41.33 percent, a CPE score of 4.13 percent, a TCE score of 1.725, and a CADE score of 2.6 percent:

Total Facility Power = 7,500 kW

IT Equipment Power = 3,100 kW

IT Utilization = 10 percent

Data Center Capacity = 5,000 kW

7500 / 3100 = 2.4 PUE

3100 / 7500 = 41.33 percent DCIE

10 percent × 3100 / 7500 = 4.13 percent CPE

7500 / 3100 × 0.71299 = 1.725 TCE

3100 / 7500 = 41.3 percent Facility Energy Efficiency

3100 / 5000 = 62 percent Facility Utilization

41.3 percent × 62 percent = 25.6 percent Facility Efficiency

25.6 percent Facility Efficiency × 10 percent IT Asset Efficiency = 2.6 percent CADE

Data Center B draws 12,250 kw of total power. Of that, 6,700 kw are consumed by its IT equipment. CPU utilization for the servers in that Data Center averages 5 percent. Say that Data Center is located in the central part of Texas, which has a carbon emissions rate of 1.32435 pounds of carbon dioxide per kWh of electricity produced.

That facility has a PUE score of 1.8, a DCIE score of 54.69 percent, a CPE score of 2.73 percent, a TCE score of 2.421, and a CADE score of 1.8 percent:

Total Facility Power = 12,250 kW

IT Equipment Power = 6,700 kW

IT Utilization = 5 percent

Data Center Capacity = 10,000 kW

12250 / 6700 = 1.8 PUE

6700 / 12250 = 54.69 percent DCIE

5 percent × 6700 / 12250 = 2.73 percent CPE

12250 / 6700 × 1.32435 = 2.421 TCE

6700 / 12250 = 54.7 percent Facility Energy Efficiency

6700 / 10000 = 67 percent Facility Utilization

54.7 percent × 67 percent = 36.6 percent Facility Efficiency

36.6 percent Facility Efficiency × 5 percent IT Asset Efficiency = 1.8 percent CADE

Data Center A and B each rate as level one on the CADE tiering system.

The IT energy efficiency factor is not included in the sample CADE calculations because that value has not yet been developed. Expect the CADE metric and tiering system to be modified to some degree when it is defined and added to the equation. If nothing else, CADE scores overall can be expected to drop because IT energy-efficiency scores are invariably going to score less than 100 percent.

Data Center Productivity (DCP)

The Green Grid in 2008 proposed a framework for future Data Center metrics under the umbrella of Data Center Productivity (DCP). DCP metrics not only measure the consumption of a Data Center-related resource, as most Data Center efficiency metrics do, but also tally that against the Data Center's output. In short, DCP looks to define what a Data Center accomplishes relative to what it consumes:

$$\text{Data Center Productivity (DCP)} = \frac{\text{Useful Work Produced by Data Center}}{\text{Resource Consumed Producing the Work}}$$

The framework is intended to be applicable for a range of Data Center capacities, from power—which is explored in the Green Grid's inaugural DCP metric, Data Center Energy Productivity—to other Data Center resources such as floor space.

Monitor www.thegreengrid.com and Data Center industry publications for the latest information about development of metrics under the DCP umbrella.

Usage of Metrics

Whatever metrics you opt to gather concerning your Data Center and whatever metric scores you come upon for Data Centers that belong to other companies, they are meaningful only when they can be viewed in context. It's not enough to see that a Data Center has a particular score, you need to understand the conditions and circumstances behind the score and any potential caveats of the metric formulas being used. Consider the following potential variables:

- **There is more than one way to collect data:** Power readings can be taken at different component levels, with different frequency, using tools with different levels of precision.

- **Scores will vary over time:** As already mentioned, the amount of power consumed by Data Center hardware changes throughout the course of a day as different processing tasks begin and end. Also, under many metric formulas, the same Data Center can register as less efficient when it is partially filled with servers than when more fully occupied. That's because some mechanical and electrical components run less efficiently when partially loaded and also because certain supporting infrastructure (minimal amounts of lighting and conditioning, for instance) inherently represent a larger percentage of total power demand in a lightly occupied facility.

- **Redundancy influences scores:** More layers of standby electrical infrastructure reduce downtime but also reduce metric scores due to additional power loss.

- **Geography influences scores:** Some Data Centers will have an easier or harder time conserving energy than others based solely on where they are located. Data Centers in warmer climates have less opportunity to improve energy efficiency by drawing upon external air than Data Centers in cooler climates, for instance. Likewise, a Data

Center in a region where commercial power is unreliable might have to provide more redundant electrical infrastructure, thereby incurring more power loss.

Data Centers aren't created equal—and are, in fact, unequal in so many ways that it's unwise to compare their metrics. The Green Grid says as much in its 2009 whitepaper, "Usage and Public Reporting Guidelines for The Green Grid's Infrastructure Metrics (PUE/DCIE)":

> "Each Data Center has individual characteristics, capabilities, and operational policies that will affect its power performance. In addition, each Data Center also has different capabilities with respect to collecting and analyzing power consumption data. Without additional information about reported results, interpretations of data collected by different organizations using different approaches over different timeframes may be meaningless or misleading."

To reduce the variation in how its PUE and DCIE metrics are calculated, The Green Grid in that 2009 document outlines standard data collection methodology, offering three levels of complexity. The most basic approach calls for taking power readings at least monthly at a Data Center's UPS equipment and the main distribution panel for its air conditioning system; the most advanced approach involves taking continuous power readings from all individual IT hardware and all facility equipment. The Green Grid further suggests annotating PUE and DCIE metrics to indicate which of the three approaches have been used.

With no value in comparing Data Center metrics across facilities, the true benefit in keeping metrics of your Data Center is to gain insight into that particular facility's efficiency relative to its unique circumstances. As Data Center conditions change in the future, either due to green improvement projects that you implement or simply as new hardware is installed over time, maintaining Data Center metrics enables you to understand how the efficiency of the facility changes and perhaps influence your future operational practices or choices for future green upgrades.

Summary

It's necessary to measure your Data Center's capacity and resource consumption to understand how green it is and the impact—financially and consumption-wise—of any upgrades that you make.

Power is the most critical element to track because it is a finite resource needed for a Data Center to function; it is a common platform across IT and facility systems; and its ongoing cost for your facility represents a tremendous opportunity for savings. Another way of quantifying a Data Center's environmental impact is to measure its carbon footprint, which is derived from the amount of energy the facility uses and the electrical mix that powers it. Generator emissions, heat waste, and water consumption are other key indicators of how green a Data Center is.

A growing number in the Data Center industry are now using environmental building assessment systems to gauge the efficiency of their server environments. The rating systems aren't configured to address Data Centers in particular, but do evaluate general green characteristics such as energy efficiency, carbon emissions, pollution, water consumption, building material selection, and more. Some cities reward projects whose facilities are built for certification by an environmental building assessment system, offering them fast-tracked permitting, green technical assistance, fee waivers, low interest loans, and tax credits.

Among the environmental building assessment systems in use worldwide are the UK's Building Research Establishment Environmental Assessment Method (BREEAM); Green Globes in the United States and Canada; France's Haute Qualité Environmentale (HQE); the Hong Kong Building Environmental Assessment Method (HK-BEAM); Taiwan's Ecology, Energy Saving, Waste Reduction and Health (EEWH); the United States' Leadership in Energy and Environmental Design (LEED); and the National Australian Built Environmental Rating System (NABERS)—also, Japan's Comprehensive Assessment System for Building Environmental Efficiency (CASBEE); Australia's Green Star; Hong Kong's Comprehensive Environmental Performance Assessment Scheme (CEPAS); Singapore's Green Mark; and the German Sustainable Building Certificate. Of those, only the BREEAM system has a Data Center-specific standard today; the U.S. Green Building Council is developing one for the LEED system.

Organizations to look to for current or future Data Center efficiency metrics include the European Commission, with its Data Center Code of Conduct; Data Center industry groups the Green Grid and the Uptime Institute; and the U.S. Environmental Protection Agency and its individual Energy Star programs for Data Centers and servers.

Informative and popular Data Center metrics used today include the following:

- **Power Usage Effectiveness (PUE):** Dividing total facility power by IT equipment power

- **Data Center Infrastructure Efficiency (DCIE):** Dividing IT equipment power by total facility power

- **Compute Power Efficiency (CPE):** Multiplying IT equipment utilization by IT equipment power and dividing by total facility power

- **Technology Carbon Efficiency (TCE):** Multiplying PUE by carbon emissions factor

- **Corporate Average Data Center Efficiency (CADE):** Multiplying facility efficiency by IT asset efficiency

- **Data Center Productivity (DCP):** Dividing the useful work produced by a Data Center by the resource consumed producing the work.

Each Data Center has unique factors that influence their metric scores. Data can be collected in different ways; scores change over time as processing loads rise and fall; and both infrastructure redundancy and geographic location influence scores. Don't compare scores among Data Centers, but instead use metrics to better understand and drive improvements within your own specific facility.

Chapter 3

Green Design and Build Strategies

This chapter discusses methods for limiting the environmental impact that occurs during the construction of a Data Center through decisions concerning physical location, choice of building materials, landscaping choices, and jobsite construction practices.

Siting the Data Center

The location of your Data Center can have a lot to do with how green it is. If your server environment is built in a region that possesses an abundance of renewable energy, for instance, you have a head start on a facility where such resources are rare.

Some companies, especially smaller ones, don't have the luxury of choosing among multiple potential sites for their Data Center. The hosting environment is, by default, going to be constructed at the same place where the rest of their operations or office space is. If you do have an ability to choose, however, consider the following local conditions when you evaluate potential Data Center sites:

- **Electrical mix:** As discussed in Chapter 2, "Measuring Green Data Centers," some energy sources spawn much more carbon dioxide when used to produce electricity than others. Deciding to locate your Data Center in a region where electricity has a lower carbon emissions factor is an excellent way to make the facility greener before design work begins. (You can find more information about electrical mix in Chapter 4, "Powering Your Way to a Greener Data Center.")

- **Weather:** Some Data Center energy-efficiency measures can be implemented only with the cooperation of Mother Nature. For instance, air side economizers that use outside air to chill a Data Center (discussed in Chapter 5, "Cooling Your Way to a Greener Data Center") are more practical to use in regions where it's cold much of the year rather than in areas where it's usually warm or mild.

- **Building codes:** Are the green measures that you intend to include in your building allowed by the regional building codes? If they aren't, can you either do without that efficiency or else invest the time and effort to negotiate for a variance for your project?

Note   The Robert Redford Building in Santa Monica, California, houses offices of the Natural Resource Defense Council and in 2004 became one of the first buildings to achieve a Leadership in Energy and Environmental Design (LEED) platinum rating. Design efforts began in 1999 but the 15,000-square foot (1,393.5-square meter), three-story building was not completed until late 2003. Part of the lengthy time for completion was because of the need to negotiate with the city for the use of green technologies that either conflicted with or else were not addressed by building codes at the time.

Green design elements included rainwater collection, the use of recycled plastic piping (in lieu of copper), and the use of waterless urinals.

- **Work-force proximity:** Although not a Data Center design issue per se, the distance that employees commute to reach your facility affects how much carbon dioxide they generate every day. It's for this reason that some environmental building assessment systems award points for features that promote alternative transportation, such as close proximity to public transit or installing bicycle storage units.

As green as you want your Data Center to be, it's impractical to select a site solely on its environmental merits. Above all else, the server environment needs to be reliable—it does your business no good to have a green Data Center if the facility doesn't adequately safeguard your hardware and mission-critical data. Other factors that you should consider when evaluating potential Data Center sites include the following:

- **Property zoning:** Is construction of a Data Center allowed at the location?

- **Natural disasters:** Is the region prone to earthquakes, ice storms, hurricanes, tornadoes, flooding, landslides, fire, or other severe events?

- **Pollution:** How is the air quality at the location? Is there any risk of IT equipment exposure to dust, industrial byproducts, or other contaminants?

- **Interference:** Are there any nearby sources of electromagnetic interference (also called radio frequency interference) such as telecommunication signal facilities or airports?

- **Vibration:** Are there any nearby sources of vibration such as railroads, major roads, or construction?

- **Political climate:** Is the region politically stable or do conditions exist that might jeopardize the safety of employees or operation of a Data Center?

- **Flight paths:** Is the property within the flight path of an airport, increasing the possibility of a plane crashing onto the site?

Note   Site selection considerations, including how to evaluate a property's risk factors and mitigate them, are discussed in greater detail in the book on Data Center physical design, *Build the Best Data Center Facility for Your Business.*

Building Design and Material Selection

Just as important as the decision of where to build your Data Center is choosing what to build it out of. Even if you've been involved in a lot of Data Center projects, this might be a new question (or series of questions) for you. Conventional Data Center Facilities are built with traditional construction materials—concrete, steel, lumber, drywall, glass, and copper, for instance. Employing different materials and streamlining their physical arrangement can result in a greener facility.

Avoiding the Landfill

One of the most straightforward strategies for making the design and build phase of your Data Center project green is to, whenever possible, avoid actions that cause anything to be thrown out.

That means employing high-quality, durable building materials. The fewer times you have to replace worn or damaged components, the fewer resources that are consumed. Also, choose materials composed of renewable resources, recycled content, or substances that would otherwise end up in a landfill.

Green options among common building materials include the following:

- **Salvaged brick and stone:** Using reclaimed brick and stone has become so popular in construction projects that businesses have emerged that are entirely devoted to collecting and providing such materials.

- **Concrete containing fly ash:** Fly ash is a fine residue created as a waste byproduct when coal is burned in electric power generation plants. Using the glass-like powder as a substitute for cement in concrete keeps it out of landfills and reduces demand for cement, the production of which generates significant carbon dioxide. Concrete containing fly ash is also stronger and easier to pump than that containing only conventional cement.

- **Synthetic gypsum board or drywall:** Like fly ash, synthetic gypsum is a waste byproduct of power plant coal combustion—in this case created when sulfur dioxide is removed from a power plant's exhaust flue gas. Such removal is required by law in many regions because sulfur dioxide contributes to acid rain. As with using fly ash in concrete, employing synthetic gypsum keeps this waste material out of landfills.

- **Green insulation:** All building insulation is inherently green because it improves energy efficiency. Cellulose insulation is considered even greener than conventional fiber glass insulation because it is made primarily from recycled newsprint. Another option is natural fiber insulation made from scrap denim, retrieved from clothing factories and otherwise bound for the trash.

- **Sustainable wood:** Wood is a renewable resource, assuming the forest it comes from is effectively managed to ensure its continued existence and replenishment. Several forest certification programs exist today that verify sustainability; the international Forest Stewardship Council is the best recognized. (FSC-certified wood is specifically referenced in the LEED rating system, for example.)

- **Rubberized asphalt:** Rubberized asphalt is a mix of regular asphalt and crumb rubber—ground up scrap tires. The material reduces tire noise and is less expensive than conventional asphalt; every lane-mile utilizes an estimated 2,000 old tires that would otherwise end up in landfills.

- **Steel:** Modern steel is made in one of two methods and, due to major cost savings of recycling steel over mining iron ore and processing new steel, both involve recycled content. Steel made through the electric arc furnace process in which an electric current is passed through scrap steel to melt and refine it, contains 25 percent to 35 percent recycled content. This type of steel can be flattened relatively easily and is used for items such as automotive body panels, exterior panels for major appliances and containers such as soup cans. Steel made through the basic oxygen furnace process, which combines molten iron from a blast furnace with pure oxygen, contains nearly 100 percent recycled content. Because of its great strength, this type of steel is typically used for items such as structural beams or plating.

What Makes a Green Building Product?

At the beginning of this book, I raised the question of how to define green and, ultimately, how to define a green Data Center.

BuildingGreen, LLC, publisher of the monthly *Environmental Building News*, maintains a database of more than 2,000 "environmentally preferable" building materials. As part of compiling that list, the *Environmental Building News* editorial staff developed standards for designating a building product as green. Their criteria fall into five categories and provide excellent benchmarks for considering when an item to use in your Data Center project is green:

1. Products made with salvaged, recycled, or agricultural waste content:

   - Salvaged products

   - Products with post-consumer recycled content

   - Products with pre-consumer recycled content

   - Products made from agricultural waste material

2. Products that conserve natural resources:

   - Products that reduce material use

   - Products with exceptional durability or low maintenance requirements

   - Certified wood products

   - Rapidly renewable products

3. Products that avoid toxic or other emissions:

   - Naturally or minimally processed products

   - Alternatives to ozone-depleting substances

   - Alternatives to hazardous products

continues

continued

- Products that reduce or eliminate pesticide treatments

- Products that reduce storm-water pollution

- Products that reduce impact from construction or demolition activities

- Products that reduce pollution or waste from operations

4. Products that save energy or water:

- Building components that reduce heating and cooling loads

- Equipment that conserves energy and manages loads

- Renewable energy and fuel cell equipment

- Fixtures and equipment that conserve water

5. Products that contribute to a safe, healthy built environment:

- Products that do not release significant pollutants into the building

- Products that block the introduction, development, or spread of indoor contaminants

- Products that remove indoor pollutants

- Products that warn occupants of health hazards in the building

- Products that improve light quality

- Products that help control noise

- Products that enhance community well-being

More information on the BuildingGreen database is located at http://www.buildinggreen.com.

Beyond employing individual recycled materials for your Data Center project, how about using a recycled building? That is, constructing your server environment within an existing structure rather than constructing entirely new. Even if you have to make major modifications for the pre-existing building to effectively house your servers, the project is still likely to consume fewer materials than a new build. Some of the environmental building assessment systems endorse this by awarding points for building reuse.

Note The building industry generally uses the term *greenfield* to describe pristine or undeveloped land, *brownfield* for abandoned properties (typically industrial or commercial facilities) believed to contain hazardous contaminants, and *grayfield* for properties containing abandoned buildings. I say "generally" because in some regions, *brownfield* merely refers to any land that has been previously developed.

So, perhaps counter intuitively, building on a greenfield site actually makes a Data Center less green.

Embodied Energy and Emissions

You can take an even deeper look at how green your building's construction materials are by considering their embodied energy. That's the total quantity of energy expended in creating and providing a given item, including the following:

- Extracting raw materials

- Processing and manufacturing an item

- Transporting it

- Installing it

Broader definitions of the term *embodied energy* include the energy needed to maintain an item and ultimately recycle or dispose of it. A similar concept, *embodied emissions* or *embodied carbon*, refers to the carbon dioxide produced during those same stages of an item's life.

Accurately gauging the embodied energy and emissions of building materials can be extremely difficult. For one, no single method or formula has been agreed upon for calculating those values. Also, even the same building materials have their own circumstances unique to your specific project. How exactly was a given item manufactured? How far did it have to be transported, first to whatever outlet it was sold from and then to the construction site? For that matter, how was it transported? Different modes of transportation consume energy and produce carbon at different rates.

Despite such variables, several studies have been performed to classify embodied energy and emissions of various materials. Embodied energy is typically measured as a quantity of energy per weighted unit of building material, for example megajoules (MJ) per pound or kilogram. Embodied emissions are expressed as a quantity of carbon dioxide per weighted unit of building material, for example pounds or kilograms of carbon dioxide per pound or kilograms.

The University of Bath has compiled an Inventory of Carbon and Energy that includes embodied energy and carbon ratings for approximately 170 construction materials. Researchers drew information from a variety of published sources and, where regional elements needed to be incorporated, generally based them on factors relevant to the United Kingdom. (For instance, using the typical mix for electricity produced in the UK to help calculate embodied emissions values.)

Table 3-1 lists values for several common building materials, based on the University of Bath's Inventory of Carbon and Energy.

Table 3.1 *Embodied Energy and Carbon of Common Building Materials*

Material	Embodied Energy		Embodied Carbon	
	MJ/lb	*MJ/kg*	*Lb CO$_2$/lb*	*Kg CO$_2$/kg*
Aggregate	0.045	0.10	0.002	0.005
Aluminum (virgin)	98.88	218.00	5.20	11.46
Aluminum (recycled)	13.06	28.80	0.77	1.69
Asphalt (road and pavement)	1.09	2.41	0.06	0.14
Brick	1.36	3.00	0.10	0.22
Cement	2.09	4.60	0.38	0.83
Cement (25 percent fly ash)	1.60	3.52	0.28	0.62
Cement (50 percent fly ash)	1.10	2.43	0.19	0.42
Glass	6.80	15.00	0.39	0.85
Insulation	20.41	45.00	0.84	1.86
Insulation (fiberglass)	12.70	28.00	0.61	1.35
Insulation (cellulose)	0.43 to 1.5	0.94 to 3.3	—	—
Paint	30.84	68.00	1.61	3.56
Plaster (gypsum)	0.82	1.80	0.05	0.12
Polyvinylchloride (PVC) pipe	30.62	67.50	1.13	2.50
Steel (virgin)	16.01	35.30	1.25	2.75
Steel (recycled)	4.31	9.50	0.20	0.43
Stone	0.45	1.00	0.025	0.056
Timber	3.86	8.50	0.21	0.46
Wallpaper	16.51	36.40	0.88	1.93

A handful of lessons can be taken away regarding embodied energy and emissions:

■ **Buy local materials:** The shorter distance that an item has to be transported, the lower its embodied energy and emissions.

■ **Buy materials with recycled content:** Reusing an item or material invariably consumes fewer resources than using something new.

■ **Get back to nature:** Goods made from natural components rather than man-made ones typically consume less energy and resources.

■ **Less is more:** The fewer materials you use in construction, the less energy and carbon emissions that are involved.

Finally, as you consider embodied energy and emissions when choosing among various building materials, don't forget to compare items based on how they are actually used in the construction of a building. For instance, although steel has higher embodied energy and emissions than brick or stone, it also has greater strength relative to its mass. If you were to build a wall out of the three materials, you can obtain the same structural strength by using a smaller amount of steel—perhaps enough less to involve less embodied energy and emissions.

Maintaining Air Quality

The building materials and fixtures you choose for your facility additionally impact air quality, both outdoor and indoor, which in turn affects the health and productivity of employees. Because green considerations often focus upon the external environment, you might not automatically think of indoor air as a consideration for how green your facility is. Nearly all environmental building assessment systems include indoor air quality as a rating criterion, though.

Numerous building-related components—from paints and adhesives to flooring and carpeting to furniture and office equipment—contain contaminants. Some, such as ceiling tiles, produce particulate matter that can cause eye, nose, and throat irritation. Others include organic chemical compounds that evaporate into the air. Known as volatile organic compounds (VOC), these substances can emit smog-forming particles and make building occupants ill. VOCs typically include carbon-based molecules, although specific regulatory definitions about what substances are VOCs and what aren't differ by region.

According to the U.S. Environmental Protection Agency, health impacts from VOCs can include the following:

■ Eye, nose, and throat irritation

■ Headaches, loss of coordination, dizziness, and nausea

■ Nosebleeds (epistaxis)

■ Shortness of breath (dyspnea)

■ Vomiting (emesis)

■ Memory impairment

■ Damage to liver, kidney, and central nervous system functions

■ Cancer in humans and animals

As when dealing with any irritating or harmful substances, the severity of symptoms can vary based on concentration and length of exposure.

To maintain good air quality at your facility, choose paints, adhesives, sealants, wood products, carpeting, and other materials that are classified as low- or no-VOCs. Several countries mandate relevant products be labeled with their VOC content, and many manufacturers provide the information even in regions where they are not required to do so. If such information is not readily available for a product you are considering purchasing, inquire with the manufacturer.

During construction, provide ample ventilation when the materials are installed. Set up fans to expel polluted air outside during construction, not to bring outside air in. When possible, air out items before they are installed.

Note A handy construction tip is to provide extra ventilation whenever building materials are used that are either wet or emit an odor. Odors are a sign that an item is releasing chemicals into the air, so don't remove fans until well after the smell is gone.

How many fans do you need to deploy to air out a building space? That depends upon three factors:

- The size of the area you're ventilating

- How frequently you want to fully replenish the area with fresh air, known as air changes per hour

- The air moving capability of your fans, which is typically listed in cubic feet per minute (cfm).

Various environmental and construction agencies recommend performing anywhere from 5 to 12 air changes per hour to maintain good air quality. To calculate the cumulative cfm fan rating you need to fully refresh the air in an area, take the size of the space in cubic feet, multiply it by the number of air changes per hour that you want, and then divide by 60.

For instance, if you have a room that is 15 feet by 15 feet wide, with a 10-foot ceiling, and you want to perform 5 air changes per hour, you need a fan rated at 187.5 cfm:

15 feet $\times$ 15 feet $\times$ 10 feet = 2250 cubic feet.

2,250 cubic feet $\times$ 5 air exchanges = 11,250 cubic feet per hour.

11,250 / 60 minutes = 187.5 cubic feet per minute.

(Using metric equivalents, that's a 63.7 cubic meter room; 63.7 cubic meters $\times$ 5 air exchanges = 318.5 cubic meters per hour. 382 / 60 minutes = 5.3 cubic meters per minute.)

As a more extreme example, say you want to air out your huge Data Center—a 100,000-square foot room with a 12-foot ceiling—at a rate of 12 air changes per hour. That room requires multiple fans with a cumulative rating of 240,000 cfm:

100,000 feet × 12 feet = 1,200,000 cubic feet.

1,200,000 × 12 air exchanges = 14,400,000 cubic feet per hour.

14,400,000 / 60 = 240,000 cubic feet per minute.

(Using metric equivalents, that's a 33,960-cubic meter room; 33,960 cubic meters × 12 air exchanges = 407,520 cubic meters per hour, and 407,520 / 60 = 6792 cubic meters per minute.)

> **Caution**   Zinc filaments have been known to grow from the underside of Data Center floor panels, a phenomenon known as *zinc whiskers*. Typically just a couple of microns wide and a few hundred microns long, the filaments are considered innocuous unless they are dislodged, at which point they can be propelled by the Data Center's cooling system and enter sensitive hardware, potentially causing an electrical short.
>
> Because zinc filaments can become airborne, are they a threat to the health of Data Center users in addition to Data Center hardware? No studies have been conducted on the issue, so for now there is no clear answer. Even just considering the nonzinc particles that can be stirred up by a Data Center's air conditioning system, I would err on the side of caution and minimize the time that employees spend working in the Data Center. Avoid setting up desks or other items inside the Data Center that facilitate employees using the space as a long-term work area.

Choosing Efficient Fixtures and Appliances

Although the vast majority of your building's resource consumption occurs in the Data Center, don't overlook other fixtures and appliances. Every watt of electricity you save, gallon (liter) of water you conserve, or pound (kilogram) of carbon dioxide that you avoid generating, the greener your facility is. It doesn't matter where in the building the savings occur.

This is especially true for mixed-use facilities, in which a notable portion of the building footprint is occupied by non-Data Center space. As mentioned in Chapter 2, it's often much easier to implement certain green practices in office spaces than hosting areas.

Efficiency opportunities can include the following:

- **Lighting:** Design office areas to maximize daylight, reducing the use of powered lights (and typically increasing the comfort and productivity of building occupants). Install timers and motion sensors so lights automatically shut off during times when employees are not present. Fluorescent T12 bulbs are the ubiquitous choice for ceiling lights, but thinner T8 and T5 bulbs use less energy—25 percent to 50 percent less by various estimates. (T indicates the tubular shape of the bulb; the number represents the diameter of the bulb in eighths of an inch.) Light emitting diode (LED) lights are used rarely in office buildings but can provide even greater energy savings.

Note Some lighting must remain on in your building, including the Data Center, at all times due to safety reasons. You don't want employees to suddenly find themselves in complete darkness.

Requirements for emergency lighting are typically spelled out in regional building codes. If they are not specified for your Data Center project for some reason, be sure to at least illuminate major walkways in your Data Center and the entire building so that a person can easily locate and walk to an exit.

- **Office electronics:** Choose energy-efficient office equipment. The U.S. Environmental Protection Agency's Energy Star program addresses computers, copiers, digital duplicators, fax machines, printers, and even water coolers. An excellent source of information about computers and monitors is the online Electronic Product Environmental Assessment Tool (EPEAT), which evaluates those devices according to 51 environmental criteria including material selection, packaging, energy efficiency, and to what degree a product's component parts can be reused or recycled at the end of its useful life. The tool is available at http://www.epeat.net.

- **Power strips:** In many workplaces, computer peripherals such as monitors, printers, and speakers are left on perpetually, even during nonbusiness hours. Several electrical power strips are on the market nowadays that detect when a primary device (that is, your computer) is either not present or not drawing power and then cut power to the other sockets that peripheral devices are plugged in to. This avoids desktop items drawing power when not needed, without having to rely on people to manually unplug them at the end of each workday.

- **Kitchen appliances:** Ideally your Data Center isn't located in a building that also contains a cafeteria or break room, due to the increased potential for a fire or water leak to occur. If it is, however, you can at least choose energy-efficient appliances.

- **Plumbing fixtures:** Even if your Data Center is located within a dedicated building that contains no office space or other regularly occupied areas, it will likely include one or more restrooms. Waterless urinals forgo the 1.5 gallons to 3.5 gallons (5.7 liters to 13.2 liters) of water per use of conventional toilets, typically saving tens of thousands of gallons (liters) per year. Auto-sensing sink fixtures can also reduce water, as do low flow shower heads if the building happens to include employee shower facilities.

Even fixtures that don't consume power or water can indirectly impact the building's energy efficiency. Designing work areas to be open or use low-height cubicle walls, for instance, improves illumination and can potentially reduce lighting needs.

Note Cisco installed more than 400 waterless urinals at its San Jose, California, campus in 2007 and 2008. Switching to these from conventional toilets saves an estimated 8.5 million gallons (32.2 million liters) of water per year.

Data Center Configuration

The physical configuration of your Data Center—where you place it in a building and how you arrange its physical infrastructure components—provides another opportunity to make the facility more efficient. Strategies to consider include the following:

- Situating your hosting space at the center of a building rather than right against an external building wall provides some isolation from outside temperatures, for instance, so your cooling system won't have to work as hard on hot days.

- Placing cooling infrastructure near heat-producing hardware, a practice known as *close-coupled cooling*. Compared to traditional Data Center designs, where large air handlers attempt to cool large sections of the hosting space, close-coupled cooling requires less fan energy to project cooling where it's needed and reduces unwanted opportunities for chilled air and server exhaust to mix. This approach and the inefficiency that comes with mixing Data Center airflows are covered in Chapter 5.

- Streamlining your structured cabling design by adopting a distributed physical hierarchy. A distributed design uses significantly fewer cabling materials and improves the cooling airflow. This design and a detailed look at the reduced length of cable runs it offers are presented in Chapter 6, "Cabling Your Way to a Greener Data Center."

Building Exterior

The outside of your Data Center building will be subjected to a variety of weather and temperatures during its lifespan. So, in addition to the green characteristics you want for other building elements—durable and preferably made from renewable or recycled content—look for external building components that can mitigate those outdoor conditions.

For instance, you can lower the temperature of your building and reduce how hard your internal cooling system must work by using surfaces that have high solar reflectance and thermal emittance. That is, they efficiently reflect sunlight and shed absorbed heat.

Both solar reflectance and thermal emittance are typically expressed as either a percentage or as a value between 0 and 1. The higher the number, the less a material absorbs and retains heat. To qualify for an Energy Star label, for example, low-slope roofs must have an initial solar reflectance of at least 0.65 and after 3 years at least 0.50. Steep slope roofs must have an initial solar reflectance of at least 0.25 and after 3 years at least 0.15.

Roofs with high-radiative properties, often called *cool roofs*, make your building greener not only because they conserve energy, but also because they decrease heat islands. *Heat islands*, where urban areas have higher temperatures than nearby rural ones, can increase peak energy demand on an electrical grid, possibly leading to brownouts or blackouts, and contribute to the creation of smog.

Heat islands are caused by the reduced quantity of trees and foliage in developed areas, airflow restrictions created by tall buildings, and exhaust heat from motor vehicles and buildings. Many cities can see a temperature difference of as much as 10 degrees

Fahrenheit (5.6 degrees Celsius) above adjoining rural areas, according to the U.S. Environmental Protection Agency.

Tip   Several government agencies have programs to reduce heat islands. Some are financial incentive programs—offering partial rebates on the installation of cool roofs, for example—whereas others are in the form of building code requirements.

Check with the regional planning department where your Data Center is to be constructed to see what programs might exist. Information regarding heat island initiatives in the United States is maintained by the Environmental Protection Agency at http://tinyurl.com/rabyat.

A subset of cool roofs, also known as green roofs or living roofs, employs live vegetation atop conventional roofing. In addition to the temperature-reducing benefits of other cool roofs, green roofs reduce storm-water runoff, act as additional building insulation, and are credited with nearly doubling a roofing system's lifespan by shielding the surface from sun and rain. Green walls or living walls, which apply the same mechanism to a building's vertical surfaces, can also be employed, although are much less common.

Whether applied to a roof or wall, a living surface requires careful engineering. Simply allowing ivy to grow up the side of your building does not equate to a green wall. A proper installation involves a protective membrane to prevent either moisture or plant roots from penetrating to the building, a drainage system to keep foliage from being flooded by pooled water, a soil layer to anchor plants and absorb nutrients and, of course, the vegetation itself—typically plants that are fast growing, drought tolerant, and low maintenance. The entire system needs to be lightweight so as to not pose structural problems for the roof.

Tip   Are you interested to know how efficiently a particular brand of roofing system reflects sunlight and sheds heat? Would you like to know how much of a difference that a more efficient roof can make upon your building's cooling (and therefore energy) usage?

The Cool Roof Rating Council maintains a listing of the solar reflectance and thermal emittance of more than 1,200 roofing materials at http://www.coolroofs.org/index.html.

The U.S. Department of Energy and U.S. EPA's Energy Star program each provide roofing comparison calculators. They estimate a roof's cooling costs based upon factors such as regional electrical prices, local weather conditions, air-conditioning efficiency, roof insulation, solar reflectance, and thermal emittance. By entering different data into the tools, you can see the potential savings associated with roofs possessing more radiative properties.

The calculators are located at (DOE) http://www.ornl.gov/sci/roofs+walls/facts/CoolCalcEnergy.htm and (Energy Star) http://www.roofcalc.com/RoofCalcBuildingInput.aspx.

External building surfaces are also, obviously, prime locations to install photovoltaic cells—devices that convert solar energy into electricity. These can include solar panels mounted on rooftops or walls or even building integrated photovoltaics, in which components are embedded within the envelope of the building. Building integrated photovoltaic systems can take the form of roofing tiles, spandrel panels (opaque glass used between floors in commercial building facades), awnings, skylights, sunshades, walls, and more.

Photovoltaics today typically generate 5 watts to 15 watts per square foot (50 watts to 150 watts per square meter) when in full sunlight. You, therefore, need from 65 square feet to 200 square feet (6 square meters to 18.6 square meters) of photovoltaics to produce one kilowatt of power.

Exactly how much energy can be harvested by a solar array varies by product, because some are more efficient than others, and by environmental conditions, including the following:

- **Latitude:** Various parts of the world receive more or less sun exposure than others, which affects how much solar energy can be collected.

- **Climate:** Overcast or stormy weather reduces the amount of sun that a photovoltaic system is exposed to. Nearby snowy surfaces can actually boost performance by reflecting more light onto a solar array, but only if the array itself isn't covered with snow.

- **Orientation:** Photovoltaic components should be installed to receive maximum exposure to the sun. Avoid obstructions to the system such as trees or other structures especially during peak collection hours, when the sun appears highest in the sky.

- **External air quality:** The more contaminants in the air, the less solar energy that reaches a solar array.

Note   RoofRay, a solar array modeling service based in Walnut Creek, California, offers an online tool that calculates the solar potential of specific buildings. Along with entering your building address and key information such as the tilt angle of the roof, you trace a solar array onto an actual satellite image of the roof of the building.

The tool then calculates the size of the solar array and, by incorporating regional factors such as typical weather conditions, projects how much energy it can capture and the impact upon your electrical bill. The tool is available at http://www.roofray.com.

If you install a photovoltaic system and employ a cool roof on your building, clean their surfaces frequently. Any dirt or debris that covers them reduces their efficiency, reducing how much energy you collect.

Landscaping

Although not frequently given much consideration when planning a Data Center project, landscaping—encompassing not only lawns and vegetation but also the artificial surfaces on a property—has a significant effect on how green your facility is, influencing building heat loads, water usage, air quality, and other conditions.

Be strategic about what you plant on your land and where. That means not only using drought tolerant and low maintenance plants, but also placing trees in key locations to shade buildings and areas that can otherwise absorb and store unwanted heat, such as parking lots.

If your Data Center project involves building new structures, or expanding existing ones, don't indiscriminately move earth and demolish trees and other vegetation. The goal is to minimize disruption to the land and, where possible, reintegrate natural components. For instance, if you need to remove trees during construction, try to replant them elsewhere on the site.

Figure 3.1 shows workers relocating a tree to make way for Data Center construction. The tree was moved to a makeshift tree farm on the building site, shown in Figure 3.2.

Image provided by courtesy of Scott Smith.

Figure 3.1 *Relocating a Tree*

Image provided by courtesy of Scott Smith.

Figure 3.2 *Temporary Tree Farm*

In Figure 3.3, a few feet (one meter) of dirt is excavated from the ground floor of a building to make room for a sunken Data Center raised floor. Figure 3.4 shows the amount of soil removed from the building in a period of 24 hours.

Image provided by courtesy of Andy Broer.

Figure 3.3 *Backhoe in the Data Center*

Image provided by courtesy of Andy Broer.

Figure 3.4 *Reusable Soil*

Note Figures 3.1 through 3.4 are from a Cisco Data Center project in Richardson, Texas, completed in 2007.

We built the Data Center in a pre-existing cold shell building, which is an empty building with an unfinished interior. We opted to forgo entrance ramps and sink the Data Center's raised floor so that its top surface would be level with the corridors leading to it, which required excavating the ground floor. The extracted dirt was reused on the property as land berms.

Installation of a security fence around the perimeter of the building necessitated the removal of about 45 trees, including bald cypress, crepe myrtle, live oak, magnolia, and red oak trees. Half of them were replanted in the immediate vicinity of the Data Center building; others were placed in key locations on the campus or donated for use on other (non-Cisco) properties.

To reduce water usage, avoid pollution, and reduce your maintenance costs, you need to implement good landscape management practices, including the following:

- **Irrigate efficiently:** Don't overwater, which not only consumes more water, but can also cause vegetation to grow faster and, therefore, require additional maintenance.

- **Use mulch:** Place mulch in planting areas to insulate foliage, reduce water usage, and limit erosion. Where possible, reuse plant clippings or wood waste from your own property as mulch.

- **Leave grass clippings on lawns:** Grass clippings decompose over time. This is good for the lawn, providing nutrients from the clippings, avoiding the need to dispose of the green waste, and reducing water and fertilizer usage.

- **Limit pesticide usage:** Consider solutions for controlling unwanted weeds and insects that don't involve chemicals so as to maintain good air quality.

- **Avoid excessive pruning:** Pruning can trigger faster growth, requiring additional maintenance activity.

Be aware that many green elements that are effective for the exterior of your building can also be incorporated onto your overall property. For instance, the same advantages of implementing a cool roof—lowering energy consumption to cool a building and reducing heat islands—can be gained by implementing cool pavement, consisting of materials with high solar reflectance and thermal emittance.

Likewise, photovoltaic components can be installed on your property to harvest solar energy. Solar canopies for parking lots can perform double duty at a building site, both generating electricity and providing shade for employee vehicles. Street lamps are also available that can be powered by solar energy alone or by a combination of wind and solar energy.

Consider using pervious concrete or porous asphalt for paved locations on your property such as sidewalks, parking areas, and curb and gutter systems. Unlike conventional paving, pervious materials enable water to seep through. This reduces storm-water runoff, helps recharge groundwater, and better transfers cooler temperatures from the earth below to the pavement, reducing heat island effects. Rubberized asphalt, mentioned at the beginning of this chapter as a green material because it uses ground up scrap tires that would otherwise end up in landfills, is available in pervious form.

You can reduce water usage at your site by collecting and storing rainwater, using it for nondrinking activities such as watering vegetation and (after treating the water) flushing toilets. Rainwater harvesting equipment consists of a catchment (typically atop a building roof) to collect the water, a distribution system (angled roof features, gutters, down-spouts), and a container to store it (a cistern).

How much water can you expect to collect? That depends upon the size of the catchment and how much rain falls in the region. To make an estimate, multiply the size of the collection area by the average amount of rainfall for a given period.

For instance, if your catchment area is 20 feet long by 50 feet wide and the area receives 24 inches of rain per year, that's 20 feet × 50 feet × (24 inches / 12) = 2000 cubic feet of water. Multiply by 7.48 to convert to gallons; 2000 cubic feet × 7.48 = 14,960 gallons.

Using metric figures, that's a 6.1 meters × 15.2 meters × (61 centimeters / 100) = 56.6 cubic meters of water. Multiply by 1,000 to convert to liters; 56.6 cubic meters × 1000 = 56,600 liters. (Note: The end calculations of 14,960 gallons and 56,600 liters don't convert exactly due to rounding of metric measurements.)

This is an idealized number because it does not account for water spillage or evaporation, both of which reduce the total water yield.

Note   Before installing a rainwater harvesting system on your site, make sure it's legal to do so. Due to water rights regulations and laws that prohibit standing water because it's a breeding ground for disease-carrying mosquitoes, some government agencies either outright prohibit rainwater collection or at least require a permit to do so.

In the United States, Colorado and Utah prohibit the practice whereas—as of this writing—Arizona, Hawaii, Kentucky, Ohio, Texas, Washington, and West Virginia either have or are considering regulations concerning rainwater harvesting.

Strategies for a Greener Construction Site

Construction sites have an inherent messiness to them. Dirt is kicked up as heavy machinery rumbles across the property. Mountains of packaging material form as building fixtures are unwrapped. Scrap building materials accumulate as items are cut to specific sizes. Even the minor leavings of lunches, multiplied by hundreds of people working on site for months, can have a significant impact upon the surrounding environment if not managed in some way.

It's therefore important that just as you design your Data Center to have less environmental impact, so too plan your construction site. Designate separate areas to store building materials, unpackage and assemble building fixtures and appliances, deposit recyclable items (packaging, bottles, and the like), deposit salvageable items (such as leftover building materials), and dispose of construction waste. If the property is undeveloped, carefully choose the makeshift roads that construction vehicles carve in to the property to limit disruption of the soil. Define vulnerable areas on the job site where construction activity is not allowed.

Other approaches to make the construction phase of your Data Center project greener include the following:

- **Mitigating dust, smoke, and odors:** Effective dust control measures include limiting site traffic, reducing vehicle speeds, installing wind fencing, covering dirt piles, and watering regularly at the site.

■ **Controlling erosion and waste-water runoff:** Prevent sediment, debris, or other pollutants from entering nearby streams or storm drains by employing diversion ditches,
silt fencing, and other retention structures. Minimize soil disturbance, limit grading
to small areas, and place ground coverings over exposed areas.

■ **Minimizing noise and vibrations:** Newer construction equipment bearing muffling
devices can be notably quieter and generate less-powerful vibrations than older systems. Install barriers, such as chain-link fencing mounted with plywood and sound-
absorbing mats, at the start of the project. Set up temporary barriers around stationary
construction activities known to generate noise (for example, a worker cutting
notches in panels for a Data Center raised floor). Include noise-related financial
incentives and penalties in your construction contracts so that on-site workers are
accountable for noise mitigation. Measure on-site noise periodically.

■ **Managing construction waste:** Save money and make your Data Center project
greener by reducing how much construction waste is produced and then reusing or
recycling what is created. To reduce waste, standardize on building material sizes to
make leftover stock less likely. Ask suppliers to consolidate packaging and take back
transport materials such as pallets. Separate construction debris into recyclable and
nonrecyclable materials; then seek out a local company that buys and resells second-
hand construction materials to reuse your leftover materials.

Building Commissioning

Modern buildings are complex entities—those housing Data Centers are especially so.
An effective way to ensure that a facility's various infrastructure systems are all working
well is to have the building commissioned.

Commissioning involves a systematic review of equipment to make sure all components
work according to their specifications and that interactions between equipment happens
properly. The scope of commissioning can vary, both in terms of what phases of a project
that a commissioning authority is involved in and what equipment is reviewed.
Commissioning can be done on either new or existing buildings (sometimes called
retrocommissioning).

For a new building, the process ideally begins with the initial planning of the project and
continues through design, construction, and then post-construction stages, typically continuing for about a year after a building comes online so that potential warranty issues
are identified and addressed. Simply commissioning at the end of a project is less effective because it does not allow potential shortcomings to be addressed in the planning or
design stage.

Systems that are commonly commissioned include the following:

■ **Heating, ventilation, and air conditioning (HVAC) systems:** Air conditioning and
distribution, central heating and cooling, water-cooling delivery elements, pressure
management systems, and variable frequency drives

- **Building management systems:** Controls interfacing with HVAC, electrical, fire alarm, and security systems

- **Primary and standby electrical systems:** Power distribution systems, lighting controls, automatic transfer switches, uninterruptible power supply systems, and generators

- **Fire detection and suppression systems:** Fire detection equipment and alarms, notification systems, wet or dry sprinkler systems, gaseous fire suppression system, and the interface between detection and suppression components

- **Plumbing systems:** Hot and cold water, sanitary waste, and storm drainage systems

- **Specialty systems:** Elevators and escalators

- **Building elements:** Building envelope, exterior curtain walls, and roofing structure

- **Voice and data distribution systems:** Cabling, telephony systems, and networking equipment

How valuable is commissioning? An analysis of building commissioning projects sponsored by the U.S. Department of Energy determined that commissioning uncovers an average of 28 deficiencies per new building and 11 per existing building. HVAC systems accounted for the most problems.

The 2004 study, *The Cost-Effectiveness of Commercial-Buildings Commissioning*, reviewed 175 commissioning projects conducted across the United States between 1984 and 2003 involving 224 buildings. It was conducted by Lawrence Berkeley National Laboratory, Portland Energy Conservation, Inc., and Texas A&M University's Energy Systems Laboratory. Its authors concluded that "commissioning is one of the most cost-effective means of improving energy efficiency in commercial buildings" and estimated that buildings in the United States alone could realize $18 billion per year in energy savings.

Retrofitting an Existing Data Center

Although this chapter is written predominantly from the perspective of constructing an all-new Data Center, don't overlook green design and build possibilities for projects that involve upgrading your existing server environments. Although you won't be making a site selection decision, green strategies around building materials, building exteriors, and landscaping are still valid, and it's even more important to maintain good air quality around an already populated building than at a construction site.

Existing roofing systems can certainly be retrofitted with cool roofs, living roofs, or photovoltaic systems, and building commissioning can be done as easily on existing structures as on new ones.

Remember that if you retrofit a pre-existing server environment, you have already implemented one green element. You're reusing a structure rather than constructing something new and have, therefore, avoided consuming even more resources.

Summary

When evaluating a potential Data Center site, consider local factors including electrical mix, weather conditions, building codes, and work-force proximity because each of these influence how green your facility can be.

Durable building materials need replacement less often and, therefore, consume fewer resources. Pick materials composed of renewable resources, recycled content, or substances that would otherwise end up in a landfill. Also choose items with less-embodied energy and embodied emissions.

Maintain good air quality by using building components such as paints, carpeting, and office equipment that have little or no volatile organic compounds, and be sure to thoroughly ventilate the building during construction.

Choose energy-efficient building fixtures and appliances such as lighting components, office electronics, power strips, kitchen appliances, and plumbing fixtures.

Insulate the Data Center from external temperatures by placing it at the center of the building. Employing a distributed design for the Data Center's structured cabling requires less cabling, thereby reducing the amount of materials that are consumed, than a direct-connect design.

Several green features can be incorporated into the exterior of your building including highly reflective cool roofs or vegetation-bearing living roofs, each of which reduce heat island effects. A photovoltaic system can also be installed—either on a rooftop or integrated into building surfaces—with its efficiency influenced by location, climate, sun exposure, and air quality.

Landscaping affects the thermal load, water usage, air quality, and other green elements of your building. Choose drought tolerant and low maintenance plants and strategically place trees to shade buildings and parking lots. Irrigate efficiently, use mulch to save water and reduce erosion, allow grass clippings to decompose on lawn areas, limit the use of pesticides, and avoid excess pruning.

Consider photovoltaic installations on the grounds of your site as well. Pervious concrete and porous asphalt allow water to pass through, reducing storm-water runoff and heat islands. You can use a rainwater collection system to gather an alternate source of water for nonpotable uses such as landscaping.

Reduce the environmental impact of your building construction site by establishing separate areas to store materials, unpackage fixtures, sort recyclables, collect salvageable items, and dispose of construction waste. Prohibit construction activity in sensitive portions of the site. Mitigate dust, smoke, and odors; control erosion and wastewater runoff; minimize noise and vibrations; and manage construction waste.

Have your building commissioned to ensure that its infrastructure systems work correctly in conjunction with one another. The scope of commissioning can vary, but systems that are commonly reviewed include HVAC, building management, primary and standby electrical, fire detection and suppression, plumbing, elevators, building envelope, roofing, and voice and data distribution.

You can implement several green design and build approaches just as effectively during the retrofit of an existing Data Center as during construction of a new facility.

Chapter 4

Powering Your Way to a Greener Data Center

This chapter discusses how energy is used in Data Centers, traces the potential for power savings along the electrical delivery chain, and presents carbon emission factors for different regions of the world. The chapter additionally presents alternative energy options and offers design strategies, technology solutions, and operational methods for reducing Data Center energy usage.

How a Data Center Consumes Energy

Although there are hundreds of ways, large and small, to make your Data Center greener, nothing has a greater impact than optimizing its energy consumption. Conventional methods for producing electricity consume finite resources (fossil fuels), emit greenhouse gases, and pollute the air, so every action that leads to your facility using less energy makes it markedly greener. Because power usage is the most expensive operational cost for Data Centers, energy efficiency improvements also present the greatest savings opportunities among green solutions.

To begin making your Data Center more energy efficient, it helps to have a clear picture of how power is used in the server environment. By knowing what elements either consume the most power or are the farthest downstream in the power delivery chain, you can determine the prime targets for making efficiency improvements.

Table 4.1 shows the proportional use of power in a typical server environment, according to research by Emerson Network Power, which manufactures Data Center power and cooling system components.

Emerson determined these proportions after modeling the energy consumption of what it considers a typical 5,000-square foot (464.5 square-meter) Data Center. The hypothetical facility features 210 equipment racks, oriented in a hot- and cold-aisle configuration, and uses 2.8 kW of cooling per rack. It draws slightly more than 1.1 MW of power overall, has about 350 tons of cooling capacity, and has two redundant 750 kva UPS systems. Emerson's analysis, published in the 2008 paper "Energy Logic: Reducing Data Center

Energy Consumption by Creating Savings that Cascade Across Systems," shows an almost even division of power consumed by IT equipment (52 percent) and facilities equipment (48 percent).

A glance at Table 4.1 shows that servers (totaling 44 percent of power usage, from various components) and cooling infrastructure (38 percent) are excellent candidates to pursue energy-efficiency measures because they each use more energy by far than any other Data Center system. Chapter 8, "Choosing Greener Gear," Chapter 9, "Greening Your Data Center Through Consolidation, Virtualization, and Automation," and Chapter 5, "Cooling Your Way to a Greener Data Center," present energy-efficiency strategies for those two Data Center elements (servers and cooling infrastructure).

In addition to identifying which systems consume the most power in your Data Center, it's also useful to know how much energy is involved with conveying electricity through your facility to the destination IT equipment. By reducing energy consumption at the point farthest downstream in the Data Center, you actually achieve cumulative savings all the way upstream. If a server draws less power, there's an even greater benefit due to the smaller quantity of electricity that has to be conditioned, cooled, distributed, converted, and delivered across the Data Center.

Table 4.1 *Breakdown of Data Center Energy Consumption*

Data Center System	Proportional Use
Cooling	38%
Processor	15%
Other server components	15%
Server Power Supply	14%
UPS	5%
Networking equipment	4%
Storage	4%
Building switchgear and medium voltage transformer	3%
Lighting	1%
PDU	1%

According to the same Energy Logic paper by Emerson, saving 1 watt of energy at the server level accumulates to nearly 3 watts in total, as shown in Figure 4.1.

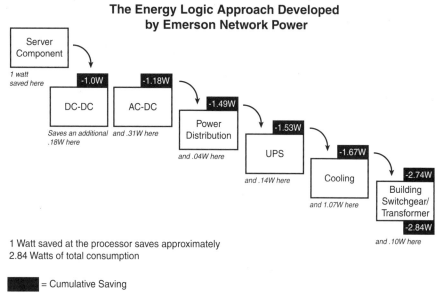

1 Watt saved at the processor saves approximately
2.84 Watts of total consumption

= Cumulative Saving

Figure 4.1   *Accumulating Data Center Power Savings*

Note   Believe it or not, the cumulative benefit from reducing how much power your servers consume is not unlike a health benefit that occurs from losing weight.

A 2004 study by researchers at Wake Forest University showed that for every 1 pound of weight that a person loses, there is a 4-pound reduction in stress on the knees. (Using rounded metric measurements, that's for every half a kilogram a person loses, there is a 2-kilogram reduction in stress on the knees.) A person walking 1 mile (1.6 kilometers) would save 4,800 lbs (2,177.2 kilograms) of compressive load from each of the knees, and the effect scales, meaning a person walking 10 miles (16.1 kilometers) saves 48,000 pounds (21,772.4 kilograms).

Researchers measured stress on the joints of 142 overweight and obese adults suffering from osteoarthritis of the knee. Measurements were taken before and after an 18-month weight loss program, during which participants lost an average 2 percent in body weight.

Just as slimming pounds (or kilograms) takes pressure off of a person's knees, so does slimming power consumption take pressure off a Data Center's electrical system.

The Carbon Factor

As mentioned in Chapter 2, "Measuring Green Data Centers," and Chapter 3, "Green Design and Build Strategies," electricity comes from many sources, each of which generates different quantities of carbon dioxide and other greenhouse gases. Electrical mixes vary by region, so if you build two Data Centers that are physically identical, but in locations fed by different utility providers, those server environments can have carbon footprints that are quite similar or extremely different. In extreme cases, one site might involve several times the associated greenhouse gases of its twin. Knowing the electrical mix of different regions can enable you to choose a greener location for your future Data Center or at least understand the emissions of your existing server environments and assess the quantity of emissions you can save by making your facility more energy efficient.

Table 4.2 shows the energy-related carbon dioxide emissions per megawatt hour in 2006 for 25 countries and regions, based upon data compiled by the International Energy Agency. (Original source material is published in CO2 Emissions from Fuel Combustion, © OECD/IEA, 2008, Pages II.61–II.63.)

Looking at Table 4.2 you can see that building the same Data Center in Iceland rather than India can result in a dramatically smaller carbon footprint, for instance, strictly due to electrical mix. The IEA maintains data on carbon emissions associated with fuel combustion for more than 140 countries and regions. Data used in Table 4.2 is the most recent available at the time of this book's publication. You can find updated information at www.iea.org.

Although some countries have either just one major commercial power provider or else a few suppliers with little variety among their electrical mix, others have many regional suppliers, each with their own power profile.

Tables 4.3 and 4.4 show energy-related regional emissions data for the United States, which has more than two dozen regional variations. Information comes from the Emissions & Generation Resource Integrated Database (eGRID), which is maintained by the U.S. Environmental Protection Agency. Locations of the eGRID subregions are represented in Figure 4.2.

Tables 4.3 and 4.4 include two sets of data—one incorporating all electrical plants and their emissions for a region (the grouping at the left) and another that includes only electrical sources used during times of peak demand (the grouping at the right, labeled nonbaseload). The total mix is useful to estimate a facility's carbon footprint, whereas the nonbaseload is valuable for estimating what emissions can be avoided by reducing electrical consumption, which allows those peak-demand plants to remain offline.

Table 4.2   *2006 Carbon Dioxide Emissions from Electricity and Heat Generation, by Country and Region*

Region	Carbon Dioxide lbs/MWh	Carbon Dioxide kg/MWh
Brazil	178.57	81
Canada	405.65	184
China	1,737.24	788
Denmark	751.78	341
France	187.39	85
Germany	890.67	404
Hong Kong, China	1,884.95	855
Iceland	2.20	1

Region	Carbon Dioxide lbs/MWh	Carbon Dioxide kg/MWh
India	2,081.16	944
Italy	890.67	404
Japan	921.53	418
Korea	1,022.94	464
Netherlands	868.62	394
Russia	725.32	329
Singapore	1,181.68	536
Spain	771.62	350
Sweden	105.82	48
Switzerland	57.32	26
Thailand	1,126.56	511
Turkey	965.62	438
United Arab Emirates	1,807.79	820
United Kingdom	1,113.33	505
United States	1,232.38·	559
Vietnam	873.03	396
World	1,113.33	505

The source material for data in Table 4.2 is originally presented by the International Energy Agency in grams per kilowatt hour (g/kWh). Data has been adjusted using common conversion rates, so it appears in the same scale as similar content presented in Tables 4.3 and 4.4. Similarly, data appearing in Table 4.4 has been converted from the EPA's original listings that are shown in Table 4.3.

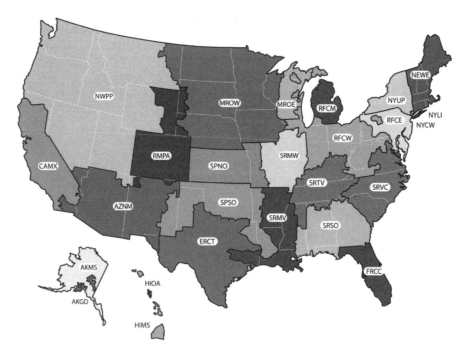

Figure 4.2   *United States eGRID Subregions*

Tip   Data used in Tables 4.2, 4.3, and 4.4 are the most recent available at the time of this book's publication, which is 2006 data from the IEA and 2005 data from the U.S. EPA. Updated information can be found at http://www.iea.org/ for multiple countries and at http://www.epa.gov/cleanenergy/energy-resources/egrid/index.html for regions within the United States.

The EPA has also incorporated the eGRID data into an online tool, called the Power Profiler. By entering the ZIP code of your Data Center site, you can see the emissions associated with your energy consumption compared to the average for the United States. The EPA Power Profiler is at http://www.epa.gov/grnpower/buygp/powerprofiler.htm.

Looking at Tables 4.3 and 4.4, you can determine that building the same Data Center in most areas of New York State (NYUP subregion) rather than Michigan (RFCM subregion) can result in a smaller carbon footprint, for instance.

Note that eGRID emission rates are calculated based upon generation at the power plant, and therefore don't include electrical losses during transmission. Greenhouse gas emissions relative to the net power received by a customer would be higher per megawatt hour or gigawatt hour.

Table 4.3 *2005 Greenhouse Gas Annual Output Emission Rates (in pounds)*

eGRID Subregion Acronym	eGRID Subregion Name	Annual Output Emission Rates			Annual Non-Baseload Output Emission Rates		
		Carbon Dioxide lb/MWh	Methane lb/GWh	Nitrous Oxide lb/GWh	Carbon Dioxide lb/MWh	Methane lb/GWh	Nitrous Oxide lb/GWh
AKGD	ASCC Alaska Grid	1,213.49	25.60	6.51	1,423.97	36.41	8.24
AKMS	ASCC Miscellaneous	498.86	20.75	4.08	1,457.11	60.47	11.87
AZNM	WECC Southwest	1,311.05	17.45	17.94	1,201.44	20.80	8.50
CAMX	WECC California	712.99	30.24	8.08	1,071.56	39.24	5.55
ERCT	ERCOT All	1,324.35	18.65	15.11	1,118.86	20.15	5.68
FRCC	FRCC All	1,264.50	45.92	16.94	1,331.52	48.16	12.95
HIMS	HICC Miscellaneous	1,415.73	314.68	46.88	1,535.57	338.44	51.42
HIOA	HICC Oahu	1,737.38	109.47	23.62	1,759.89	120.11	20.79
MROE	MRO East	1,812.91	27.59	30.36	1,797.60	28.82	25.20
MROW	MRO West	1,810.47	28.00	30.71	2,131.99	45.57	35.22
NEWE	NPCC New England	829.41	86.49	17.01	1,256.11	77.47	16.02
NWPP	WECC Northwest	898.04	19.13	14.90	1,323.68	49.28	18.73
NYCW	NPCC NYC/Westchester	781.11	36.02	5.46	1,496.57	56.80	9.08
NYLI	NPCC Long Island	1,353.45	115.41	18.09	1,492.65	60.32	10.78
NYUP	NPCC Upstate NY	699.63	24.82	11.19	1,491.43	45.30	18.41
RFCE	RFC East	1,090.50	30.27	18.71	1,756.59	41.61	24.36
RFCM	RFC Michigan	1,543.33	33.93	27.17	1,649.82	29.40	26.24
RFCW	RFC West	1,536.99	18.23	25.71	1,991.95	24.49	31.72
RMPA	WECC Rockies	1,870.19	22.88	28.75	1,613.03	22.42	20.14
SPNO	SPP North	1,960.94	23.82	32.09	2,169.74	31.18	31.99
SPSO	SPP South	1,655.25	24.98	22.61	1,376.74	24.40	12.04

continues

Table 4.3   *2005 Greenhouse Gas Annual Output Emission Rates (in pounds) (continued)*

eGRID Subregion Acronym	eGRID Subregion Name	Annual Output Emission Rates			Annual Non-Baseload Output Emission Rates		
		Carbon Dioxide lb/MWh	Methane lb/GWh	Nitrous Oxide lb/GWh	Carbon Dioxide lb/MWh	Methane lb/GWh	Nitrous Oxide lb/GWh
SRMV	SERV Mississippi Valley	1,017.49	24.31	11.71	1,255.79	29.50	9.82
SRMW	SERC Midwest	1,830.27	21.15	30.50	2,100.44	25.66	32.92
SRSO	SERC South	1,476.99	26.27	25.47	1,674.83	35.20	26.41
SRTV	SERC Tennessee Valley	1,509.94	20.05	25.64	1,997.83	28.25	32.86
SRVC	SERV Virginia/Carolina	1,118.40	23.77	19.79	1,747.29	40.09	27.46

Table 4.4   *2005 Greenhouse Gas Annual Output Emission Rates (in kilograms)*

eGRID Subregion Acronym	eGRID Subregion Name	Annual Output Emission Rates			Annual Non-Baseload Output Emission Rates		
		Carbon Dioxide kg/MWh	Methane kg/GWh	Nitrous Oxide kg/GWh	Carbon Dioxide kg/MWh	Methane kg/GWh	Nitrous Oxide kg/GWh
AKGD	ASCC Alaska Grid	550.43	11.61	2.95	645.90	16.52	3.74
AKMS	ASCC Miscellaneous	226.28	9.41	1.85	660.93	27.43	5.38
AZNM	WECC Southwest	594.68	7.92	8.14	544.96	9.43	3.86
CAMX	WECC California	323.41	13.72	3.67	486.05	17.80	2.52
ERCT	ERCOT All	600.71	8.46	6.85	507.51	9.14	2.58
FRCC	FRCC All	573.57	20.83	7.68	603.97	21.85	5.87
HIMS	HICC Miscellaneous	642.16	142.74	21.26	696.52	153.51	23.32
HIOA	HICC Oahu	788.06	49.65	10.71	798.27	54.48	9.43
MROE	MRO East	822.32	12.51	13.77	815.38	13.07	11.43
MROW	MRO West	821.22	12.70	13.93	967.05	20.67	15.98
NEWE	NPCC New England	376.21	39.23	7.72	569.76	35.14	7.27
NWPP	WECC Northwest	407.34	8.68	6.76	600.41	22.35	8.50

eGRID Subregion Acronym	eGRID Subregion Name	Annual Output Emission Rates			Annual Non-Baseload Output Emission Rates		
		Carbon Dioxide kg/MWh	Methane kg/GWh	Nitrous Oxide kg/GWh	Carbon Dioxide kg/MWh	Methane kg/GWh	Nitrous Oxide kg/GWh
NYCW	NPCC NYC/Westchester	354.31	16.34	2.48	678.83	25.76	4.12
NYLI	NPCC Long Island	613.91	52.35	8.21	677.05	27.36	4.89
NYUP	NPCC Upstate NY	317.35	11.26	5.08	676.50	20.55	8.35
RFCE	RFC East	494.64	13.73	8.49	796.78	18.87	11.05
RFCM	RFC Michigan	700.04	15.39	12.32	748.35	13.34	11.90
RFCW	RFC West	697.17	8.27	11.66	903.53	11.11	14.38
RMPA	WECC Rockies	848.30	10.38	13.04	731.66	10.17	9.14
SPNO	SPP North	889.47	10.80	14.56	984.18	14.14	14.51
SPSO	SPP South	750.81	11.33	10.26	283.26	11.07	5.46
SRMV	SERV Mississippi Valley	461.53	11.03	5.31	569.62	13.38	4.45
SRMW	SERC Midwest	830.20	9.59	13.83	952.74	11.64	14.93
SRSO	SERC South	669.95	11.92	11.55	759.69	15.97	11.98
SRTV	SERC Tennessee Valley	684.90	9.09	11.63	906.20	12.81	14.91
SRVC	SERV Virginia/Carolina	507.30	10.78	8.98	792.56	18.18	12.46

Alternative Energy Sources

Knowing that the most common methods for producing electricity today consume finite resources—fossil fuels—and generate greenhouse gases, you can make your Data Center greener by seeking alternative sources for both its day-to-day energy needs and its stand-by power system.

The best alternatives are, obviously, those that are renewable, generate the fewest emissions, and are reliable. Most can at least lessen your Data Center's consumption of conventional energy from regional utility providers. For those forms of alternative energy that aren't practical to deploy directly in support of your Data Center, consider purchasing green power credits.

Biofuels

Biofuels, which are made from biomass materials, can be used for Data Center standby generators as an alternative to conventional diesel fuel or gasoline.

The two most common forms of biofuel are biodiesel, made from vegetable oils or fats such as recycled cooking oil; and ethanol, an alcohol fuel made from crops such corn or sugar cane. Both substances can be mixed with their traditional counterparts—biodiesel with standard diesel fuel and ethanol with gasoline—or else used as standalone fuel. Biofuels produce fewer carbon emissions than conventional fuel although also typically generate somewhat less power, so are often used as a blend rather than at full concentration.

Biodiesel can be used in most diesel generators without having to modify the machinery and so is more commonly used. Generators that use ethanol are much rarer.

Fuel Cells

Another approach for greening your Data Center's power system is to supplement or outright replace the electricity you receive from your utility provider with a cleaner source. Hydrogen fuel cells, for instance, combine hydrogen and oxygen to create electricity and produce heat and water as byproducts.

Oxygen used by a hydrogen fuel cell typically comes from the surrounding air whereas the hydrogen can come from a variety of sources that typically involve fewer carbon emissions than conventional electrical mixes and are, therefore, greener. Many stationary fuel cells run on natural gas, for instance, which, although it is a fossil fuel, emits less carbon, sulfur, and nitrogen than others. Because a fuel cell is installed directly on your property, they also avoid the transmission loss that utility-provided electricity incurs.

Note Energy transmission and distribution losses vary greatly by region. Losses of approximately 10 percent are common in many developed countries, with much higher losses in some developing nations. Published reports indicate India has transmission and distribution losses of more than 30 percent, for instance, even reaching 50 percent in some cities where illegal tapping of power lines is rampant.

A fuel cell consists of two electrodes, an anode and a cathode, with an electrolyte between them. Incoming hydrogen passes through the anode and is separated into protons and electrons by way of a catalyst. The electrolyte enables protons to pass through to the cathode, whereas electrons are blocked and instead flow through an external circuit in the form of electricity before reaching the cathode. Incoming oxygen, meanwhile, passes through the cathode, where another catalyst combines it with the protons and electrons to form water and heat.

The several types of fuel cells are alkaline, direct methanol, metal air, molten carbonate, phosphoric acid, proton exchange membrane/polymer electrolyte, and solid oxide. Each fuel cell type has its own features, including different form factors, electrolyte substance, operating temperatures, and fuel characteristics they require, making some more suitable to power a Data Center than others.

Note   For a visual representation of how a fuel cell functions, visit the Northern Alberta Institute of Technology's website at http://www.nait.ca/38348.htm. The site includes an interactive diagram of a fuel cell and a game that involves placing fuel cell components in the correct sequence for the system to function correctly.

Fuel cell products are available as large stationary units that can provide hundreds of kilowatts of electricity to a Data Center or as smaller, cabinet-sized components. Fuels cells can be used in place of a Data Center's primary power from a utility provider or standby power that typically comes from a generator.

The energy efficiency of a fuel cell—how much of its fuel is converted to electricity versus what is lost as waste heat—depends upon the type of fuel cell and how much power is drawn from it. Generally, the greater current that is drawn, the less efficient a fuel cell is. Using the heat produced by a fuel cell, making its waste byproduct a usable resource, obviously improves its relative efficiency.

A database of incentive programs offered in the United States to encourage the deployment of hydrogen fuel cells is available at http://www.fuelcells.org/info/statedatabase.html.

Fujitsu's Data Center Fuel Cell

Electronics manufacturer Fujitsu began partially powering the chiller plant that supports 48,000 square feet (4,459.3 square meters) of Data Center space on its Sunnyvale, California, campus with a fuel cell in 2007. The 200-kW unit provides one-third of the power for the Data Center's chiller plant. In addition, a portion of the fuel cell's waste heat is circulated through the non-Data Center area of that same building in the form of hot water, helping warm about 78,000 square feet (7,246.4 square meters) of office space.

continues

continued

Interested in finding a green power source to reduce its carbon emissions, Fujitsu representatives initially researched photovoltaic components but determined that its building roofs had limited sun exposure due to shade from several mature trees on the campus, which was constructed in the 1970s. The fuel cell proved to be a better fit for the legacy campus, according to building operations manager Ted Viviani, because of its greater energy output and smaller physical footprint.

Greater financial incentives were also available for a fuel cell installation than photovoltaics. Fujitsu received a $2,500 per kilowatt rebate from the state of California, through Pacific Gas and Electric and a federal tax credit of $1,000 per kilowatt. Together, the incentives brought the net cost for the fuel project below $500,000, an amount that Fujitsu expects to recover through energy savings within 3 1/2 years. According to Viviani, costs for the natural gas for the fuel cell have averaged 7 cents to 7.5 cents per kWh, compared to 10.5 cents to 11 cents per kWh wholesale price it pays for electricity.

Fujitsu estimates that capturing and using much of the waste heat from the fuel cell has roughly doubled its energy efficiency, to between 85 percent and 90 percent.

Fujitsu officials have been so satisfied with the fuel cell that when the company eventually expands the Data Center to twice its existing footprint, it intends to fully supply the electrical needs of the expansion area with fuel cells. Two 400-kW and one 200-kW fuel cell are to be installed as the server environment's primary power source; utility power will serve as its standby power source; and diesel generators will be a third-power supply.

As shown in Figure 4.3, installation of a fuel cell at Fujitsu's Sunnyvale campus involved transporting the unit by crane.

Image provided by courtesy of Fujitsu

Figure 4.3 *Moving a Fuel Cell for Installation*

Figure 4.4 shows the installed fuel cell.

Image provided by courtesy of Fujitsu

Figure 4.4   *A 200-Kilowatt Fuel Cell Supporting a Data Center Chiller Plant*

Hydropower

Hydropower involves using the momentum of water to generate electricity and has long been considered green because it is renewable and generates less carbon dioxide than producing electricity from fossil fuels. The three major commercial applications of hydropower include hydroelectricity produced by dams, tidal power, and wave power.

Hydroelectric Dams

Hydroelectric dams involve blocking rivers and then using the force of the captured water to turn a turbine, which in turn drives a generator rotor that creates electricity. Hydropower's green cachet, combined with its low cost, has in recent years lured businesses with significant computing needs to build server environments in locations in which hydroelectricity is abundant.

For instance, Google, Microsoft, and Yahoo all launched Data Center construction projects in Quincy, Washington, a farming town of approximately 6,000 people, in 2006 to take advantage of hydroelectric power provided by the nearby Columbia River. Local power costs are about 2 cents per kilowatt hour, which is a fraction of the nearly 14 cents per kilowatt hour for electricity in Silicon Valley and 9 cents per kWh average across the United States. According to published reports, by 2008 Quincy had more than 2 million square feet (185,806 square meters) of Data Center space either online or under construction.

Unfortunately, although hydropower is a renewable, often low-cost source of energy, hydroelectric dams come with some caveats to being green. First, building a dam to convert water's momentum into electricity has a major impact upon the local environment. It changes the behavior of the dammed waterway and floods the surrounding land with the formation of a new reservoir. Both of these disrupt the habitats of animals that live in the river or on land.

Second, dams have been identified as major producers of methane, a greenhouse gas with 20 to 25 times the global warming potential of carbon dioxide. When a body of water is dammed, decaying vegetation and other organic material get trapped within the reservoir where they break down and emit methane into the water. Water is churned as it passes through a dam's turbine, releasing the methane into the air. Without the presence of the dam, the organic material would continue along the waterway and whatever distributed quantities of methane that form in the water are oxidized and released as less intensive carbon dioxide.

A 2007 report by Brazil's National Institute for Space Research estimates that major dams of the world emit 229.3 billion pounds (104 million metric tons) of methane. That amount, detailed in "Methane Emissions from Large Dams as Renewable Energy Resources: A Developing Nation Perspective," equals more than 4 percent of the estimated warming impact on the entire world from human activities.

What does this all mean when considering hydroelectricity to power your green Data Center? Hydropower from dams probably shouldn't be considered as green as other alternative sources.

Tidal Power

A second approach to hydropower is to use ocean tides to drive turbines. Tidal power is gathered by way of turbines that are either submerged underwater or else embedded in large dams known as *barrages*.

Although tidal power has not been extensively developed to date, it is considered a promising source of renewable energy. Tidal energy comes from the sun and moon's gravitational pull and can be accurately predicted, making it a more reliable source of energy than solar or wind power. Water is also much denser than air and needs to move at a much lower velocity to generate significant energy by way of a turbine than wind does.

Note that barrages have similar impacts upon surrounding ecosystems as river-based hydroelectric dams, so barrage-based tidal energy should also be considered less green than other alternative energy sources.

Note   Financial institution Morgan Stanley announced in 2008 plans for a Data Center in northern Scotland powered solely by tidal power. The Data Center is to be online and drawing 20 MW of power by 2011 and 150 MW by 2013, entirely independent of Scotland's national power grid.

Turbines to capture tidal energy for the Data Center are to be installed in the Pentland Firth area, between the Scottish mainland and the Orkney Islands.

Wave Power

Yet another form of hydropower comes from ocean surface waves. Wave power is captured by placing equipment in the ocean that, thanks to the rise and fall of the water, bobs up and down and acts as a hydraulic pump to drive a generator to create electricity.

Wave power isn't as cost-effective today as some other alternative energy sources, and you probably can't directly incorporate it into the design of your Data Center, but it's an interesting renewable energy source to watch for future developments.

The first commercial wave farm of its kind, Aguçadoura Wave Park, opened off the coast of Portugal in 2008. The facility initially produced 2.25 MW of power and expansion plans call for it to ultimately provide 21 MW. Other wave farm projects have been planned for locations off the coast of England, Scotland, Spain, Brazil, and Hawaii.

Note   Although the company hasn't built it, Google submitted an application with the U.S. Patent and Trademark Office in 2007 for a floating server environment that would be cooled by ocean water and powered by wave power generators and wind turbines. As proposed, the Data Center would be located 3 miles to 7 miles (4.8 kilometers to 11.3 kilometers) offshore.

Google indicates in the patent application that a shipboard Data Center's mobility would enable it to be positioned closer to end users, thereby alleviating latency. The Data Center could even sail into an area that has been struck by a natural disaster in which traditional telecommunications infrastructure is unavailable, as part of a military deployment, or simply to provide additional computing or communication capabilities during a major event.

The patent was awarded to Google in 2009.

Solar

Harvesting energy from sunlight was discussed in Chapter 3 in the context of free-standing solar panels and building integrated photovoltaic systems. As mentioned there, photovoltaics today typically generate 5 watts to 15 watts of electricity per square foot (50 watts to 150 watts per square meter) when in full sunlight, meaning that one kilowatt of power can be produced from 65 square feet to 200 square feet (6 square meters to 18.6 square meters) of solar array.

Solar energy is renewable and doesn't emit any greenhouse gases when producing electricity. The chief barrier to using it as a primary source of power, whether to operate Data Center systems or for other purposes, has always been the inability to efficiently store its energy for later use. Even in regions that receive maximum possible sun exposure due to location and an agreeable climate, solar energy can only be collected for a limited number of hours per day.

Rechargeable batteries are generally used to store solar energy for devices that are disconnected from a utility power source. Alternatively, thermal mass systems using substances such as water, rock, earth, or molten salt store solar energy in the form of heat.

Wind

Last but not least is the option of harnessing wind power through the use of electricity-producing turbines. Wind-powered electrical capacity has grown dramatically in recent years, from 7,600 MW worldwide in 1997 to 93,864 MW in 2007, and is projected to reach 240,000 MW (240 GW) by 2012 according to the Global Wind Energy Council.

Much like solar, wind energy is renewable and nonpolluting yet challenging to store, and unpredictable enough to make it more appropriate as a complement to a Data Center's commercial power rather than a full-fledged replacement. Google and Yahoo are among the operators of major Data Centers that are supplementing some of their conventional energy usage with wind farms and photovoltaic devices.

Table 4.5 shows the top 10 countries in term of wind-powered electrical production, according to the GWEC's Global Wind 2007 Report.

Table 4.5 *Top 10 Installed Wind Capacity in 2007, by Country*

Region	Megawatts	Percentage
Germany	22,247	23.7
United States	16,818	17.9
Spain	15,145	16.1
India	7,845	8.4
China	5,906	6.3
Denmark	3,125	3.3
Italy	2,726	2.9
France	2,454	2.6
United Kingdom	2,389	2.5
Portugal	2,150	2.3
Total Top 10	80,805	86.1
Rest of the world	13,060	13.9
Total	93,864	100

The United States had the greatest increase in wind-powered electricity in 2007, adding 5,244 MW of capacity, and the GWEC anticipates it will become the top producer worldwide by the end of 2009. Thirty-four U.S. states were generating electricity from wind power by 2007, with Texas (4,356 MW), California (2,439 MW), Minnesota (1,299 MW), Iowa (1,273 MW), and Washington (1,163 MW) constituting the top producers.

Designing a Data Center Power System for Maximum Efficiency

Regardless of what source you draw upon to power your Data Center, you want to design the facility's electrical system to maximize capacity, reduce waste, and optimize consumption. Many of the components within your Data Center's power system offer opportunities for this.

As you begin to design the various physical elements, carefully determine their sizing and degree of redundancy. For sizing, avoid components that are oversized, providing superfluous capacity that goes unused or else consumes more resources than are strictly necessary, or undersized and prone to be a choke point for providing power. For redundancy, provide suitable layers of standby infrastructure without overbuilding and consuming resources, increasing electrical waste, and incurring capital costs unnecessarily.

Direct Current Versus Alternating Current

As mentioned at the beginning of this chapter, a certain amount of power is lost as electricity is conveyed from utility provider to Data Center to individual servers within that Data Center. One strategy that has been suggested for reducing this electrical waste is to avoid some of the multiple power conversions that occur within a Data Center by using direct current (DC) power instead of alternating current (AC). Eliminating electrical conversions lowers energy consumption, both by saving the electricity that is otherwise lost but also by reducing the need for cooling to deal with heat that is generated during conversion. Lowering energy consumption in turn cuts carbon emissions and operational costs for the Data Center.

AC power involves sending electrons back and forth across a wire, hence the term *alternating*. The reversal of direction occurs between 50 and 60 times per second; the exact rate, known as the frequency and expressed in Hertz, varies from among the electrical systems of different countries. It's 60 times per second (60 Hz) in the United States and 50 times per second (50 Hz) throughout Europe, for example. DC power sends the flow or current continuously in one direction. Batteries, which have positive and negative poles, use DC power.

Note   The terms direct current and Data Center are both commonly abbreviated as DC, so the phrase "DC power" in a conversation about Data Center power can be confusing unless it is obvious what DC represents. In this book the term *Data Center* is spelled out in all instances. Any use of the abbreviation DC refers to direct current.

AC power voltage can be changed by way of a transformer. This enables utility companies to transmit AC power across long distances over a high-voltage, low-amp wire and then convert it to lower voltages for final distribution to homes, businesses, and other uses. The alternative method, transmitting in a low-voltage, high-amp configuration requires much thicker and much more expensive wire.

For conventional Data Centers, power is delivered from the utility provider in AC format, converted to DC at the uninterruptible power source (UPS), converted back to AC for delivery throughout the Data Center and converted at the server yet again to DC. (Utility power is typically delivered at 600 volts or 480 volts in the United States and then stepped down to 208 volts or 120 volts for distribution to Data Center cabinets.) If a Data Center were to employ DC power instead of AC, most of those internal conversions could be avoided.

The key green question, then, is how great a gain in efficiency can the use of DC power provide? There is disagreement in the Data Center industry as to the answer.

Lawrence Berkeley National Laboratory (LBNL) suggests that implementing a DC electrical system in a Data Center can be more efficient than AC power by 20 percent or more, following a side-by-side comparison of rack-mounted servers powered by AC and DC. The demonstration project, conducted in 2006, included three configurations:

- **A conventional Data Center power delivery system:** AC-powered servers were provided with 208/120-volt AC power.

- **DC conversion/distribution at the rack:** A rectifier unit converted 208/120-volt AC at the rack and delivered 380-volt DC power to DC-powered servers.

- **DC conversion/distribution at the building/Data Center:** A system-level rectifier unit converted 480-volt AC to 380-volt DC and delivered it to DC-powered servers in the rack.

Results from the demonstration, summarized in the 2008 report "DC Power for Improved Data Center Efficiency," showed energy savings of 5 percent to 7 percent for the two DC configurations over the conventional AC configuration. Authors of the report state that the AC distribution systems used in the project were "best in class" and that the performance of the DC configurations actually represents a 28-percent efficiency improvement over the AC systems found in an average Data Center.

Note   The 2006 demonstration project by LBNL used 380-volt DC power, although that's not the only DC configuration considered for use in Data Centers. There are two other approaches commonly discussed:

- Stepping 480-volt AC power down to 48 volt-DC by way of a rectifier at the UPS, delivering the 48 volt power through the Data Center's power distribution units to rack power supplies

- Converting that 480-volt AC power to 550-volt DC in a rectifier, sending it to a power distribution unit, stepping it down to 48 volt in a DC-DC converter and then distributing it to rack power supplies

American Power Conversion (APC), manufacturer of Data Center electrical infrastructure systems, has a different view on DC power distribution, however. In a pair of whitepapers published in 2007, APC says "Many of the benefits commonly stated for DC distribution are unfounded or exaggerated" and "The latest high efficiency AC and DC power distribution architectures are shown to have virtually the same efficiency."

In its papers "AC vs. DC Power Distribution for Data Centers" and "A Quantitative Comparison of High Efficiency AC vs. DC Power Distribution for Data Centers," APC says that the LBNL study had "skewed" results from comparing legacy AC power distribution systems with hypothetical DC power distribution efficiency. APC's findings are that DC power distribution leads to only approximately a 1-percent gain in efficiency over existing high-efficiency AC distribution, and even achieving that would require the implementation of 380-volt DC architecture not in use today.

Even if DC power distribution can offer greater efficiency than APC concludes, other factors have largely precluded its use in the Data Center industry:

- Not all hardware deployed in Data Centers can operate on direct current power. If you want to pursue DC power in your Data Center, check with the vendors you typically buy machines from to confirm the models you want are available in a DC configuration. If they are, also determine whether you need to pay a premium for the DC power supplies as they are likely to be less common.

- Direct current power distribution often involves higher voltages than alternating current, posing a greater safety risk for facilities personnel. At minimum, this can require changing policies around the performance of electrical-related Data Center work, curtailing what activities can be done hot, that is with systems energized rather than turned off.

- Fewer people are trained on direct current power systems than AC power. With DC systems used less frequently, less people have experience servicing and maintaining them.

As long as those conditions exist, it's unlikely that most companies will use DC power for their Data Center. Expect the topic to continue to be discussed, however, and watch for future developments.

Power Distribution Units

Power distribution units (PDU) perform the final step in the power delivery chain of a Data Center, converting electricity to a voltage suitable for IT server cabinets and hardware. Although it's inevitable for some power to be lost during that conversion process, you can reduce that loss by using high-efficiency PDUs.

Greater PDU performance was actually mandated by law in North America beginning in 2005, when the United States and Canada each enacted legislation requiring low-voltage, dry-type transformers of the kind normally used in Data Centers to meet certain efficiency benchmarks. In the United States, it was the U.S. Energy Policy Act of 2005 requiring transformers to meet standards spelled out in the National Electrical Manufacturers Association's (NEMA) "Guide for Determining Energy Efficiency for Distribution Transformers, TP-1-2002," beginning in 2007. In Canada, it was the Canadian Standards Association's (CSA) own Minimum Efficiency Values for Dry-Type Transformers, C802.2.

Table 4.6 shows the minimum transformer efficiency levels required under those laws.

The efficiency levels are for when the transformers are carrying 35 percent of their nameplate-rated load.

Improving transformer efficiency among your Data Center PDUs by just a few percent adds up to significant cost and energy savings over time. PDU models with even greater electrical efficiency than mandated by U.S. and Canadian law are available on the marketplace and are certainly worth employing.

Table 4.6 *Efficiency Levels for Dry-Type Distribution Transformers (Three Phase, Low Voltage)*

kVA	Required Efficiency
30	97.5%
45	97.7%
75	98.0%
112.5	98.2%
125	98.2%
150	98.3%
225	98.5%
300	98.6%
500	98.7%
750	98.8%
1,000	98.9%

Note   A comparison study of PDUs operating in a 33,000-square foot (3,065.8-square meter) Data Center for the United States Postal Service (USPS) showed that replacing even relatively modern PDUs in the facility with more efficient models could save more than 780,000 kWh of energy, 1 million pounds (450 metric tons) of carbon dioxide and $100,000 per year in electricity.

The study, published in the 2008 paper "Opportunity for Transformer Energy Savings in Data Center PDUs" by Powersmiths was performed at the USPS' Data Center in San Mateo, California. Conversion losses were measured for three existing and six new PDUs. The existing PDUs included two 125 kVA units purchased less than 2 years prior and a third 150 kVA unit installed in the 1980s; the new PDUs included two 225 kVA and four 150 kVA units that exceed the efficiency levels listed in Table 4.6.

Measurements of the units are shown in Table 4.7.

The older equipment had electrical losses of nearly four times that of the new systems. (Interestingly, the PDU that was more than 20 years old showed greater efficiency than models less than 2 years old.) Assuming that all 36 existing PDUs at the USPS Data Center shared the average efficiency of those tested (94.6 percent), replacing them with newer, more efficient (98.4 percent) PDUs would save 787,418 kWh of energy, reduce 24,400 pounds (11.1 metric tons) of cooling load and avoid the production of 1,058,400 pounds (480 metric tons).

Based on regional power costs of $0.13 per kWh, the more efficient systems would also provide $107,700 per year in cost savings. Extrapolated for a 20-year lifespan, that amounts to $3.89 million.

Table 4.7   *Performance of PDUs in USPS Data Center*

	PDU	kVA	Average Load	Efficiency	Losses (kW)	Averages
Existing	1	125	42.0%	95.8%	2.094	94.6% efficiency 1.76 kW loss
	2	125	26.3%	91.1%	2.593	
	3	150	16.8%	97.0%	0.619	
New	4	225	16.9%	98.5%	0.600	98.4% efficiency 0.47 kW loss
	5	225	17.8%	98.5%	0.603	
	6	150	19.9%	98.5%	0.443	
	7	150	19.3%	98.5%	0.476	
	8	150	15.0%	98.1%	0.419	
	9	150	12.8%	98.3%	0.310	

Uninterruptible Power Sources

For decades, Data Center standby power systems have consisted of a generator paired with a bank of batteries. The battery bank, known as an uninterruptible power source or uninterruptible power supply (UPS), bridges the gap when commercial power fails and a Data Center's electrical load must be supported by its own on-site generator. The UPS carries the load for mere seconds; first when the load is transferred between the commercial feed and the generator at the onset of the outage and then again when the outage is over and the load is transferred back again. This is known as *ride-through power.*

Data Center designers usually equip a server environment with a UPS with sufficient capacity to handle the room's maximum possible power needs for at least a few minutes—much more than the handful of seconds that are needed for ride-through. Designers who want to provide a safety margin, if a malfunction occurs during the transfer of electrical load between UPS and generator, provide more capacity. If a commercial power fails and for some reason the load doesn't transition correctly to the standby generator, this additional UPS capacity gives Data Center IT personnel extra minutes to deliberately shut down servers, which is gentler on them than the "crash" that occurs when power to them fails abruptly. Occasionally, the extra time is enough to either permit Data Center facilities staff to fix whatever problem prevented the electrical load from transferring to the generator or even for commercial power to return.

As ubiquitous as batteries are in Data Center standby power systems, they have their drawbacks. For one, they're not infallible. Batteries sometimes fail to adequately hold a charge, exposing the Data Center to downtime whenever a commercial outage occurs.

They're also not particularly eco-friendly. Conventional UPS batteries contain toxic lead, sulfuric acid, fiberglass, and thermoplastic polymers, and under certain conditions they can emit highly flammable hydrogen gas. Like PDUs, UPS systems also waste a certain amount of energy. Finally, batteries need to be replaced every few years, although most manufacturers do take them back and at least partially recycle their components.

Fortunately, you can take some steps to make the UPS for your Data Center more energy-efficient and therefore greener. To start, design your UPS system to be modular, consisting of a series of smaller components rather than just a few large components that are lightly loaded. Different UPS models and configurations provide different levels of energy efficiency from one another, but all generally perform more efficiently when carrying a higher electrical load.

A modular design also provides greater redundancy—if a UPS fails for some reason, the failure has less impact if the unit accounts for a smaller portion of your overall standby power system.

A 2005 report on UPS efficiency, "High Performance Buildings: Data Centers Uninterruptible Power Supplies," measured a variety of UPS types and saw average efficiency levels of 86 percent for units carrying 25 percent of their maximum electrical load, 89 percent for units carrying a 50 percent load, and 90 percent for units carrying a load of 75 percent or higher.

The report, featuring research performed by Ecos Consulting and EPRI Solutions for Lawrence Berkeley National Laboratory, notes that UPS systems are typically operated between 30 percent and 50 percent of maximum load—even less in newer facilities that are only lightly populated with IT hardware.

Figure 4.5 shows a generic efficiency curve for a UPS and illustrates how they perform better when carrying more electrical load.

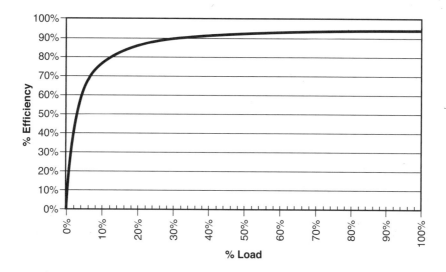

Figure 4.5   *UPS Efficiency Curve*

Because UPS efficiency does vary by model, configuration, and how heavily loaded the unit is, you can additionally make a greener UPS system by requesting efficiency curves from the manufacturer for the specific models you are considering purchasing. If you can accurately estimate how heavily the unit will be loaded in your Data Center, you can then choose a UPS that performs most efficiently under those conditions.

A much greener alternative to batteries is a rotary or dynamic UPS. In a rotary UPS, a flywheel is connected to the Data Center's commercial power source, building up kinetic energy based upon the mass of the flywheel and how quickly it rotates. (Some systems use a heavy flywheel moving at relatively low speed; others use a lighter flywheel moving at higher speed.) When commercial power fails, stored kinetic energy from the rotary UPS is tapped to support the Data Center electrical load for the few critical seconds needed for the facility's standby generator to engage.

Flywheels lack the toxic materials of batteries and require less maintenance, making them notably greener. Although rotary systems can have a higher initial price tag than conventional batteries, that additional upfront expense is more than offset over time through reduced costs for maintenance and disposing of batteries. Flywheel solutions also occupy a smaller footprint than equivalent battery banks, which can offer more options when designing a Data Center facility.

The major caveat that comes with having a flywheel standby power system is that it can only hold a Data Center's electrical load for a fraction of the time of a battery bank—seconds instead of minutes. That's sufficient to provide ride-through power but offers no cushion if for some reason power fails to transition correctly.

In 2003, the U.S. Department of Energy's Federal Energy Management Program issued a "Federal Technology Alert" document (DOE/EE-0286) about flywheel energy storage. The agency pronounced flywheel systems "generally more reliable than batteries" and recommended their use in conjunction with a generator that can be brought online within 10 seconds or else paired with batteries. The flywheel could handle common, momentary power disruptions and extend the life of the batteries, which can be harmed by frequent discharging and recharging.

If you're comfortable with your Data Center not having that additional runtime for ride-through power, a rotary system provides a classic green solution—gentler on the environment and with less expensive operational costs.

Note   Cisco historically used battery UPS systems at its major Data Centers, sizing them to provide 20 minutes of runtime when a room operates at maximum electrical load. They're coupled with generators that have 8 hours of runtime. (When an outage occurs generators are refueled every 4 hours, allowing them to operate for days at a time if needed.)

Beginning in 2009, though, the company began using flywheel technology in place of UPS batteries in new Data Center designs. The rationale for the change was that not only are dynamic UPS systems greener, but also the 20-minute runtime from UPS batteries doesn't buy much during an outage involving a major Data Center. Much of that time is inevitably consumed as the IT and facilities staffs that support the Data Center work to determine that the room's electrical load hasn't been picked up by the standby generator as expected. How many servers can realistically be shut down in the remaining time offered by the UPS?

Generators

Diesel generators, the hallmark of Data Center standby power systems, aren't known for being particularly eco-friendly because they emit carbon monoxide, hydrocarbons, nitrogen oxides, and particulate matter. It's no surprise, then, that government and air quality agencies in certain regions of the world restrict how many hours per year or quarter that generators can operate or else what level of emissions they are allowed to produce.

The U.S. Environmental Protection Agency in 2006 issued New Source Performance Standards (NSPS) that steadily increase emissions restrictions on all types of stationary diesel engines, including those found in Data Centers. By 2014 the standards for new generators with capacity greater than 560 kilowatts and 751 horsepower—the category that Data Center generators fall within—mandate 60 percent fewer nitrous oxides, 85 percent fewer hydrocarbons, 70 percent less carbon monoxide, and 90 percent less particulate matter than standards in effect before 2006.

Table 4.8 shows past, present, and future emission restrictions in the United States for generators greater than 560 kilowatts and 751 horsepower. Emission maximums are listed in grams per kilowatt hour (g/kWh) and come from the U.S. Environmental Protection Agency.

Table 4.8   *U.S. EPA Emissions Restrictions for Data Center Generators*

Emission Material	2000–2005	2006–2010	2011–2013	2014–2017
Nitrous oxides	9.2	6.4	3.5	3.5
Hydrocarbons	1.3	6.4	0.40	0.19
Carbon monoxide	11.4	3.5	3.5	3.5
Particulate matter	0.54	0.20	0.10	.04

France and Germany regulate stationary generator emissions as well. France's standards, spelled out in its Directive 2910, address the same pollutants as the U.S. EPA and vary based upon how many hours per year a generator operates (more or less than 500 hours), its megawatt thermal rating, and for some emissions the fuel it operates on. Germany's standards, under its Technische Anleitung zur Reinhaltung der Luft (TA-Luft) regulation, address nitrous oxides, carbon monoxide, and dust and also vary based upon a generator's megawatt thermal rating and fuel type.

Although the European Union and several individual countries including Chile, China, India, Japan, and Singapore have emissions standards for certain types of diesel engines, their regulations do not apply to stationary generators. Generator manufacturers and related industry organizations are strong lobbyists for consistent standards, however—none want to supply different products from country to country—so if future regulations are introduced for stationary generators, they are likely to align with the U.S. standards.

When choosing a commercial generator, you obviously want to be greener by choosing a model that generates minimal emissions. Lower emissions are typically accomplished through engine controls that govern fuel quantity, injection timing and pressure, and turbocharging.

Other approaches for reducing emissions involve treating a generator's exhaust gas. For instance, nitrogen oxide emissions can be greatly reduced by way of a selective catalytic reduction system. The system injects urea into the exhaust stream as it passes over a catalyst, which then converts the mixture into nitrogen and water vapor. Another option is to employ a soot trap that captures particulate matter from a generator's exhaust. Such traps either deploy mechanical filters or catalytic filters that transform particulate matter into carbon dioxide.

Lighting

Lighting accounts for only a small fraction of the power consumed in a Data Center, but it still provides another opportunity to make the facility greener through energy efficiency.

Daylighting, the practice of using natural light within a building, is quite green because it not only avoids the energy demand and cooling associated with operating artificial lighting, it's also considered an environmental improvement for people working in the area. Properly diffused daylighting actually improves people's comfort and productivity. (A series of studies performed by the Heschong Mahone Group for Pacific Gas and Electric in 1999 and then the California Energy Commission's Public Interest Energy Research program in 2003 showed improved worker performance, higher student test scores, and even greater sales of retail items in store areas under natural lighting conditions.)

Daylighting has generally been considered impractical for Data Centers due to physical security constraints—no one wants an exterior window or skylight on a Data Center. However, you still can supplement your server environment's conventional lighting during the day through the use of solar tubes. Solar tubes collect and redirect light along their length, allowing daylight to penetrate an otherwise enclosed interior space. Solar tubes vary in size, with larger installations being about 14 inches (35.6 centimeters) in diameter and up to 40 feet (12.2 meters) in length. A transparent dome at the top (roofside) of the tube enables light to pour in; a diffuser at the bottom distributes light into the interior space. Note that solar tubes don't store light or convert it to electricity as a photovoltaic component does. Just like a window or skylight, the solar tube simply enables whatever daylight is available to pass through.

Fluorescent ceiling lights are a mainstay of Data Centers as much as office areas, so the same lighting efficiency suggestions offered in Chapter 3 apply: Deploy thinner T8 or T5 fluorescent bulbs or even light emitting diode (LED) installations to reduce energy usage compared to traditional T12 bulbs, and install timers and motion sensors so lights automatically shut off when employees are not present.

Whatever lighting system you employ in your Data Center, be careful when laying out the room's physical infrastructure so as to not obstruct the output of light in the area. Potential obstructions include

- Cable trays suspended from the ceiling

- Patch panels mounted above racks

- Busbars suspended from the ceiling

- Ceiling-mounted cooling units

- Exhaust chimneys for server cabinets

- Limited clearance between the Data Center ceiling and the tops of server cabinets

Call out the location of these Data Center items as part of your Data Center design documents to ensure they don't accidentally obstruct the room's overhead lighting.

Finally, consider deploying light-colored server cabinets in your Data Center rather than dark ones. They better reflect light, brightening the room.

Power Monitoring

When a new server or networking device is installed in your Data Center, how do you know how much power it draws and, therefore, how much of your Data Center's electrical capacity it consumes? Ratings on hardware power supplies are no gauge. They represent a maximum limit for the unit, not typical consumption. Data Center industry assumptions around what a server will actually consume compared to its nameplate rating vary from 40 percent to 65 percent.

If you chose a particular hardware model for the promise of energy efficiency, how can you verify it is delivering on the manufacturer's claims? Even assuming the energy consumption data published in a hardware maker's marketing materials are entirely accurate, it's unlikely that conditions in your Data Center are identical to the environment in which that data was collected.

Consider employing branch circuit monitors that track the level of current at the circuits and breakers of a Data Center's electrical panels, and amp-reading power strips that monitor power draw at server cabinets and network racks.

Although these tools don't make your Data Center greener by themselves, they provide up-to-the-moment visibility of how your Data Center is consuming energy. This can help you identify the most power-hungry hardware in your facility and gauge the effectiveness of green improvements you make.

Overhead Versus Under-Floor Distribution

A key decision to make when designing a Data Center is whether to route its electrical conduits and structured cabling overhead or below a raised floor. Both approaches have been implemented to good effect in server environments around the world.

Raised floors have been prevalent in Data Centers for years, serving as the plenum in which to deliver cold air from a room's air handlers. Many Data Center designers also place electrical and structured cabling in this space, terminating them below cabinet locations, so they can be accessed by simply raising a floor panel. Proponents of this approach like having cabling and electrical conduits out of sight yet easily accessible and also the capability to guide airflow by strategically positioning perforated tiles. Ample under-floor depth can also readily accommodate large quantities of cabling and other physical infrastructure.

Figure 4.6 shows the area below a Data Center raised floor, with structured cabling and electrical conduits routed there. The raised floor shown in the image is 36 inches (91 centimeters) deep.

Image provided by courtesy of Scott Smith

Figure 4.6   *Below a Data Center's Raised Floor*

A more recent preference among some Data Center designers has been to forgo a raised floor and instead route power and cabling infrastructure above server rows. Proponents of this approach find it more convenient to make cabling changes in an overhead tray and believe the visibility of the overhead installation reduces the likelihood of Data Center users routing cables in a sloppy manner. This approach is also likely to be less expensive during initial installation because you avoid the cost of the raised floor's support grid and floor tiles. The key challenge in implementing an overhead installation is, as touched on in the "Lighting" section of this chapter, gracefully fitting power, cabling, fire suppression, lighting, and cooling elements in the limited space.

Which approach has less environmental impact? Eliminating a raised flooring system results in the use of fewer materials, which is certainly greener. Beyond that, focus on how efficiently air can be distributed within the specific Data Center. This impacts the room's energy consumption and can depend upon multiple factors including the size and shape of the room, what cooling design is used, what hardware is deployed, and the resulting quantity and physical footprint of structured cabling and electrical conduits.

Summary

Improving energy efficiency represents the greatest opportunity for making your Data Center greener, conserving energy, reducing carbon emissions, and saving money. Data Center elements that consume the most energy, such as the cooling system, and those at the end of the delivery chain like IT hardware, can provide some of the most significant improvements.

Knowing the electrical mix of different geographic regions enables you to choose a greener location for your future Data Center or understand the emissions of your existing server environment and assess the potential carbon savings that can be gained if you make your facility more energy-efficient. Look to the International Energy Agency for information about the energy-related carbon emissions of various countries and to the U.S. Environmental Protection Agency for those of regions within the United States.

Several greener forms of energy are available to either supplement or replace a Data Center's commercial or standby power sources. These include biofuels usable in Data Center standby generators, fuel cells that burn natural gas and can substitute for commercial power, hydropower that harnesses the motion of water and avoids the emissions of conventional energy sources, solar power that can supplement commercial power during daylight hours, and wind power that can also complement utility power.

Optimize your Data Center power system by not overbuilding it—base the size and number of components on the capacity and availability needs of the facility.

Powering a Data Center with direct current (DC) rather than alternating current (AC) power is frequently proposed as a method for improving energy efficiency as it avoids multiple conversions and the electrical losses that come with them. Despite the energy-savings potential, DC power distribution has not been implemented due to doubt that it can provide notable energy savings beyond AC power distribution, not all servers being available in DC configurations, worker safety concerns regarding the higher voltage typically employed with DC, and fewer people being trained on DC power systems.

Choose highly efficient power distribution units in your Data Center. Employing PDUs that are just a few percent more efficient than other models can conserve tens of thousands of kilowatt hours of energy per year, which translates to avoiding tens of thousands of pounds of carbon dioxide and saving thousands of dollars per year in electrical costs.

Uninterruptible power source batteries aren't generally green because they incorporate materials such as lead and sulfuric acid, they waste energy during operation, and they require replacement every few years. UPS systems operate more efficiently when carrying a larger load, so design a modular system consisting of smaller components rather than a large system that is bound to be lightly loaded and, therefore, perform less efficiently. When looking to buy a UPS, obtain efficiency curves from the manufacturer and choose a model that performs the best under the load conditions you anticipate for your specific Data Center.

An alternative to UPS batteries is a rotary UPS that uses flywheel technology to store kinetic energy. Rotary systems are greener than conventional battery designs and less expensive to maintain, although they can provide only several seconds of ride-through power instead of the minutes offered by batteries.

Data Center standby generators can be made greener by implementing technologies to limit the carbon monoxide, hydrocarbons, nitrogen oxides, and particulate matter that they emit. Look for generator models that incorporate engine controls to minimize emissions by controlling fuel quantity, injection timing, and pressure and turbocharging, and those that use selective catalytic reduction systems and soot traps.

Improve Data Center lighting efficiency by using solar tubes to bring daylight into the facility, by deploying thinner T8 or T5 fluorescent bulbs or light emitting diodes in place of conventional T12 fluorescent bulbs, and by installing timers and motion sensors to shut off overhead lights when employees are not present.

Use branch circuit monitoring and amp-reading power strips to tell how much energy is consumed and at which specific locations within your Data Center.

Power and cabling can be effectively routed overhead or under-floor in a Data Center. Strategically position physical infrastructure components to avoid interfering with airflow efficiency.

Chapter 5

Cooling Your Way to a Greener Data Center

This chapter discusses how Data Center temperature settings impact energy usage and offers design strategies, technology solutions, and operational methods for improving cooling efficiency.

Setting Data Center Temperatures

Part of what determines how hard your Data Center cooling system has to work, and therefore how much energy it consumes, is the temperature at which you maintain the room. Operating a server environment at 65 degrees Fahrenheit (18.3 degrees Celsius) obviously requires more electricity for cooling than operating it at 75 degrees Fahrenheit (23.9 degrees Celsius), for instance.

For decades, Data Center managers sought to maintain server environments at temperatures slightly below that of office building space, applying time-proven wisdom that computing equipment performs better in cool conditions than warm. (It's an observation confirmed by physics—circuit speeds are faster due to lower resistance, components degrade slower, and heat removal is more efficient at cooler temperatures.)

As server densities increased, however, causing Data Center cooling capacities to shrink and energy consumption of Data Center cooling systems to grow, many people in IT, facilities, and even the air-conditioning industry began considering the energy and cost savings to be gained by raising operational temperatures.

The American Society of Heating, Refrigerating and Air-Conditioning Engineers (ASHRAE), for instance, in 2008 widened its recommended temperature range for IT hardware, "to provide greater flexibility in facility operations, particularly with the goal of reduced energy consumption in Data Centers." The 2008 ASHRAE Environmental Guidelines for Datacom Equipment recommends a temperature range of 64.4 degrees to 80.6 degrees Fahrenheit (18 degrees to 27 degrees Celsius), measured at the server inlet, nearly twice the span of its 2004 recommendation of 68 degrees to 77 degrees

Fahrenheit (20 degrees to 25 degrees Celsius). Even broader ranges are reportedly being considered for the future.

Data Center industry publications meanwhile reported in various articles in 2007 and 2008 that Google, Hewlett-Packard, Microsoft, Sun Microsystems, and Washington Mutual have each opted to raise temperature settings in their server environments as a way to reduce energy consumption and lower costs. The Gartner Research's 2008 report, "How to Save a Million Kilowatt Hours in your Data Center," includes raising operational temperatures as a recommended practice to reduce Data Center power consumption.

The most dramatic benefits from higher operational temperatures are realized by Data Centers that have economizers—energy-saving devices discussed later in this chapter. The warmer that it is acceptable for a Data Center to function, the more days per year that economizers can supplement the facility's conventional cooling system, thereby lowering energy consumption, electrical costs, and carbon emissions.

Data Centers without economizers can see lesser energy reductions. They benefit from raising the supply air or chilled water temperature for the Data Center cooling system, which increases the efficiency of the chiller. Every 1 degree Fahrenheit (0.56 Celsius) increase in the temperature of the chilled water supply leads to a 1 percent to 2 percent increase in chiller efficiency; therefore, a chiller that can supply a Data Center with chilled water at 55 degrees Fahrenheit (12.8 degrees Celsius) will be 10 percent to 20 percent more efficient than one required to produce chilled water at 45 degrees Fahrenheit (7.2 degrees Celsius).

Before you rush to raise the set points of your Data Center air handlers, though, you need to carefully balance potential energy, cost, and carbon savings against the ultimate purpose of your server environment—to protect IT hardware and ensure high availability. Consider the following caveats that come with a higher Data Center operating temperature:

- **The higher the overall temperature in your server environment, the less buffer you have against a cooling malfunction:** If one or more air handlers go offline, temperatures can skyrocket—especially in a room with high equipment density and power consumption. A cooling malfunction in a room operating near 80 degrees Fahrenheit (26.7 degrees Celsius) is obviously going to bring servers to thermal shutdown faster than one operating at 68 degrees Fahrenheit (20 degrees Celsius).

- **Data Center temperatures vary:** Setting your Data Center temperature at 75 degrees Fahrenheit (23.9 degrees Celsius) might mean some systems are actually at 80 degrees Fahrenheit (26.7 degrees Celsius). Temperatures often vary across a server environment, especially along the height of a cabinet. In a Data Center that has open server rows arranged in hot and cold aisles, the coldest air enters the bottom front of a server cabinet, but how much warmer is what enters at the top front of that cabinet?

Note If a Data Center loses its cooling capability, the impact upon its hardware can be swift and severe. A study by Opengate Data Systems shows that servers housed in a Data Center operating at 10 kw of load per server cabinet suffers thermal shutdown in just 1 minute when cooling goes offline during a commercial power outage. In a Data Center operating at 5 kw per cabinet, thermal shutdown occurs in just over 3 minutes.

The Data Center Emergency Cooling Study was performed in 2007 through computer modeling and represented a utility power failure at a small Data Center in which standby power kept hardware operational but did not support the room's cooling system—a common arrangement in small facilities supported solely by a UPS and no generator. The study simulated an 840-square foot (78-square meter) server environment possessing a 10-foot (3-square-meter) high ceiling and an 18-inch (45.7-centimeter) deep raised floor. Electrical load was divided evenly among 14 racks, which were represented in a hot- and cold-aisle configuration and supplied with cooling suitable to achieve a temperature of 64.4 degrees Fahrenheit (18 degrees Celsius) at the server intake.

When cooling was taken offline, with 5 kw of load per cabinet, temperatures climbed 1 degree Fahrenheit every 2.4 seconds (1 degree Celsius every 4.3 seconds), reaching 114.8 Fahrenheit (46 Celsius) in 2 minutes and 165.2 Fahrenheit (74 Celsius) in 4 minutes. Figure 5.1 illustrates the temperature changes, measured at the intake and exhaust points of hardware.

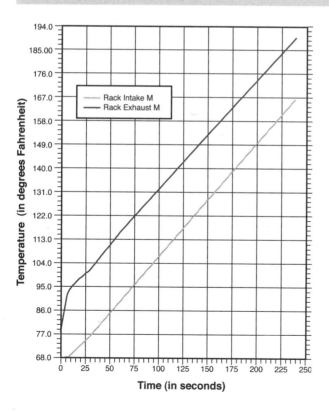

Figure 5.1 *Temperature Climb During a Commercial Power Failure*

Note Hardware manufacturer Dell explored temperature variation within a server cabinet by installing 29 of its 1U servers into a 42U cabinet along with a 1U keyboard/monitor tray and three portable UPSs. According to its 2002 whitepaper, "Rack Impacts on Cooling for High Density Servers," server inlet temperatures varied by as much as 11 degrees Fahrenheit (6 degrees Celsius) based upon how high or low they were positioned within the cabinet.

- **Fans on Data Center hardware might begin working harder:** Some models of hardware feature variable speed fans, which at cooler temperatures adopt a lower flow rate and therefore use less energy. Those fans could respond to a Data Center's higher temperatures by running faster, consuming more energy, and being noisier. ASHRAE, in its 2008 Environmental Guidelines document, suggests that a 3.6 degrees Fahrenheit (2 degrees Celsius) increase in Data Center temperatures could see a corresponding rise in noise of 3 to 5 decibels. Many existing Data Centers are already so loud from air handlers and hardware fans that it's impossible to converse with another person just a couple of steps away; raising the noise level even higher can potentially cause hearing loss among those who work in the Data Center for extended periods of time.

- **Hot aisles will get hotter:** It's not unusual for the aisle behind a bank of servers to reach 100 degrees Fahrenheit (37.8 degrees Celsius). A higher Data Center operational temperature can raise that threshold—up to 130 degrees Fahrenheit (54.4 degrees Celsius) according to some estimates. That's an uncomfortable and potentially unsafe condition for Data Center users to work in unless mechanisms are in place to evacuate the heat.

- **Equipment makers might balk at honoring warranties for hardware housed in warmer environments:** When an IT engineer calls a manufacturer about a malfunction and there's no clear cause, it's not unheard of for the service representative to question the environment in which the device resides. Specification sheets for Data Center hardware often list operating temperatures of 95 degrees Fahrenheit (35 degrees Celsius) or hotter, but that won't stop someone from pointing at the ambient temperature as the source of a mystery malfunction.

So, it's valid to raise the operational temperature of your Data Center to make it greener, but be sure you're comfortable with the reduced thermal buffer and other conditions that come with the higher set point. If you have suitable monitoring tools to do so, consider slightly raising your Data Center temperature every couple of months and then measuring the energy consumption involved with your cooling system functioning at that level. Over time, you can get a good idea of what energy and cost reductions you achieve for each incremental temperature change and can then determine weather the savings are worth the trade-offs.

Heat Recovery and Reuse

Much of this chapter involves design and operational strategies for cooling a server environment more effectively. That is, how to offset the room's heat load as efficiently as possible. The greenest improvement you can make to your Data Center cooling isn't to overcome the facility's heat load, though. It's to transform that heat load from something that consumes resources to something that is a resource. In other words, put the heat generated by your Data Center to good use.

Using Waste Heat *from* the Data Center

By capturing Data Center waste heat and reusing it elsewhere, you save energy, carbon emissions, and money on two different fronts at the same time. You save where the waste heat is applied, using less energy and fuel to warm that location, and you save in the Data Center where you don't have to cool that waste heat.

Data Center waste heat is used in several creative applications these days:

■   A 2,150-square foot (200-square meter) Data Center in Uitikon, Switzerland, warms a nearby community swimming pool with some of its waste heat. Heat from the server environment is routed through a heat exchanger that warms water that is then pumped into the pool. The Data Center, operated by GIB-Services and designed by IBM, is estimated to generate 2,800 MWh of waste per year when operating at full capacity.

■   Intel built a 10,000-square foot (929-square meter) Data Center in Israel in which waste heat warms the 11-floor building in which it resides, providing office heating during the winter and hot water for onsite kitchens and showers throughout the year. Heated condenser water, which in a conventional Data Center is released into the air by way of a cooling tower, is captured by heat recovery chillers, providing hot water for building heating systems. Recovering the waste heat is estimated to save $235,000 per year compared to a conventional infrastructure design to cool the Data Center and heat the office space. The design, meanwhile, eliminates the need for additional boilers to heat the overall building, avoiding the carbon dioxide and nitrogen oxides that would otherwise be emitted.

■   Canada's *Winnipeg Sun* newspaper has its newsroom warmed by a 2500-square foot (232.3-square meter) Data Center that is owned and operated by its parent company, Quebecor Media, and located on the ground floor directly below. On cold days, which can easily account for 6 to 8 months per year in Winnipeg, about two-thirds of the server environment's waste heat warms the newspaper's editorial offices while the remainder is diverted into the adjacent warehouse area containing the paper's printing presses and receiving dock. Delivery of the waste heat is directed using automated baffles controlled by temperature sensors. On warm days, surplus waste heat is diverted outside.

■   The University of Notre Dame's Center for Research Computing is using racks of servers installed in a converted shipping container to warm a greenhouse and botanical garden maintained by the city of South Bend, Indiana. The 8-foot long by 20-foot wide by 8-foot high (2.4-meters long by 6.1-meters wide by 2.4-meters high) container features a single row of 8 racks drawing up to 45 kilowatts of power and generating 150,000 BTUs per hour of usable heat according to Paul Brenner, high-performance computing scientist for the university. Using the waste heat saves about $35,000 per year to warm the Ella Morris and Muessel-Ellison Botanical Conservatories and Potawatomi Greenhouse and cuts equivalent cooling costs for the hardware. The reduced energy costs from the project enables the Center to extend the usable operational life of the servers, which are used for activities including atomic modeling, molecular dynamics simulations of chemical or nuclear reactions, and data mining of genetic patterns.

Figure 5.2 shows a sketch of the Sustainable Distributed Data Center used by the University of Notre Dame's Center for Research Computing to warm a community greenhouse.

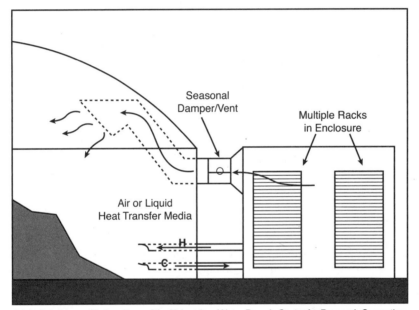

Original sketch provided courtesy of the University of Notre Dame's Center for Research Computing

Figure 5.2 *Warming a Facility with Server Exhaust*

Using Waste Heat *for* the Data Center

Using the heat from a server environment to warm another space isn't the only way to strategically reuse waste heat in a Data Center project. You can reverse that approach, using heat from another source to help cool your server environment. This can be done by employing chillers that use heat as part of their cooling process rather than the mechanical compression that conventional Data Center chillers use.

A traditional Data Center chiller contains an evaporator, a compressor, and a condenser. The evaporator transforms liquid refrigerant into gas and in the process chills the water that circulates to and from Data Center air handlers. The compressor draws in this gas, changing it into high-pressure, high-temperature vapor that can be condensed easily. The condenser transforms this vapor back into liquid, discharging heat, and then returns the liquid refrigerant back to the evaporator.

The compression and delivery of the refrigerant vapor to the condenser is driven by an electric motor, which obviously consumes electricity. Two other forms of chillers, absorption and adsorption chillers, instead use heat—in the form of steam, hot water, or combustion—to perform the compression.

An absorption chiller, the more common of the two heat-driven chillers, also features an evaporator and condenser but a generator and absorber in place of the compressor. Thermal compression occurs by combining heat with a mixture of a refrigerant and absorbing material—most commonly water and lithium bromide although ammonia and water are also used. The chiller's cooling effect occurs when the refrigerant is evaporated at low pressure conditions. The vaporized refrigerant is then absorbed, pumped into the generator, and regenerated by applying heat. Refrigerant exits the generator and is chilled by cooling water, such as that provided by a cooling tower, and then circulated back to the evaporator.

An adsorption chiller features two absorbing chambers, the evaporator and condenser, and employs a solid absorbing material—typically silica gel. The chiller's cooling effect occurs in the evaporator when the refrigerant is evaporated at low pressure, by adsorption of the silica gel. Heat in the form of hot water regenerates the silica gel in the other chamber. The resulting water vapor is condensed and then cooled by cooling water such as provided by a cooling tower.

Although absorption and adsorption chillers produce less cooling relative to their incoming energy than mechanical chillers, they're ultimately a greener choice when the source of their energy is waste heat rather than the electricity used by a conventional chiller.

Mechanical System Opportunities for Efficiency

Several green approaches can be applied to the major components of a Data Center's cooling system. These encompass the mechanical infrastructure elements that are maintained by the facilities organization and are predominantly located outside of the hosting space.

Economizers

An excellent way to green your Data Center cooling system is to reduce the hours of operation for its most power-hungry component—the chiller. This can be done through the use of economizers that, when temperature and humidity are right, allow you to leverage outside conditions to cool your Data Center rather than running the chiller.

There are two types of economizers:

- **Airside:** An airside economizer works by drawing cool outside air into the Data Center cooling system. Instead of chilling the Data Center's heated return air and re-cycling it back into the hosting space, the process that normally happens, filtered outside air is used.

- **Waterside:** A waterside economizer works by using your facility's cooling towers to cool the chilled water through evaporation.

Both types of economizers avoid running the compressor within your Data Center chiller, saving energy. Because economizers rely upon cool external temperatures, they can obviously be used more frequently in regions where colder temperatures are prevalent for longer periods of time and in Data Centers that have higher operational temperature settings.

Cooling with Outside Air

One of the ways that Data Centers traditionally protect the hardware they house is to limit their exposure to outside air conditions. The temperature extremes, humidity ranges, and contaminants of external air are all considered unhealthy for servers, so Data Centers expend a notable amount of power to regulate those conditions.

What if you could forgo those controls and simply draw in outside air—warm or cold, moist or dry, clean or dirty—and use it to cool your Data Center while expelling server exhaust outside? How bad would it be for your hardware and how much power could you save by simplifying your cooling infrastructure?

Intel explored these questions in a proof of concept test in which it tracked the operational performance of hardware during a 10-month period in 2007 and 2008. They installed 900 blade servers into two compartments of a 1,000-square foot (92.9-square meter) server environment in New Mexico, loading each space with a power density of more than 200 watts per square foot (2,153 watts per square meter). One compartment used a conventional cooling design, recirculating and cooling internal air. The other space used an air economizer, drawing in outside air as warm as 92 degrees Fahrenheit (33.3 degrees Celsius) while venting heated air outside.

A few controls were placed upon the compartment using outside air. The air chiller engaged when temperatures exceeded 90 degrees Fahrenheit (32.2 degrees Celsius) and supply air was warmed when temperature conditions dipped below 65 degrees Fahrenheit (18.3 degrees Celsius). A household air filter blocked major air particles although did not prevent dust from covering servers. Humidity was uncontrolled and fluctuated from 4 percent to 90 percent during the test.

Continues

Continued

According to the Intel whitepaper, "Reducing Data Center Cost with an Air Economizer," when the economizer was in use in the compartment that used outside air, it reduced cooling-related energy consumption by 74 percent. With New Mexico's climate, which remains below 90 degrees Fahrenheit (32.2 degrees Celsius) 91 percent of the year, this equates to a 67 percent reduction in cooling-related power usage per year. Intel estimates that for a 10-MW Data Center that extrapolates to $2.87 million per year in cooling costs (assuming 8 cents per kWh for electricity) and, by simultaneously avoiding the need for evaporative cooling measures, 76 million gallons (287.7 million liters) per year in makeup water can be conserved.

How did hardware perform in the dusty, minimally controlled environment? Servers in the compartment using outside air incurred a 4.46-percent failure rate, compared to a 2.45-percent failure rate in the other compartment. Depending upon your point of view, that either represents a minor variation (a mere 2.01 percent between the two environments) or a major disparity (4.46 percent is 82 percent higher than 2.45).

Personally, I'm not quite ready to throw open the proverbial windows of my Data Centers and turn off the conventional cooling system, but I think this study raises interesting questions:

- Where is the ideal balance point when it comes to expending energy to insulate hardware from external conditions? Are we overprotecting servers and therefore wasting a tremendous amount of energy and money?

- What if the test continued for a longer period of time? Under its dusty conditions, would the server failure rates have risen?

- Might unregulated outside air be a viable option for cooling a lab environment or Data Center that has lower availability requirements?

The Green Grid consortium offers an online calculator for estimating how many hours per year that airside or waterside economizers can be used, along with the associated energy and cost savings, at locations across Canada and the United States. Users enter key information about their Data Center site such as the IT electrical load, facility electrical load, local energy costs, and ZIP code.

For instance, a Data Center with 3 MW of electrical load—2 MW for IT load and 1 MW for supporting infrastructure—based in San Jose, California, (ZIP code 95134) and paying 13 cents per kWh can operate an air economizer for 1,358 hours for a savings of $84,000 or a waterside economizer for 3,296 hours for a savings of $200,000, according to the tool. Meanwhile, a Data Center with the same electrical load based in Research Triangle Park, North Carolina (ZIP code 27709) and paying 8.5 cents per kWh is projected to operate an air economizer for 617 hours for a savings of $25,000 or a waterside economizer for 3,457 hours for a savings of $140,000.

The calculator contains data from hourly observations from 2,186 weather stations in the United States and Canada, collected from 1999 through 2008. It is available at the Library and Tool section of the Green Grid website: http://www.thegreengrid.org/.

Heat Wheel

Another method of leveraging cool outside temperatures is to employ a rotary heat exchanger, also known as a *heat wheel*. The wheel rotates slowly between cool outside air and warm Data Center air. Panels within the wheel are cooled by the outside air and then, once inside, absorb heat from the server environment.

Although heat wheel technology isn't new, it has only recently begun to be implemented within server environments. As with economizers, the heat wheel saves energy by avoiding the need to operate the Data Center's compressors. The heat wheel also has an advantage over economizers in that it minimally mixes internal and external air, reducing the need to filter contaminants or control humidity.

Note   Telecommunications company KPN and Intel tested heat wheel performance in a KPN server environment in Amsterdam, Netherlands, in 2007. (Amsterdam is an ideal location to implement a heat wheel because of its cool climate most of the year.)

For the test, which is outlined in the Intel case study document, "The Coolest Data Centre," the companies installed 54 servers and powered on about 300 household heaters to generate a thermal load in the 1,076-square foot (100-square meter) Data Center.

Exhaust air ranging from 82.4 degrees to 98.6 degrees Fahrenheit (28 degrees to 37 degrees Celsius) was passed through the heat wheel, which succeeded in maintaining the Data Center at a temperature range of 68 degrees to 77 degrees Fahrenheit (20 degrees to 25 degrees Celsius).

Geothermal Cooling

A different method of using your Data Center's surroundings to help cool the facility is to implement a geothermal system. That is, embed piping below the surface of your property and use the cool underground temperature to chill liquid that passes through the piping. (Piping can be arranged in a horizontal or vertical pattern, depending upon the ground space available on the Data Center property.)

Geothermal cooling involves less energy than conventional Data Center cooling design because it uses the ground temperature and because it enjoys some insulation from seasonal temperature variations. A geothermal system can either be implemented in conjunction with a traditional Data Center cooling tower or built as a self-contained, closed-loop system. The closed-loop system provides the additional green benefit of avoiding the need for copious amounts of makeup water—the water needed to replace what is typically lost from a cooling tower due to evaporation—from the local municipal supply.

Like many green technologies, a geothermal system is more costly upfront than a conventional cooling system for a Data Center, but is ultimately less expensive over time, due to reduced energy costs and maintenance.

The ultimate implementation of geothermal cooling for your Data Center is to build the facility underground, causing the surrounding earth to serve as a large heat sink. In addition to their cooling benefit, such facilities also provide notable physical protection from attack or natural disaster.

Notable Below-Ground Data Centers

Although underground Data Centers aren't exactly commonplace, they aren't unheard of either. Several such facilities are in operation today and many have interesting histories:

- A decades-old nuclear bunker built below Stockholm, Sweden, was converted in 2007 and 2008 into a futuristic-looking Data Center facility that has drawn comparisons to a super-villain's lair. The 11,950-square foot (1,110-square meter) facility, owned by Internet service provider Bahnof, is situated below 98.4 feet (30 meters) of bedrock, protected by 15.7-inch (40-centimeter) thick doors, and capable of withstanding a hydrogen bomb. Staff work areas such as a network operations center have amenities including artificial daylight, greenhouses, waterfalls, and a 687-gallon (2,600-liter) salt-water fish tank. A glass-walled conference room overlooks the server environment and standby power is provided by a pair of diesel engines originally designed to power submarines.

- A former coal mine in Japan's Honshu island is being transformed into a server environment through the installation of 30 portable Data Center containers some 328 feet (100 meters) below the surface. Local groundwater and cool ambient temperatures are to be employed to keep the hardware—about 250 servers per container—cool. The project was initiated by a consortium of 12 companies, including Sun Microsystems. The Data Center is to be online in 2010.

- An underground Data Center near Houston, Texas, was originally constructed as a 38,000-square foot (3,530-square meter) secret nuclear fallout shelter by Louis Kung, nephew of famed Chinese political figure Madam Chang Kai Shek and founder of Westlin Oil. The facility, originally built in 1982, was converted to a Data Center in 2004, and two 100,000-square feet (9,290-square meter) expansions of the underground server environment were announced in 2007.

- Two former nuclear missile silos in New Mexico were purchased by Strategic Data Services in 2000 with plans to convert its 1,200,000-square foot (111,484-square meter), 22-stories of space into server environments.

Minimizing Partial Loads

Most discussions around Data Center cooling these days focus on the challenge of providing sufficient capacity to meet demand. That's understandable, as the greater processing capabilities and smaller footprints of modern servers translate to greater power consumption and increased thermal load within a server environment. Meeting the growing cooling needs of IT hardware presents a major challenge for server environments, especially legacy Data Centers originally built to lower capacity specifications.

To green your Data Center, however, you need to also look at a cooling challenge at the other end of the spectrum. What do you do about a Data Center whose cooling infrastructure, rather than being pushed to the breaking point, only carries a fraction of the thermal load it was designed to accommodate? This scenario doesn't get the same attention as that of a nearly overheated Data Center, yet it happens frequently and can have a significant operational impact.

The challenge that a partial thermal load presents for a Data Center is that, much like some of its electrical components, certain cooling components run less efficiently when not operating at full capacity. Or more accurately, some cooling components can fail while carrying a partial thermal load, and the method often employed to avoid such a malfunction results in a less-efficient cooling system. For instance, if your Data Center cooling system uses an air-cooled chiller and operates only at a partial load, an imbalance can occur between the compressor and evaporator and cause the compressor to stall.

Newly opened Data Centers are certainly vulnerable to this partial load condition. For a major Data Center facility equipped with hundreds of server cabinets, megawatts of power by the score, and hundreds of tons of cooling, it can take years to house enough hardware to fully draw upon its capacities.

A common strategy to avoid the instability that comes with a partial load is to recycle heated, high-pressure refrigerant vapor back into the chiller. This is known as *hot gas bypass*. In essence, you eliminate the instability that a partial thermal load creates by deliberately putting additional load on the system.

Although this solution helps avoid a chiller malfunction, it is counterproductive to being green. Your chiller consumes energy to process the refrigerant vapor that is recycled rather than used to cool anything. Hot gas bypass results in greater energy consumption than if that artificial load weren't added. If you're greening your Data Center in part by making your hardware more energy efficient, hot gas bypass offsets some of the energy savings that you should otherwise realize.

Say you upgrade to more power-efficient equipment (see Chapter 8, "Choosing Greener Gear") or reduce the number of machines in your Data Center by way of virtualization (see Chapter 9, "Greening Your Data Center Through Consolidation, Virtualization, and Automation"). This upgrade reduces both power and cooling demand in your server environment. With hot gas bypass being used, however, the thermal load on your chiller remains high, causing you to miss out on the energy savings that you should earn from your reduced cooling needs. (You would still see the direct energy savings from cutting the number of servers demanding power.)

Note   If you work in your company's facilities department, you're likely familiar with hot gas bypass, which is a mechanism that has been implemented in refrigerant systems for decades.

If you work in the IT department, however, you might not be aware of it. (Why would you be?) Talk with your peers in facilities to see if your Data Center chiller can accommodate a partial thermal load without resorting to a hot gas bypass.

How, then, can you either minimize the likelihood of a partial thermal load in your Data Center or else improve efficiency of your cooling system when it is at partial load? Consider the following solutions:

- **Build smaller:** If the Data Center you plan isn't expected to draw significantly upon its cooling capacity for years, maybe you don't need to build all of it immediately. Consider building a segment of the server environment with plans to expand it as later growth and demand warrant. For instance, instead of constructing a 20,000-square foot (1,858-square meter) Data Center, you might construct a 5,000-square foot (464.5-square meter) module and then build other modules, identical to the first, in the future. Building the facility and its cooling system on a smaller scale means that incoming hardware provides a proportionately larger thermal load. Designing a Data Center in such a modular fashion is an excellent practice because it fosters scalability and standardization. It also spreads the capital cost for the facility over a longer period of time, which might be advantageous for your business.

- **Downsize your baseline cooling:** Another method to increase the thermal load of incoming equipment relative to your Data Center cooling system is to limit the initial cooling capacity of the facility, while allowing for future expansion. For instance, rather than providing 200 watts per square foot (2,153 watts per square meter) of cooling to the Data Center, begin by providing 100 watts per square foot (1,076 watts per square meter) and have supplemental cooling measures ready to install or bring online when there is sufficient heat load to warrant it.

- **Employ cooling infrastructure with variable capacity:** Recognizing the instability and inefficiency that comes from supporting a partial thermal load, cooling system manufacturers have developed technologies that better align chiller capacity to the heat load. For instance, there are compressors that allow for shutting off the supply of refrigerant to some cylinders in the system, lowering the relative capacity of the compressor and allowing it to operate more efficiently with less thermal load.

Variable Frequency Drives

Another mechanism for making your Data Center cooling system greener, whether it's operating at partial load or near maximum capacity, is a variable frequency drive.

Several components in a Data Center cooling system are powered by electric motors. These include chillers, secondary pumps, cooling tower fans, and air handlers. For years, such motors had only two settings—off and on.

However, you now can install variable frequency drives on these motor-driven components. Variable frequency drives allow the speed of an electric motor to match the demand load placed upon it, rather than operating at full power whenever turned on. Changing the frequency of the power fed to the motor changes the motor's operating speed.

Thanks to some underlying mechanical principles for fans and pumps, known as *affinity laws*, variable frequency drives can provide energy savings in a Data Center that are better than linear. To put it another way, reducing the speed of the pumps and fans in your Data Center cooling might save more energy than you would expect.

The affinity laws state

■   Airflow from a fan is proportional to the fan's motor speed.

■   The pressure generated by a fan is proportional to the change in the fan's motor speed, squared.

■   The horsepower needed to run a fan is proportional to change in the motor speed cubed.

By these principles, when you double a fan's speed, for instance, it produces twice as much airflow and produces four times the pressure, yet requires eight times the power. Turn that around and you realize that by cutting fan speed by half, you reduce airflow in half, lower pressure to one-fourth of what it was, and draw only one-eighth (12.5 percent) of the power.

Figure 5.3 illustrates the affinity laws and how energy consumption relates to fan speed, pressure, and horsepower.

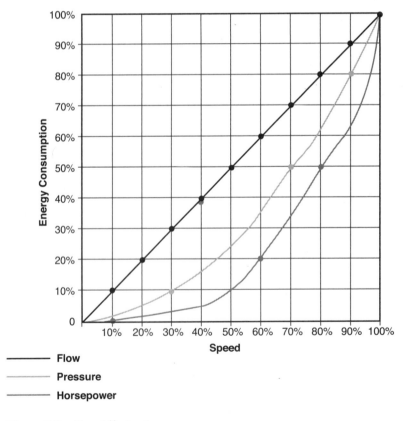

Figure 5.3   *Fan Affinity Laws*

Note   Curious to know how much energy and money you can save by implementing variable frequency drives? Alliant Energy Corporation, an electric holding company that provides electricity and natural gas to parts of the Midwest United States, offers an online calculator that estimates both forms of savings for when variable frequency drives are applied to cooling components including hot- or chilled-water pumps, fan motors, pump motors, and cooling tower fans.

Users enter key data such as the horsepower of the motor, how many hours per week the item is in operation, and local energy cost. The tool is available at http://www.alliantenergy.com/docs/groups/public/documents/pub/p010794.hcsp.

Cooling Tower Water

Data Center cooling systems typically employ evaporative cooling, by way of large cooling towers, to help vent the prodigious heat that the facility produces. This process can involve vaporizing millions of gallons/liters of water per month, which must then be replenished with makeup water.

Makeup water most often comes from the local municipal supply. You can make your Data Center notably greener, greatly reducing its impact upon the local water supply, if you can draw upon recycled water rather than fresh.

Note   Multiple Data Centers in Quincy, Washington, are or soon will be using reclaimed water in their Data Center cooling towers courtesy of a water recycling facility that the city opened in 2009. Quincy built the pumping station and miles of pipelines to deliver approximately 1 million gallons (3.79 million liters) of waste water to nearby Data Centers owned by Microsoft, Yahoo, Intuit, and Sabey Corporation and irrigate local parks and school properties. The waste water, which comes from area homes and businesses, is captured and treated at an existing municipal water reclamation plant.

Having the Data Centers use the reclaimed water conserves local ground water, which is the lone source of the city's drinking water. Prior to construction of the water recycling facility, the treated water was simply allowed to percolate back into the ground.

Phase one of the project, which brought water to the Microsoft Data Center, was completed in 2009 and paid by a $4.5 million grant from the Washington State Legislature. Phase two, scheduled for completion in 2010, is estimated to cost $5 million and will bring water to the Yahoo, Intuit, and Sabey facilities.

Regardless of the source of your makeup water, you can help reduce how much your Data Center consumes by limiting the amount of water lost through cooling tower *drift* and *blow-down.*

Drift, or windage, is when exhaust air leaving a cooling tower also carries away droplets of water. This phenomenon can be reduced by installing appropriately named drift eliminators, which are panels for the outgoing air to pass through. Drift eliminators come in several form factors, including blade and cellular honeycomb designs, and are made from a range of materials including ceramics, metal, plastic, and fiberglass.

Blow-down involves intentionally draining water from a cooling tower to reduce contaminants. When water evaporates and exits a cooling tower, minerals and particulate matter are left behind in the water that remains. Air that passes through the cooling tower is also known to deposit contaminants such as dirt or sand. Over time, these can accumulate and interfere with the efficient operation of the system. A common method to reduce the amount of contaminants is to regularly drain off a portion of the recirculated water. (Even if you don't work directly with your Data Center cooling tower, you might be familiar with the blow-down process. Draining off water to remove sediment buildup is a recommended practice for many home water heaters.)

Employ good filtration systems and biocides in the cooling tower to diminish particulate buildup, thereby reducing the need for blow-down and maintaining the efficient performance of your Data Center cooling. Test condenser water quality and carefully manage blow-down activity to avoid draining more than necessary.

Note   You need to use drift eliminators and biocides for your Data Center cooling towers not only to reduce the facility's water consumption but also to avoid health risks.

Cooling towers have been identified as a source for Legionnaire's disease, a severe form of pneumonia. (The disease was named for an outbreak that occurred at the site of an American Legion convention in Philadelphia, Pennsylvania, in 1976, in which 221 people were infected and 34 of them died.)

Legionaella bacteria can grow in almost any source for warm water, and the disease is transmitted through the inhalation of fine mist that contains the bacteria. Drift eliminators reduce the amount of water droplets that escape from a cooling tower whereas biocides help eliminate the source bacteria.

Hosting Environment Opportunities for Efficiency

Several green cooling solutions are additionally available for inside the Data Center. Depending upon how responsibility for the design and operation of your server environments are assigned, these technologies and approaches are likely to be implemented as a joint effort between the facilities and IT organizations.

Air- Versus Liquid-Based Cooling

When designing your Data Center's cooling system, a key decision to make is what medium you want to use to cool your hardware—air or liquid.

Early Data Centers, built in the 1960s, featured chilled water systems to cool the large, centralized mainframe computers they housed. Liquid-based cooling continued to be prevalent in server environments for decades, finally tapering off in the 1990s as smaller, rack-mounted servers became popular. Data Center managers found they could cool the distributed hardware with ambient air, eliminating the risk of fluid leaks, and began confining the liquid element of cooling to air handlers typically installed around the edges of Data Center floor space. As hardware density and, therefore, thermal loads increased in Data Centers during the 2000s, interest in liquid-cooling technologies reemerged due to its greater capacity for removing heat than air.

With both air- and liquid-based cooling technologies now available, what approach is the greenest—and best overall—for your server environment? Each solution has its own advantages and disadvantages.

Air-based cooling in Data Centers involves the aforementioned air handlers and often additional measures to efficiently channel chilled air to servers while drawing their hot exhaust away. (These mechanisms are discussed in the "Optimizing Airflow" section of this chapter.) The advantages of air cooling are that today's facilities engineers are extremely familiar with the technology, chances of a leak are lower than liquid cooling, and air is readily available, which avoids the need to run piping to deliver it to cabinets.

Although liquid-based cooling is sometimes referred to under the umbrella term "water-cooled cabinets," the cooling material is as likely to be Freon or glycol as water, and the delivery mechanism might not even directly involve a cabinet. (Liquid carbon dioxide has begun to appear as a refrigerant as well.) The three common forms of cooling in which liquid is incorporated at or adjacent to Data Center cabinets follow:

- **A vertical panel installed directly behind the back of a server cabinet:** The panel- or door-mounted cooling coil neutralizes hot exhaust generated by hardware inside the cabinet, preventing it from impacting the rest of the server environment.

- **A sealed server cabinet in which airflow passes through a heat exchanger at the bottom or side of the cabinet:** This solution likewise offsets heat generated by hardware within the cabinet.

- **In-row cooling:** A portable cooling unit installed between server cabinets or mounted onto the ceiling above them. Designed to work with a hot and cold aisle server row configuration, the unit draws warm air from the hot aisle while projecting chilled air into the cold aisle.

Figure 5.4 shows ceiling-mounted cooling units in operation within one of Cisco's Data Centers in San Jose, California.

Figure 5.4 *Overhead Cooling Units*

Liquids are more efficient at removing heat than air, which means liquid-based cooling solutions can support greater hardware density than air-based cooling and are more energy-efficient. Despite these advantages, liquid cooling hasn't returned as the favored approach to cooling Data Centers. The upfront costs to implement liquid cooling are significantly more expensive than air cooling, and many Data Center personnel are hesitant to bring liquids back extensively into their server environments.

Note I typically present at a few major Data Center industry conferences each year, discussing various physical design strategies. During one such presentation in San Jose, California, in 2008, I asked the audience of approximately 150 Data Center managers how many of them were comfortable implementing a liquid-cooling solution at their server cabinets.

Only three people raised their hands.

As with many Data Center design options, you need to review the advantages and disadvantages of available cooling technologies to determine which is most appropriate for your needs. The deciding factor likely depends upon your overall design strategy:

■ Do you intend to fill every rack unit in your server cabinets with equipment, and do you have adequate power available to support those systems? If so, liquid cooling is probably an apt choice because it supports the high density of equipment that you want.

■ Do you have ample Data Center floor space and therefore plan to spread out hardware to minimize impact upon your physical infrastructure (structural loading, hot spots, cabling density, and so on) and provide a large temperature buffer if a cooling system failure occurs? If so, air cooling is optimal because it can support your needs while avoiding the costs and risks of a liquid-cooling solution.

It might even be appropriate to use a mix of the two approaches, perhaps providing air cooling across most of your Data Center while running liquid cooling to select rows where hardware is installed at much greater density. With some careful planning, you can design your Data Center in such a way that isolates piping for the liquid cooling so that if a leak does occur, other server rows are not impacted.

Optimizing Airflow

One of the biggest challenges for Data Centers is effectively cooling everything in the hosting space. Even server environments that aren't overfilled with hardware and possess sufficient cooling capacity overall can have problems with hot spots. The difficulty typically isn't making cold air for the Data Center, it's precisely delivering that cold air where it's needed while removing the hot air generated by servers.

Air is, fundamentally, lazy. Your Data Center expends significant energy to move it—both incoming chilled and exhaust hot—to where it needs to be. The more that you can optimize airflow in your Data Center, the less energy it takes to run your cooling system and the greener your facility can be.

Isolating Hot and Cold Airflow

An excellent way to improve the efficiency of your Data Center cooling system, thereby consuming less energy and making the server environment greener, is to isolate airflow in the room. That is, prevent hot exhaust vented from IT hardware from mixing with the chilled air that is pumped in to cool them.

Data Center designers and managers began implementing hot and cold aisle designs more than a decade ago, realizing that if you alternate the direction of adjacent server rows in a Data Center that the performance of the room's cooling system improves. Subsequent experience has shown that hot and cold aisle configuration can be improved upon further, by preventing warm and cool air from combining above server cabinets or at the end of rows.

One approach is to employ enclosed server cabinets that have an attached chimney to guide hardware exhaust into an overhead plenum space above. This not only avoids the mixing of hot and cold air, it precludes heated air from entering the hosting area, easing how hard that the room's air handlers need to work to cool your servers.

Figure 5.5 illustrates an enclosed cabinet configuration in which hot exhaust vents directly into an overhead plenum space, preventing it from entering the hosting area where equipment is housed.

Figure 5.6 shows the real-life implementation of the enclosed cabinet configuration. The image is from a Cisco Data Center in Richardson, Texas, in which all server cabinets have been deployed with chimneys. The heated air is propelled away from the servers entirely by their fans; no extra fans are used.

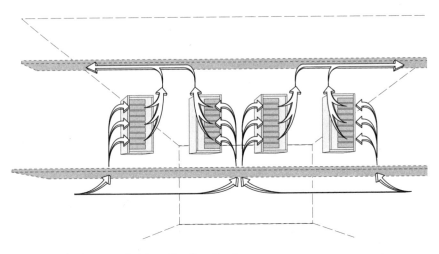

Figure 5.5   *Enclosed Chimney Cabinet Cooling Design*

Note   Even though cabinets are deployed with chimneys, the server rows in this Data Center are still arranged in a hot and cold aisle design (as shown in Figure 5-5).

Although cabinet orientation doesn't matter when chimneys are used, we opted to use the hot/cold layout to accommodate any future equipment that might need to be installed in the Data Center and yet not fit within a traditional cabinet footprint.

Another method for isolating hot and cold air in your Data Center is to enclose entire server rows. For this approach, build a chamber that encompasses the back halves of adjacent rows. Just as cabinet chimneys isolate and remove exhaust air, so do the chambers perform that function for multiple cabinets.

Figure 5.6 *Enclosed Chimney Cabinet Implementation*

Figure 5.7 shows the exterior of multiple server row enclosures, each possessing transparent doors on either side to enable both visibility and physical access into the space. The front halves of several server cabinets are visible, protruding from the chamber in the foreground of the image.

Figure 5.8 shows the inside of a server row cooling enclosure. The back halves of server cabinets extend into the enclosure, ensuring that hardware exhaust is isolated and does not mix with the cool air.

Plenum

By definition, Data Center plenum space is intended for air distribution. There's no rule about how deep that plenum space should be, either below a raised floor or above a false ceiling, so server environments have been constructed with plenum spaces of all sizes—from too shallow for a flashlight to fit under a floor tile to deep enough for a person to walk through.

From an energy-efficiency perspective, however, bigger is definitely better. Deeper plenum enables air to flow through more easily, requiring less energy from Data Center air handlers. Plenum space should also have minimal obstructions. It does little good to have a large plenum if the area is packed with items such as cable trays or ducting.

Photo courtesy of Intel Corporation

Figure 5.7   *Enclosed Row Cooling—External Chamber View*

Photo courtesy of Intel Corporation

Figure 5.8   *Enclosed Row Cooling—Internal Chamber View*

Note   Early Cisco Data Centers were typically built with 12 inches to 18 inches (30 centimeters to 46 centimeters) of plenum space below their raised floors. This was done in part because the rooms were constructed in buildings not specifically designed to house a Data Center, so vertical space was tight, and in part because the facilities were intended to cool only 50 watts per square foot (538 watts per square meter).

Modern Cisco Data Centers are now generally constructed in purpose-built facilities and, when equipped with a raised floor, include a 36-inch (91.4-centimeter) below-floor plenum. This additional depth has helped us quadruple our earlier cooling capabilities.

Sealing Unwanted Gaps

Just as you don't want hot exhaust mixing with the chilled air in your Data Center, you also don't want that chilled air leaking out as it travels to its destination. The more cool air that fails to reach your servers, the harder your cooling system has to work and the more energy your Data Center consumes.

To put it another way, the more thoroughly that you seal gaps throughout your Data Center, the better your cooling system can perform and the less energy it draws, leading to a greener facility.

Those gaps can take several forms:

- **Open floor tile notches:** If you route power or cabling under your Data Center raised floor, you undoubtedly use notched tiles to thread electrical cords or patch cords through. Cap off those notched tiles to prevent air from leaking out. Several products are sold commercially to help accomplish this, such as solid caps to cover the openings, foam padding to fill the notches, or bristle brushes that restrict air while allowing cabling through.

- **Misplaced or improperly opened perforated panels:** You obviously want to strategically implement perforated panels in your Data Center, such as floor tiles in a raised flooring system or ceiling tiles to maximize airflow. Some perforated tiles have adjustable dampers that enable the user to alter how much air passes through them. Close tiles where airflow is unnecessary, and fully open them where it is needed.

- **Spaces between servers:** After you seal unwanted openings across your Data Center, make sure the cool air that is delivered is reaching a machine. There's no need to spend energy and money to cool rack space that is unoccupied. Fill empty rack space with blanking panels.

Care for a simple, real-world example of how much impact it makes on a cooling system to seal off nonessential openings? The next time you are in your car, turn on the air-conditioning system. Place your hand over one of the vents for the front passenger seat and make note of how much more cool air is suddenly projected through the vents for the driver's seat.

Cabinet Solutions

A key decision to make when designing your Data Center cooling system is what type of cabinets you want to house your hardware in. Don't underestimate the significance of this choice. Cabinets aren't simply glorified shelving to stack servers on, they're the final instrument for enabling the effective and efficient cooling of your hardware.

As already mentioned, enclosed cabinets with chimneys help isolate hot and cold airflow whereas liquid-cooled cabinets incorporate a cooling medium more capable than air.

Cabinet solutions are also available that can modify the airflow of hardware within them, changing a side-venting pattern to one that is front-to-back (cooling intake at the front; heated exhaust vented out of the back). This can be helpful for Data Centers designed with hot and cold aisles, which are most efficient when used with front-to-back cooling hardware.

Mapping and Managing Hot Spots

Even if your Data Center is supplied with adequate cooling overall to accommodate the room's thermal load, it's likely that there are hot spots. It's challenging to provide uniform flows of air throughout an entire Data Center, especially those that don't have isolation measures such as enclosed chambers. Even in server environments where airflow is well controlled, the myriad combinations of IT hardware among server cabinets provide different heat loads.

Knowing the location and intensity of hot spots in your Data Center makes it easier for you to take steps to dissipate them. You can identify hot spots by using any of several temperature sensing technologies:

- Portable sensors that measure ambient temperatures
- Server cabinet power strips that include temperature-sensor features
- Temperature-reading capabilities offered in many server models and networking devices

For a truly revealing look at your Data Center's temperature conditions, have your hosting space analyzed using *computational fluid dynamics (CFD)*. Several companies offer CFD modeling, which gives a three-dimensional view of temperature distribution. CFD modeling can reveal hot spots and cooling inefficiencies that are otherwise almost impossible to detect.

For example, Data Center air handlers in some instances can propel cool air at such high velocity that the air misses the hardware it's supposed to cool. Reducing that velocity, perhaps by even reducing how many air handlers are operating in a given area, might actually provide more effective cooling. In another example, Data Centers equipped with hot and cold aisles that aren't enclosed in some manner are likely to have intermingling of warm and cool somewhere—probably at the ends of each server row and perhaps in the space between the top of the server cabinets and the ceiling. Each of these conditions can be readily seen using CFD modeling.

Equipment Choices and Distribution

The servers, networking devices, and storage units you choose to install in your Data Center and how you arrange them can impact the efficiency of your cooling system. Although it's probably unrealistic to base your hardware purchasing decisions on how well-suited that equipment is to your Data Center cooling design, it's useful to understand what elements make a machine less compatible and to try, where possible, to mitigate those factors.

The following details can determine whether your computing systems (and how you deploy them) complement your mechanical infrastructure or create mismatches that foster cooling inefficiencies:

- **Is the hardware designed to go into a Data Center?** That might seem like a simplistic question, but a surprising number of systems never intended for use in a server environment end up installed in such facilities. (Desktop computers are probably the most common example.) The most obvious indication that a machine isn't built with a Data Center in mind is when the system can't be installed in an industry-standard server cabinet, either due to its unusual shape (too wide, for example) or because it can't be equipped with mounting brackets.

- **What is the airflow pattern of the hardware?** If you design your Data Center with hot and cold aisles, either choose equipment that has the same airflow pattern (cooled in the front, venting exhaust out the back) or be sure to install side-venting hardware into enclosed cabinets that can reroute the airflow to match the room's front-to-back pattern.

- **Do you intend to group similar hardware together?** A common approach to arranging Data Center equipment is to cluster models by manufacturer. This does have an operational benefit: You can conceivably limit vendor access in the Data Center to just the rows where its brand of hardware resides. Unfortunately, this arrangement can also create peaks and valleys of infrastructure demand across the Data Center because you end up grouping the hottest hardware together, the heaviest hardware together, the equipment that needs the most cabling together, and so on. Dispersing high heat-producing systems can help reduce the occurrence of Data Center hot spots.

This list touches upon the general physical compatibility of IT equipment with a Data Center's cooling system. Chapter 8 takes a deeper look at the environmental impact of individual equipment models.

Note   Would you consider banning equipment from your Data Center that fails to meet certain physical criteria so that you can maximize the facility's cooling performance? If you're like most Data Center managers, that's not an option—No matter how much you might want to restrict nonconforming hardware, the room's job is ultimately to host whatever systems are deemed critical for your company.

I toured a Data Center in the United States in 2006 that achieves significant cooling performance and equipment density in part by only hosting small-profile hardware that uses front-to-back airflow and fits within industry-standard server cabinets. The Data Center operators, who prefer not to publicize the room by name, reportedly achieve more than 500 watts per square foot (5,382 watts per square meter) of cooling in the facility and fully populate its enclosed server cabinets.

Any equipment that doesn't fit into its chosen cabinet profile is placed in a different facility on the same campus. It certainly contributes to the cooling efficiency of the exclusive space, although I wonder what the net cooling and energy efficiency is for both the optimized hosting area and the other server environment that contains the cast-off equipment.

Cooling Distribution

When you decide which cooling technologies you want to employ in your Data Center, it's time to green the system further by optimizing how you place components and implement cooling functions. Several fundamental strategies can make your mechanical system more efficient and therefore greener:

- **Place cooling near its target:** Generating cold air at or near the systems you want cooled is more effective than expending significant fan energy to propel the cold air there. You can accomplish this through a variety of cooling solutions, air or liquid, installed at the server row or cabinet level.

- **Use large piping:** If you need to drive somewhere, would your travel be easier by taking a wide, straight highway or a narrow, twisting street? Install large pipes with as few turns as possible. This reduces friction loss and lessens how hard the pumps in your cooling system need to work. In many cases, this can enable you to shrink the size of your pumps, further reducing energy consumption.

- **Coordinate air handlers:** As mentioned in this chapter's section concerning mapping and managing hot spots, temperature conditions vary within a Data Center. This can lead to air handlers in the same server environment operating in different modes and fighting one another rather than helping—airflow from one handler either interfering with airflow of another or wrongly influencing its temperature readings, for instance, or even one handler adding humidity into the Data Center while another unit removes it. Employing an intelligent control system that coordinates all air handler activity improves the performance of the cooling system and reduces energy consumption.

Summary

Several major companies have begun raising the operational temperatures of their Data Centers as a way to reduce energy consumption and thereby save money. The downsides of this practice are less time for your server environment to overheat during a cooling system malfunction, warmer conditions for hardware already subject to Data Center temperature variations, potential increase in noise levels, and possible warranty challenges for your IT hardware.

Using Data Center waste heat to warm another space is an excellent way to make your facility greener because it reduces two sources of energy consumption—cooling in the Data Center and heating of the destination space. Employing absorption or adsorption chillers, which use heat to produce cooling rather than mechanical compression of conventional chillers, is another way to put otherwise unwanted heat to good use.

If the local climate is suitable, economizers can be employed to use outside air to provide some or all cooling to your Data Center, saving energy and money by not running the compressor within the chiller. A heat wheel can similarly help cool a Data Center during cold weather because its panels are chilled outside and then slowly rotated into the server environment where they absorb heat.

If you install external piping for your Data Center cooling system underground, you can use the cool temperature of the earth to help chill the water that passes through the piping. A more extreme approach to using such geothermal cooling is to build your Data Center underground.

Some Data Center chillers can become unstable and malfunction when operating at only partial capacity, prompting many facilities engineers to artificially increase the thermal load to the chiller through a hot gas bypass technique. You can limit the use of hot gas bypass—and its added energy demand—by building your large Data Center in smaller modules, downsizing the initial capacity of your cooling system, and using variable capacity cooling components.

Implement variable frequency drives on the motor-driven components of your Data Center cooling system so that they draw enough energy to meet demand and no more. This can lead to substantial savings because fans require only one-eighth the horsepower to operate at half speed.

Data Centers consume large amounts of water to replace what is lost during its evaporative cooling process. Seek a source of recycled water to serve as makeup water so that your facility doesn't need to draw fresh water from the municipal supply. Install drift eliminators and a good filtration system in your Data Center cooling tower and employ biocides; these measures can inhibit water loss from windage and reduce the need to purposefully drain water to remove particulate matter.

Liquid-cooling solutions offer greater heat-removal efficiency and support higher hardware density than air cooling but are significantly more expensive and bring more potential for a fluid leak in the Data Center.

Isolate airflow in your Data Center to avoid mixing hot exhaust from hardware with incoming chilled air. Hot and cold aisles are a basic implementation of this principle; server cabinet and row enclosures provide more complete isolation.

When designing plenum space, increase its depth to facilitate airflow. Also seal gaps—covering floor tile notches, closing superfluous perforated tiles, and installing blanking panels in cabinets—to ensure chilled air fully reaches the hardware it is to cool.

A variety of cabinet solutions are available to help maximize the cooling of your hardware, such as enclosed cabinets with an exhaust chimney or models that redirect the airflow of side-venting hardware so that it matches a hot and cold aisle design.

It's useful to employ tools to monitor temperatures in your Data Center. Computational fluid dynamics modeling is the most-sophisticated option, but even deploying simple ambient temperature sensors can be helpful in identifying where hot spots have formed in your server environment.

Not all hardware is well matched with Data Center cooling infrastructure, typically due to physical features such as being too large to fit in a standard server cabinet or having an airflow pattern other than front-to-back. When arranging hardware in your Data Center, you can ease hot spots by spreading out servers that produce the most heat.

Optimize your Data Center cooling efficiency further by generating cooling close to servers, installing larger cooling pipes, and coordinating the operation of your air handlers so that they complement rather than work against one another.

Chapter 6

Cabling Your Way to a Greener Data Center

This chapter compares the environmental impacts of cabling media and illustrates the benefits of streamlining both structured cabling and patch cord installations in a Data Center to improve airflow and reduce energy consumption.

Cabling Choices

When considering approaches to greening a Data Center, scant attention is normally paid to cabling infrastructure. That's understandable because electrical components, cooling systems, and computing hardware all have higher green profiles due to their direct consumption of energy. However, the choice of what cabling media to employ and in what quantities contributes to your Data Center's environmental impact as well, from how cable types are manufactured to how much power must be consumed to provide connectivity through them.

Data Centers employ two broad types of cabling, copper and fiber optic, in different ratios, and each are available in various grades that provide different levels of performance.

Category 6 and 6A (augmented) cabling are the de facto copper implementation for Data Centers today, whereas older facilities built in the 1990s typically used Category 5 and 5E (enhanced). Copper wiring can be shielded, incorporating metal to prevent electromatic interference, or unshielded. Twinaxial cable, often simply called twinax, is another copper configuration—excellent for providing high-speed connectivity with minimal power consumption, but less widely used due to distance limitations.

Likewise, today's Data Centers are typically installed with 50/125 μm laser–optimized, multimode optical fiber rated OM3, OM3+, or OM4, and in some cases 8.3/125 μm zero or low water peak, single-mode optical fiber. Older facilities were equipped with 62.5/125 μm (OM1) or 50/125 μm (OM2) fiber optic cable and 8.3/125 μm single-mode fiber. (The numbers separated by a slash represent the diameter of the cable's core followed by the size of its cladding, measured in microns. OM stands for optical multi-mode.)

> **Note**   The fastest performing Ethernet standard as of this writing is 10 Gigabits per second (Gbps), so examples in this chapter are written for cabling that provides that rate of connectivity.
>
> Standards for 40 Gbps and 100 Gbps are under development by IEEE (the Institute of Electrical and Electronics Engineers) and projected to be approved during 2010.

Most commonly, in the modern Data Center, cable runs of copper and multimode fiber are installed between server cabinet locations and a main network row or intermediate network substation, whereas multimode and single-mode fiber are installed between the Data Center and other associated facilities, such as a campus distribution room.

With both copper and fiber capable of providing connectivity within your Data Center, which is your greenest option? The following sections provide you with the information you need to answer that question.

Manufacturing Considerations

Building materials used to construct your Data Center and the associated resources consumed to manufacture them obviously define, in part, how green your facility is. (The remainder of that definition comes from what resources the Data Center then consumes on an ongoing basis when it is operational.) Likewise, the materials used in data cabling and consumed resources that make them help define how green they are. That's primarily glass for fiber optic cable, copper (obviously) for copper cable, and plastic used inside and for the jacket of both types of cable.

In a 2008 article published in the European Union edition of *CXO* magazine, headlined "The Data Centre Future Is Green with Fiber Optics," author Andreas Koll of Corning Cable Systems offered several data points concerning the manufacture of cabling:

- General elements of a cable's anatomy, such as their protective jacket and internal plastics, require 62 pounds (28 kilograms) of raw material to produce copper cabling and 12 pounds (5.4 kilograms) for fiber cabling.

- Extracting 2.2 pounds (1 kilogram) of copper involves about 1,102 pounds (500 kilograms) of natural resources such as excavated ground material and water, whereas extracting glass involves just 6.6 pounds (3 kilograms) of natural resources.

- A bundle of 24 10-Gbps copper cables, 136 feet (41.5 meters) in length, requires 72.8 pounds (33 kilograms) of copper, whereas a 48-strand fiber cable run that provides the same connectivity involves only .12 pounds (56 grams) of glass.

- Applying the ratios suggested for extracting copper and fiber, that 24-connection, 136-foot (41.5 meter) cable run would involve 36,376 pounds (16.5 metric tons) of natural resources if copper is installed while just .37 pounds (168 grams) if fiber is used.

The numbers in that last bullet point indicate that providing the same connectivity in a Data Center by way of copper cabling instead of fiber cabling involves more than 98,000 times the natural resources! As Koll, Manager Data Centre Solutions for Corning, noted with some understatement, "an impressive contrast."

Form Factor

As anyone who has ever worked with copper and fiber cabling knows, fiber cabling has a much smaller diameter than copper cabling. That translates to smaller cable bundles for fiber than copper, which in turn means fiber can be accommodated with smaller cable trays and narrower wire management and terminate into patching fields that occupy less physical space. In a network row to which a Data Center's entire cabling system connects, fiber connections occupy only a fraction of the rack space needed for the same quantity of copper connections. As a whole, a fiber cabling system, therefore, requires less material for its supporting components than a copper cabling system.

Fiber's smaller form factor additionally reduces its potential to obstruct airflow in the Data Center. Fiber cabling also weighs less than copper. This isn't a green consideration but might be a factor at major termination points in your Data Center, where large deployments of copper can equate to notable amounts of weight.

Usable Lifespan

Another green consideration when choosing cabling is how long a particular cable type can meet your company's connectivity needs. The greater the useful life of your cabling infrastructure, the longer you can defer spending money to replace it and avoid discarding materials into the landfill and consuming more. In practice, this means you should buy the highest-performing cable available that you believe you will ever need in your Data Center.

For instance, if the performance demand on your cabling and networking infrastructure is projected to be 1 Gbps when your Data Center is constructed and you're comfortable that demand won't increase—ever—you can install any of the Data Center cabling media options available today and not worry about upgrading it. If, however, 1 Gbps is acceptable performance today but 10 Gbps might be needed at some time in the future, it's better to design your Data Center to have 10 Gbps or more capability when it first opens.

"Design and buy for the performance you'll eventually need" might seem to be an obvious recommendation, but a strong (and understandable) desire to limit construction costs can sometimes compel a Data Center project manager to choose lower-rated cabling. Although that approach does reduce the initial price tag for the Data Center, it costs your company much more money in the long run—and is certainly not green—if a handful of years later that cabling needs to be removed and replaced to accommodate increased performance demand. In that case, your business pays installation costs twice, materials costs twice, plus costs to remove the outdated system. Retrofitting your Data Center with new structured cabling might also require downtime, impacting your business even further.

Cabling manufacturer Siemon in 2006 examined the useful lifespan and annual costs for multiple types of plenum-rated copper cabling, from Category 5E through Category 7, in a whitepaper titled "Cabling Lifecycles and Total Cost of Ownership." The analysis of a 24-channel system was done in light of the then-recent adoption of 10GBASE-T standard IEEE 802.3an-2006 and in anticipation that hardware using that technology would begin appearing in Data Centers within 2 to 5 years.

Predictably, the higher the performance level of the cable, the greater total installed cost, including labor and materials (per Siemon):

- $13,483 for Category 7 (Class F) cabling

- $9,026 for 10G Category 6A (F/UTP) cabling

- $8,130 for 10G Category 6A (UTP) cabling

- $5,561 for Category 6 (Class E UTP) cabling

- $4,104 for Category 5E (Class D/UTP) cabling

However, looking at the cost of the cabling system over time, Siemon determined that the lower-performing cabling actually costs significantly more than the others. This is due to the greater number of years that higher performing cable could support future applications: 15 years for Category 7, 10 years for Category 6A, 7 years for Category 6, and just 5 years for Category 5E.

Factoring in the expense of removing any cables that couldn't provide the 10 Gbps performance, the annual cost of the cabling system became $899 for 24-channel Category 7 (Class F) cabling, $903 for 10G Category 6A (F/UTP), $813 for 10G Category 6A (UTP), $1,363 for Category 6 (Class E UTP), and $1,445 for Category 5E (Class D/UTP).

Table 6.1 summarizes Siemon's cost analysis.

The lower-performing cabling system is approximately 50 percent to 60 percent more expensive in the long run than higher-performing cables, even without including the cost for new cabling to replace it when obsolete or considering the business impact of downtime needed to do the retrofit work.

Power Consumption

Last but not least, to evaluate a cable's inherent green qualities, you need to be familiar with the power dissipation that occurs in conjunction with copper and fiber media.

Data Center hardware manufacturers and cabling vendors offer different estimates for power consumption per port, in part because of continuous improvements made to optical transceivers and copper switches. Published data on the topic can rapidly become outdated, so when assessing the energy consumed in conjunction with your Data Center cabling system, be sure to research current technology.

Table 6.1 *Cabling System Cost Comparison (24 Channel)*

Type of Cabling	Total Installed Cost	Estimated Lifespan (Support for Future Applications)	Annualized Cost
Category 7 (Class F)	$13,483	15	$899
10G Category 6A (F/UTP)	$9,026	10	$903
10G Category 6A (UTP)	$8,130	10	$813
Category 6 (Class E UTP)	$5,561	7	$1,363
Category 5E (Class D/UTP)	$4,104	5	$1,445

Factoring in the expense of removing any cables that can't provide the 10-Gbps performance

As of this writing, 10-Gbps performance is estimated to consume anywhere from 4 watts to 8 watts per copper port and approximately .5 watt to 1 watt per fiber port. (Twinax copper is estimated at as little as .1 watt per port.) Consuming a few more watts of power on a connection might not sound significant, but it can be when multiplied by the thousands of connections provided in most Data Centers. Consider a moderate Data Center with 20,000 ports. According to those power consumption estimates, providing 10-Gbps connectivity through fiber would consume 10 kilowatts to 20 kilowatts of power, versus 40 kilowatts to 80 kilowatts for using copper connections.

Copper connections generally use more power than fiber because they employ a high-voltage electrical transmitter to overcome signal degradation. Further contributing to the difference in power consumption between 10-Gbps fiber and copper cabling systems is that more fiber connections can be fit onto a networking device's line cards than copper. This allows the same connectivity to be provided with fewer devices, resulting in less demand for power and cooling in your Data Center.

Corning Cable Systems, in its 2008 whitepaper, "The Green Advantage of 10G Optical Fiber," estimates that using a 48-port, 10-Gbps fiber switch provides 76 percent in cumulative energy savings and carbon dioxide emissions over an equivalent copper switch. That's approximately 30,375 kWh and 48,600 pounds (22 metric tons) of carbon dioxide per year for fiber compared to more than 126,000 kWh and 201,900 pounds (91.6 metric tons) per year for copper.

The disparity becomes even more dramatic for greater port counts, as shown in Figure 6.1.

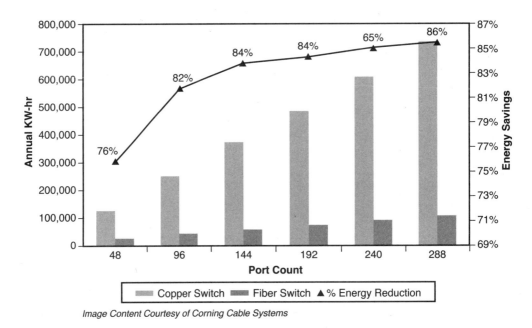

Image Content Courtesy of Corning Cable Systems

Figure 6.1   *Annual Connected Switch Total Energy and Savings Comparison for 10 Gbps Over Copper and Fiber*

Manufacturers are continually pursuing the development of more energy-efficient transceiver chipsets, so power consumption rates for both fiber and copper are expected to decline in the future.

Note   I have spent the last few pages tallying the green superiority of fiber cabling, so you might think I oppose the use of copper cabling. I don't. I do believe that a business needs to take a comprehensive look at the total cost—environmental and monetary—of how connectivity is provided in its Data Centers, though. That includes the entire cabling system (structured cable, patch cords, and even supporting products such as patching fields and cable tray) and the hardware that connect to it, including network interface cards, line cards, and other components that vary by cabling media type.

That analysis might not lead you to build a fiber-only Data Center, because copper remains a less expensive and more appropriate solution when used with some hardware. However, it will possibly make you rethink the quantities of fiber and copper that you provide in your facility and consider linking a greater percentage of your hardware over fiber.

Streamlining Cabling

Regardless of whether cabling is routed overhead or below a raised floor, you also need to determine the specific paths it follows and the quantities. Choosing optimal paths for your cable runs, installing appropriate port quantities (not too many, not too few), and limiting patching clutter all contribute to the efficiency and operational ease of use of your server environment.

Structured Cabling

Data Centers inherently use large quantities of structured cabling—tens of thousands of cables are not unusual for Data Centers of moderate size whereas major facilities can incorporate hundreds of thousands of cables. Carefully designing how your structured cabling is laid out can make your Data Center greener by requiring fewer cabling materials and easing airflow throughout the room.

An effective approach to streamline a Data Center's cabling is to implement a distributed physical hierarchy. That is, rather than run structured cabling from all server cabinet locations in your Data Center back to a main network row, establish network substations at intervals throughout the room. Run structured cabling for server cabinets to a nearby network substation and then run a subset of connections back to the main network row. Such a distributed cabling design can result in dramatically less cabling material within a Data Center.

Figures 6.2 and 6.3 show the same sample Data Center with two different physical cabling designs. The hosting environment encompasses 5,000 square feet (464.5) square meters) and includes 10 server rows of 12 server cabinet locations each. Server cabinets are shown in white; networking cabinets are shaded.

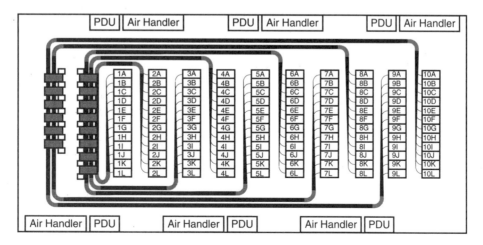

Figure 6.2 *Direct-Connect Cabling*

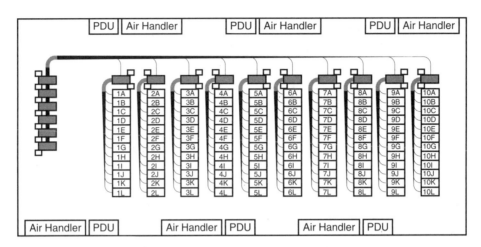

Figure 6.3 *Distributed Cabling Hierarchy*

In Figure 6.2, structured cabling is routed from each server cabinet location back to a main network row. In Figure 6.3, cabling is routed from server cabinets to a network substation at the end of each server row, and a smaller set of connections continue back to the main network row.

The distributed hierarchy dramatically reduces how much cabling is installed in the Data Center by limiting the number of cables that traverse long distances in the room.

How dramatically? If 48 ports of structured cabling (fiber or copper, it doesn't matter) are provided to every server cabinet location, the direct-connect design uses about 80 miles (129 kilometers) of cabling. Under the distributed design, 48 ports are still provided at each server cabinet location, but not all 576 of them (48 ports × 12 server cabinets = 576) continue on to the main network row. They terminate into a network substation at the end of the server row, and only 48 connections are then run from each network substation to the main network row. This streamlined design uses 23 miles (37 kilometers) of cabling—less than one-third of the other design.

Tables 6.2 and 6.3 illustrate how those cable run lengths and quantities were calculated for the sample Data Center. Table 6.2 lists cable runs for the direct-connect approach (Figure 6.2), and Table 6.3 lists cable runs for the distributed cabling (Figure 6.3) approach.

Converting 424,412 feet and 122,880 feet results in measurements of 80 miles (129 kilometers) and 23 miles (37 kilometers), respectively.

If you opt to use a distributed hierarchy for your Data Center's structured cabling, the quantity of cabling that you avoid using will obviously vary depending on the specific layout of the room and the number of cable runs (ports) involved. The larger the Data Center and the greater number of cabling connections involved, the more material at stake.

Table 6.2 *Data Center Cable Run Lengths: Direct-Connect Design*

	Cable Runs from Server Cabinet Locations to Main Network Row												Totals (in Feet)
Row 1	*1A*	*1B*	*1C*	*1D*	*1E*	*1F*	*1G*	*1H*	*1I*	*1J*	*1K*	*1L*	*13,824*
Distance (in Feet)	35	33	31	29	27	25	23	21	19	17	15	13	
x 48 Ports	1680	1584	1488	1392	1296	1200	1104	1008	912	816	720	624	
Row 2	*2A*	*2B*	*2C*	*2D*	*2E*	*2F*	*2G*	*2H*	*2I*	*2J*	*2K*	*2L*	*19,008*
Distance (in Feet)	22	24	26	28	30	32	34	36	38	40	42	44	
x 48 Ports	1056	1152	1248	1344	1440	1536	1632	1728	1824	1920	2016	2112	
Row 3	*3A*	*3B*	*3C*	*3D*	*3E*	*3F*	*3G*	*3H*	*3I*	*3J*	*3K*	*3L*	*25,344*
Distance (in Feet)	55	53	51	49	47	45	43	41	39	37	35	33	
x 48 Ports	2640	2544	2448	2352	2256	2160	2064	1968	1872	1776	1680	1581	
Row 4	*4A*	*4B*	*4C*	*4D*	*4E*	*4F*	*4G*	*4H*	*4I*	*4J*	*4K*	*4L*	*30,528*
Distance (in feet)	42	44	46	48	50	52	54	56	58	60	62	64	
x 48 Ports	2016	2112	2208	2304	2400	2496	2592	2688	2784	2880	2976	3072	
Row 5	*5A*	*5B*	*5C*	*5D*	*5E*	*5F*	*5G*	*5H*	*5I*	*5J*	*5K*	*5L*	*36,864*
Distance (in Feet)	75	73	71	69	67	65	63	61	59	57	55	53	
x 48 Ports	3600	3504	3408	3312	3216	3120	3024	2928	2832	2736	2640	2544	

Continues

Table 6.2   *Data Center Cable Run Lengths: Direct-Connect Design (Continued)*

	Cable Runs from Server Cabinet Locations to Main Network Row												Totals (in Feet)
Row 6	6A	6B	6C	6D	6E	6F	6G	6H	6I	6J	6K	6L	42,048
Distance (in Feet)	62	64	66	68	70	72	74	76	78	80	82	84	
x 48 Ports	2976	3072	3168	3264	3360	3456	3552	3648	3744	3840	3936	4032	
Row 7	7A	7B	7C	7D	7E	7F	7G	7H	7I	7J	7K	7L	55,872
Distance (in Feet)	108	106	104	102	100	98	96	94	92	90	88	86	
x 48 ports	5184	5088	4992	4896	4800	4704	4608	4512	4416	4320	4224	4128	
Row 8	8A	8B	8C	8D	8E	8F	8G	8H	8I	8J	8K	8L	61,056
Distance (in feet)	95	97	99	101	103	105	107	109	111	113	115	117	
x 48 Ports	4560	4656	4752	4848	4944	5040	5136	5232	5328	5424	5520	5616	
Row 9	9A	9B	9C	9D	9E	9F	9G	9H	9I	9J	9K	9L	67,392
Distance (in Feet)	128	126	124	122	120	118	116	114	112	110	108	106	
x 48 Ports	6144	6048	5952	5856	5760	5664	5568	5472	5376	5280	5184	5088	
Row 10	10A	10B	10C	10D	10E	10F	10G	10H	10I	10J	10K	10L	72,576
Distance (in Feet)	115	117	119	121	123	125	127	129	131	133	135	137	
x 48 Ports	5520	5616	5712	5808	5904	6000	6096	6192	6288	6384	6480	6576	
Total													424,512

Note   An alternative direct-connect cabling scenario to what is shown in Figure 6.2 involves all cables running in straight lines from each server cabinet back to the network row. (Imagine a large room full of people, with everyone trying to leave through a single exit.)

This "design" typically emerges in makeshift or undermanaged server rooms where users run out of connections and resort to stringing connections under the raised floor from whatever cabinet their server is housed in back to the network row. Little thought is given to the path of the cable other than making a successful connection.

Although this shortest-distance-between-two-points approach involves shorter cable lengths than in Figure 6.2, there are still more cables overall than in Figure 6.3. Plus, the resulting mess of overlapping cables inhibits airflow and makes troubleshooting difficult.

Table 6.3   *Data Center Cable Run Lengths—Distributed Design*

	Cable Runs to Main Network Row	Cable Runs from Server Cabinet Locations to Network Substation												Totals (in Feet)
Row 1		1A	1B	1C	1D	1E	1F	1G	1H	1I	1J	1K	1L	*10,560*
Distance (in Feet)	15	6	8	10	12	14	16	18	20	22	24	27	28	
x 48 Ports	720	288	384	480	576	672	768	864	960	1056	1152	1296	1344	
Row 2		2A	2B	2C	2D	2E	2F	2G	2H	2I	2J	2K	2L	*10,944*
Distance (in Feet)	23	6	8	10	12	14	16	18	20	22	24	27	28	
x 48 Ports	1104	288	384	480	576	672	768	864	960	1056	1152	1296	1344	

Continues

Table 6.3 *Data Center Cable Run Lengths—Distributed Design (Continued)*

	Cable Runs to Main Network Row	Cable Runs from Server Cabinet Locations to Network Substation												Totals (in Feet)
Row 3		3A	3B	3C	3D	3E	3F	3G	3H	3I	3J	3K	3L	11,328
Distance (in Feet)	31	6	8	10	12	14	16	18	20	22	24	27	28	
x 48 Ports	1488	288	384	480	576	672	768	864	960	1056	1152	1296	1344	
Row 4		4A	4B	4C	4D	4E	4F	4G	4H	4I	4J	4K	4L	11,712
Distance (in Feet)	39	6	8	10	12	14	16	18	20	22	24	27	28	
x 48 Ports	1872	288	384	480	576	672	768	864	960	1056	1152	1296	1344	
Row 5		5A	5B	5C	5D	5E	5F	5G	5H	5I	5J	5K	5L	12,096
Distance (in Feet)	47	6	8	10	12	14	16	18	20	22	24	27	28	
x 48 Ports	2256	288	384	480	576	672	768	864	960	1056	1152	1296	1344	
Row 6		6A	6B	6C	6D	6E	6F	6G	6H	6I	6J	6K	6L	12,480
Distance (in Feet)	55	6	8	10	12	14	16	18	20	22	24	27	28	
x 48 Ports	2640	288	384	480	576	672	768	864	960	1056	1152	1296	1344	

Continues

Table 6.3   *Data Center Cable Run Lengths—Distributed Design (Continued)*

	Cable Runs to Main Network Row	Cable Runs from Server Cabinet Locations to Network Substation												Totals (in Feet)
Row 7		*7A*	*7B*	*7C*	*7D*	*7E*	*7F*	*7G*	*7H*	*7I*	*7J*	*7K*	*7L*	*12,864*
Distance (in Feet)	63	6	8	10	12	14	16	18	20	22	24	27	28	
x 48 Ports	3024	288	384	480	576	672	768	864	960	1056	1152	1296	1344	
Row 8		*8A*	*8B*	*8C*	*8D*	*8E*	*8F*	*8G*	*8H*	*8I*	*8J*	*8K*	*8L*	*13,248*
Distance (in Feet)	71	6	8	10	12	14	16	18	20	22	24	27	28	
x 48 Ports	3408	288	384	480	576	672	768	864	960	1056	1152	1296	1344	
Row 9		*9A*	*9B*	*9C*	*9D*	*9E*	*9F*	*9G*	*9H*	*9I*	*9J*	*9K*	*9L*	*13,632*
Distance (in Feet)	79	6	8	10	12	14	16	18	20	22	24	27	28	
x 48 Ports	3792	288	384	480	576	672	768	864	960	1056	1152	1296	1344	
Row 10		*10A*	*10B*	*10C*	*10D*	*10E*	*10F*	*10G*	*10H*	*10I*	*10J*	*10K*	*10L*	*14,016*
Distance (in Feet)	87	6	8	10	12	14	16	18	20	22	24	27	28	
x 48 Ports	4176	288	384	480	576	672	768	864	960	1056	1152	1296	1344	
Total														122,880

Whatever approach you take to the design and layout of your Data Center structured cabling, be sure that it is implemented in a neat and organized manner to facilitate airflow and allow easy access for troubleshooting.

Patch Cords

The benefit of having neat and organized cabling obviously applies to patch cords as much as structured cabling. When you go beyond green considerations, it can be argued that it's more important to have neat patch cords than structured cabling. Data Center users typically interact with a patching field when installing or servicing hardware rather than structured cabling, so sloppy patch cords can impact operational activities more than sloppy structured cabling. Patching fields can be more challenging to maintain in some server environments, however, due to frequent hardware changes and sometimes minimal management of how patches are run.

You can follow several strategies to keep Data Center patch cords organized, thereby improving airflow to equipment, reducing energy consumption of your cooling infrastructure, and easing troubleshooting. (Not to mention maintaining the professional appearance of your Data Center.)

- **Employ a distributed cabling hierarchy:** Already mentioned as beneficial for structured cabling, this approach can help with patch cords as well. Having Data Center networking patch fields divided into smaller segments around the Data Center mitigates cabling density and potentially improves airflow to the associated networking equipment.

- **Right-size port counts:** Planning the correct number of ports in your Data Center— and reserving space for future expansion of patch fields—helps avoid messy cabling. Installing too many ports can result in unnecessarily large cable bundles; installing too few can trigger piecemeal cabling additions in the future that fit awkwardly with the original cabling infrastructure.

- **Use ample wire management:** However many connections you install in your network patching fields, be sure to include sufficient vertical and horizontal wire management to handle the maximum quantity of patch cords you plan for. This is of particular importance for some Category 6A patch cords because of their increased outside cable diameters and solid copper core wire construction. This type of cord promotes a cable memory that can be increasingly difficult to manage as the number of patch cords multiply.

- **Prepatch networking connections:** Hardware density in modern Data Centers can involve thousands of cable connections in a single server row. Prepatching networking devices and patch fields all together, before servers are installed, helps ensure that cabling is routed neatly.

Tip   I can't say enough about the merits of prepatching network connections in a Data Center. It is simply a neater implementation than adding cables ad hoc as new hardware is connected to the system. Although it can be expensive to buy all of the patch cords and dedicate (or temporarily contract) the staffing resources for prepatching, I believe the operational benefits are worth it.

- Provide patch cords in different lengths—and use them: Stock commonly used types of patch cords in your Data Center in multiple lengths so that whoever installs your hardware can make a neat connection between devices and patching fields. That means correctly routing cabling through the available wire management rather than making a straight-line connection that blocks access to hardware or patch panels. It also means choosing the right length of cable length, so there is no slack to be either coiled up and hidden in the wire management system or left hanging at the end of a connection.

Note   Cisco Data Centers are stocked with patch cords in multiple lengths, typically in 1-foot (30-centimeter) increments up to 6 feet (1.8 meters) and lengths of 8 feet (2.4 meters), 10 feet (3 meters), 12 feet (3.7 meters), and 15 feet (4.6 meters).

I once had an equipment vendor who, having come into one of our Data Centers for the first time to install hardware, was surprised and disappointed when I directed him to our supply of patch cords.

"You mean I can't just grab a handful of 8-foot cords and use them for all the connections?"

Figure 6.4 shows a dedicated cable bin area in one of the Cisco Data Centers. Each storage bin is stocked with copper or fiber patch cords of a different length.

Implementing these cabling practices, first when designing a new Data Center and then when operating it, doesn't just make the facility greener by improving airflow and conserving cabling material, it also makes it easier to use and less prone to accidental downtime.

Figures 6.5 and 6.6 illustrate dramatically different examples of network cabinets bearing high quantities of cabling. Figure 6.5 shows cable bundles spilled onto the floor due to a lack of sufficient wire management and bundles crossing into an adjacent cabinet because of a lack of available ports. Airflow to the hardware within the cabinet is obstructed, and it is extremely difficult to do any servicing without (intentionally or not) unplugging multiple cable connections. Figure 6.6 shows a group of networking cabinets with prepatched cabling. Airflow and physical access to the hardware remain excellent despite the presence of approximately 1,300 patch cords.

Figure 6.4   *Dedicated Cable Bin Area*

Figure 6.5   *Chaotic Cabling*

Figure 6.6   *Prepatched Cabling*

Note   I like Figure 6.5 because it represents two of the most common causes of sloppy patching in Data Centers. Either a Data Center has too few ports available, prompting users to steal connections from an adjacent cabinet, or it has plenty of connections—too many, really—but lacks the wire management to support and route the cables.

Look closely at the image, and you can see that there are tie-wraps around the cable bundles. The person who routed the cables started out trying to be neat and organized. Without the proper infrastructure in place, though, he didn't have a chance.

Summary

Your Data Center's environmental impact is influenced by the types and quantities of data cabling it features. Server environments today are typically installed with a mix of Category 6 or Category 6A (augmented) unshielded and shielded cabling, 50/125 µm laser optimized optical multimode fiber rated OM3, OM3+, or OM4, and 8.3/125 µm zero or low water peak single mode fiber.

Providing connectivity in a Data Center through copper cabling involves vastly more natural resources than doing so through fiber cabling due to the more intensive process of harvesting copper rather than glass and the greater portions of copper than glass in equivalent bundles of cabling.

The smaller diameter of fiber than copper equates to smaller bundles, which in turn mean less airflow obstruction and fewer supporting infrastructure components such as cable trays, wire management, and network racks.

Higher-performing cable is greener (and ultimately less expensive) than lower-performing cable because it has a longer usable lifespan and, therefore, delays the need to discard and replace their materials.

Fiber cabling connections consume one-quarter or less of the energy (and therefore are responsible for one-quarter the carbon dioxide) of copper cabling connections in Data Centers because they don't require the high-voltage transmitters and because their connections can be consolidated onto fewer networking devices.

Design your structured cabling infrastructure so as to minimize cabling materials and avoid obstructing airflow. Implementing a distributed cabling hierarchy can dramatically reduce the cumulative length of a Data Center's cable runs.

Streamline your Data Center's patching fields for both green benefits and operational efficiency by right-sizing port counts, providing ample wire management, prepatching network connections, and providing patch cords in multiple lengths to support neat installations.

Chapter 7

Refrigerants and Fire Suppressants

This chapter discusses the environmental impacts of refrigeration and fire suppression materials commonly employed in Data Centers, reviews government regulations concerning their usage, and suggests green approaches for deploying them.

Data Centers and the Ozone Layer

Earth's ozone layer, located predominantly in the lower portion of the stratosphere some 6 miles to 31 miles (10 kilometers to 50 kilometers) above the surface of the planet, provides a shield against ultraviolet radiation. This shield can be damaged by certain man-made chemicals, including those commonly used as fire suppressants and refrigerants in Data Centers.

Reductions in stratospheric-ozone enables more ultraviolet radiation to pass through. Although ultraviolet radiation has health benefits in low quantities, namely stimulating the production of Vitamin D and for treating diseases such as jaundice or rickets, greater exposure can cause medical problems in people and animals including

- **Skin aging and cancer:** Ultraviolet radiation can break deoxyribonucleic acid (DNA) bonds, damaging skin cells and spawning cancerous growth.

- **Immunosuppression:** Ultraviolet radiation can interfere with the proper function of the body's immune system, damaging cells that help fight viral infections and impairing the body's normal response to vaccinations.

- **Eye damage:** Vision disorders including eye pain, cataracts, pterygium (a growth on the white of the eye), photokeratitis (a burn on the clear, front surface of the eye), and ocular cancers have been linked to ultraviolet radiation.

Ultraviolet radiation can also harm marine animals during the early stages of their physical development and lead to reduced growth and photosynthesis in some plant life.

Fortunately for the environment, refrigerants and fire suppressants known to cause greater amounts of ozone damage are being phased out of use in Data Centers and other buildings thanks to international treaties and certain national regulations.

Evolution of Refrigerants

Chlorofluorocarbons (CFCs) were developed in the 1930s as a safe, nonreactive refrigerant alternative to materials such as ammonia, chloromethane, and sulfur dioxide that, although effective as refrigerants, were known to be toxic and flammable. CFCs, which contain chlorine, fluorine, and carbon, were employed extensively in cooling chillers for decades—most commonly in the form of trichlorofluoromethane (CFC-11) and dichlorodifluoromethane (CFC-12)—until studies in the 1970s determined that CFCs—specifically the chlorine within them—were significantly damaging the ozone layer. (Just one chlorine atom can destroy thousands of ozone molecules.)

Note   A substance's capability to destroy ozone, known as its *ozone depletion potential (ODP)*, is expressed relative to CFC-11. An ODP of 2.5 would represent a substance that destroys ozone 2 1/2 times as much as CFC-11, for instance.

In response to the negative environmental effects of CFCs, *hydrochlorofluorocarbons (HCFCs)* were developed as a refrigerant. Adding hydrogen to chlorofluorocarbons made the substances less stable, enabling them to break down before reaching the stratosphere and, therefore, the ozone layer. HCFCs are less damaging to ozone than CFCs, typically bearing ODP ratings of approximately .01 to 0.1. Although they represented a significant environmental improvement over CFCs, there was still a desire for a refrigerant substance that didn't damage ozone at all.

Chemists subsequently created *hydrofluorocarbons (HFCs)* consisting of hydrogen, fluorine, and carbon. Lacking the chlorine of prior refrigerants and even more capable to break down in the lower atmosphere, HFCs have an ODP of 0. Unfortunately, although they don't destroy ozone, HFCs are significant contributors to global warming.

Note   The measure of how much a greenhouse gas contributes to global warming is known as its *global warming potential (GWP)*, which signifies the capability of a gas to trap heat within the atmosphere and is based upon three factors:

- Its capability of absorbing infrared radiation

- Its lifetime in the atmosphere

- What wavelengths of infrared radiation it absorbs

The more infrared radiation that a gas absorbs and the longer it exists in the atmosphere, the higher its GWP. (Of course, some gases can absorb a lot but dissipate sooner whereas others absorb less but remain in the atmosphere for a greater period of time.)

Which particular wavelengths of infrared radiation a gas absorbs—where they are on the spectrum—influences GWP to a greater or lesser degree depending upon whether those wavelengths are readily absorbed by the Earth's atmosphere. If the atmosphere absorbs those wavelengths, there's little GWP impact. If the wavelengths would normally pass through the atmosphere but are prevented from doing so by the gas, this impacts GWP.

GWP is expressed relative to carbon dioxide and is calculated over a specific period of time. A gas with a GWP rating of 100 is, therefore, 100 times more heat-absorbing than an equivalent amount (by weight) of carbon dioxide.

Depending upon their configuration, HFCs have a global warming potential ranging from 140 to 11,700, with atmospheric lifetimes of 1 year to 260 years, according to the U.S. Environmental Protection Agency. (Most commercially available HFC products have a lifetime less than 15 years.)

Evolution of Fire Suppressants

Seeking a fire suppression substance that could extinguish a fire yet wouldn't harm sensitive electronic equipment, Data Center managers in the 1960s turned to halon 1301. The suppressant—bromotrifluoromethane—was one of four halogenated hydrocarbons developed into a commercial fire suppressant following research into approximately 60 potential agents by Purdue University and the U.S. Army Corps of Engineers in the late 1940s.

Halon 1301 was an effective extinguishant and possessed the least toxicity of the four, making it a highly desirable suppressant. Halon 1211, bromochlorodifluoromethane, was similarly used in computing environments but in portable fire extinguishers. (The other two halons were 1202 and 2402. Halon 1202 was utilized as a fire protection agent for United States military aircraft engines, whereas halon 2402 was employed in Russia.)

Following halon, HFCs—already noted for their use as refrigerants—also began to be employed as fire suppressants, extinguishing fires by absorbing their heat. Commonly used versions include HFC-227 (heptafluoropropane, known throughout the Data Center industry by its brand name, FM-200), HFC-23 (trifluromethane, known commercially as FE-13), and HFC-125 (pentafluorethane, known commercially as FE-25). As mentioned, HFCs have 0 ODP but significant GWP.

Table 7.1 shows the environmental impact of several refrigerants and fire suppression materials commonly used in Data Centers today and in the past.

Table 7.1 *Environmental Characteristics of Common Data Center Refrigerants and Fire Suppressants*

Material		Atmospheric Lifetime (Years)	Ozone Depletion Potential	Global Warming Potential (100 Years)
Chlorofluoro-carbons	CFC-11 (Freon-11) Trichlorofluoromethane	45	1	4750
	CFC-12 (Freon-12) Dichlorodifluoromethane	100	1	10,890
	CFC-113 1,1,2-Trichlorotrifluoroethane	85	1	6130
Halons	Halon-1211 Trifluorbromomethane	16	7.1	1890
	Halon-1301 Bromotrifluoromethane	65	16	7140
Hydrochloro-fluorocarbons	HCFC-22 (Freon-22) Monochlorodifluoromethane	1.7	.05	1810
	HCFC-123 Dichlorotrifluoroethane	1.3	.02	77
	HCFC-142b Monochlorodifluorethane	17.9	.07	2310

Table 7.1 *Environmental Characteristics of Common Data Center Refrigerants and Fire Suppressants   (continued)*

	Material	Atmospheric Lifetime (Years)	Ozone Depletion Potential	Global Warming Potential (100 Years)
Hydrofluoro-carbons	HFC-23 (FE-13) Trifluromethane	270	0	14,760
	HFC-32 Difluoromethane	4.9	0	675
	HFC-125 (FE-25) Pentafluorethane	29	0	3500
	HFC-134a tetrafluoroethane	14	0	1430
	HFC-143a Trifluoroethane	52	0	4470
	HFC-227ea (FM-200) Heptafluoropropane	34.2	0	3220
	HFC-236fa (FE-36) Hexafluoropropane	240	0	9810
Hydrofluoro-carbons (blends)	**HFC-404A**		0	3922
	44% HFC-125	29	—	—
	4% HFC-134a	14	—	—
	52% HFC-143a	52	—	—
	HFC-407A		0	2107
	40% HFC-125	29	—	—
	40% HFC-134a	14	—	—
	20% HFC-32	4.9	—	—
	HFC-407C		0	1774
	25% HFC-125	29	—	—
	52% HFC-134a	14	—	—
	23% HFC-32	4.9	—	—

Data in Table 7.1 is from the World Meteorological Organization's Scientific Assessment of Ozone Depletion: 2006, except for global warming potential value for HFC blends, which were calculated by aggregating proportional amounts of the constituent substances.

Refrigerant and Fire Suppressant Naming Schemes

The letters and numbers used to designate refrigerants and fire suppressants can be confusing to anyone unfamiliar with them. They are actually a complex code for the composition and properties of a compound.

Take the prefixes CFC, HCFC, and HFC, for instance. The first C stands for chlorine, F stands for fluorine, H stands for hydrogen, and the final C stands for carbon. Therefore, a compound with the prefix CFC contains chlorine, fluorine, and carbon and is known as a chlorofluorocarbon. Although not included among the substances named in Table 7.1, the letter B is used in refrigerant names for bromine, and the letter P stands for the term "per" or all and is used as part of the prefix PFC for perfluorocarbons.

Alternatively, the prefix codes for refrigerants can be replaced with the letter R. Therefore, CFC-11 in Table 7.1 is also known as R-11. The R designation was originally used as registered trade names for DuPont refrigerants but later adopted as a standard naming convention by ASHRAE.

The numbers in refrigerant codes represent other factors. Proceeding from right to left

- The right-most digit is the number of fluorine atoms.

- The second digit from the right (in the "tens" place) is one more than the number of hydrogen atoms.

- The third digit from the right (in the "hundreds" place) is one less than the number of carbon atoms in the compound. The number is omitted if it equals 0.

- The fourth digit from the right (in the "thousands" place) represents the number of double bonds in the compound. If this number has a value of 0, which is usually the case for stable compounds, it is also omitted from the code.

To quickly determine the number of carbon, hydrogen, and fluorine atoms in a compound, add 90 to the refrigerant number. For example, 90 plus 134 equals 224, so HFC-134 has four fluorine atoms, two hydrogen atoms, and two carbon atoms.

- For compounds in which chlorine has been replaced by bromine, an uppercase B and a number indicating the quantity of bromine atoms are added as a suffix.

- For compounds that can have different arrangements of atoms, referred to as *isomers*, a lowercase a, b, or c is added as a suffix to clarify the specific form of the molecule.

Refrigerant blends don't follow this code. Those that are zeotropic blends, meaning their constituent materials have different evaporation and condensation points, are assigned a number in the 400s. Those that are azeotropic blends, having just one boiling and condensation point, are assigned a number in the 500s. The right-most digit is chosen arbitrarily for specific blends. (Other series include 600 for miscellaneous organic compounds, 700 for inorganic compounds with relative molecular masses less than 100, and 1000 for unsaturated organic compounds.)

Some blends consist of the same substances but in different proportions. When this occurs, the blends are distinguished by adding an uppercase letter at the end. HFC-407A and HFC-407C in Table 7.1 are, therefore, both zeotropic blends that contain the same component materials yet in different proportions.

Halons use a more straightforward code. The four-digit number represents, from left to right, the number of carbon, flourine, chlorine, and bromine atoms. Halon 1211 therefore contains one carbon atom, two flourine atoms, one chlorine atom and one bromine atom, for instance. (A fifth digit represents the number of iodine atoms. This number is omitted when iodine is not present.)

Greener Approaches to Refrigerants

While refrigerants can have a significant effect on the environment, you can take several steps when designing and operating your Data Center to lessen that impact and, therefore, be greener:

- **Choose efficient chillers:** Just as modern, high-efficiency PDUs save energy over older equipment by reducing electrical losses, new chillers offer better performance than older systems—not only in how effectively they cool but also by better retaining refrigerant. Older chillers can leak 10 percent to 15 percent of their refrigerant per year compared to less than 1 percent for new equipment.

- **Use high-efficiency purge systems:** Some chiller models require use of a purge unit to keep the machine free of moisture and noncondensable gases such as air. (Moisture can lead to corrosion within the unit whereas noncondensable gases are undesirable because they can cause an increase in condensing pressure that reduces operating efficiency.) Choose a unit that minimizes refrigerant loss when purging air.

- **Seek out leaks and fix them promptly:** Leaks are one of the most common ways for refrigerant to enter the atmosphere.

- **Develop a refrigerant management plan:** Establish company policies and procedures that address purchase, transport, storage, venting, recovery, and disposal of refrigerants. Adopt a system for tracking refrigerant usage because this can assist in revealing leaks.

Finally, regularly inspect and maintain your Data Center chillers to ensure they remain in good working order. Routine practices such as checking filters, inspecting wiring, and confirming the correct temperature and pressure of all fluids make your Data Center greener by ultimately extending the life of its equipment, not to mention reducing what you have to spend on repairs in the long run.

Greener Fire Suppression Options

Several fire extinguishing technologies are available for use in Data Centers that have less environmental impact than the suppressant materials shown in Table 7.1.

The most basic approach is to do away with a gaseous fire suppression system altogether and simply rely upon the water-based fire sprinkler system usually required by local building codes. In many regions, even if your Data Center is equipped with a gaseous suppressant, the requirement for fire sprinklers still applies. Data Center designers sometimes deal with this by installing sensitive fire detection sensors in connection with their gaseous suppression system so that gas can automatically deploy before the fire sprinkler system becomes aware of a fire condition and discharges.

Whether you opt to use fire sprinklers as your sole fire extinguishing solution or strictly as a backup to a gas-based system, it's advisable to use a pre-action, dry-pipe configuration. This keeps water out of the piping within your Data Center until or unless a fire is detected, thereby reducing the chance of a water leak from an accidental pipe break.

Other green fire suppression options for your Data Center include

- **Water mist:** A mist system emits a fine water spray, extinguishing a fire by simultaneously cooling the flame and displacing its oxygen. A mist system employs a fraction of the water used by conventional fire sprinklers, allowing it to be used in a server environment without damaging hardware.

- **Inert gases:** These substances extinguish fires by removing oxygen from the air and have 0 OPP and GWP. Suppression products on the market of this type include IG-451 (composed of nitrogen, argon, and carbon dioxide and known by its brand name, Inergen) and IG-55 (argonite, composed of nitrogen and argon).

- **Fluoroketones:** Available commercially as Novec 1230, Sapphire, or Sevo 1230, this substance is stored as a liquid, expelled as a gas, and extinguishes flames by removing heat. It has an ODP of 0, a GWP of 1, and an atmospheric lifespan of approximately 5 days. (The fire suppression fluid made *Time* magazine's list of coolest inventions for 2004, for its attributes as a liquid that doesn't get things wet. During appearances on several television programs in the United States, various items were dunked into a tank of the material in its liquid form with no ill effect, including books, paintings, and powered-on electronic equipment such as laptop computers, cell phones, and flat-screen televisions.)

Thoroughly research whatever fire suppression material you consider installing in your Data Center. Some systems have unique requirements such as special storage requirements or needing additional floor space for their delivery components. Knowing this at the beginning of the design phase of your Data Center project makes it easier to either accommodate those needs or else decide early on to look for a different fire suppression solution.

Note   You might have heard about potassium-based suppressants that are distributed in aerosol form, available on the market under trade names such as Aero-K, FirePro, PyroGen, and Stat-X. The products are effective suppressants, interfering with the chemical reaction of a fire and are quite green having zero ODP and GWP. Unfortunately, they're generally not a good fit for Data Center installations because they reduce visibility when discharged, which can interfere with the ability of personnel to exit the area and can leave a residue behind. Such materials are, therefore, typically limited to use in nonoccupied areas.

Changing Environmental Regulations

Employing refrigerants and fire suppressants that are gentler on the environment isn't just an admirable approach to make your Data Center greener; in many regions of the world, it's required by law.

Concerned about the depletion of ozone in the atmosphere, 24 countries in 1987 signed the Montreal Protocol on Substances That Deplete the Ozone Layer, pledging to phase out CFCs. Amendments to the treaty in the subsequent 20-plus years added commitments to eliminate halons and HCFCs and repeatedly shortened timelines to phase out various substances.

As of 2009, 193 countries had ratified the Montreal Protocol and agreed to its provisions, which include

- Developed countries halted halon production by 1994 and developing countries do so by 2010.

- Production of CFC refrigerants stopped by 1996.

- HCFC refrigerants are phased out over a 26-year period in developed countries. Compared to 1989 levels, HCFC production was to be reduced 35 percent by 2004, 75 percent by 2010, 90 percent by 2015, 99.5 percent by 2020, and halted entirely by 2030.

- In developing countries, HCFC production is frozen in 2013 at an average of 2009 and 2010 levels. HCFC production is then reduced 10 percent in 2015, 35 percent in 2020, 67.5 percent in 2025, 97.5 percent in 2030, and halted entirely in 2040.

Several countries have gone beyond the Montreal Protocol requirements, adopting more aggressive timelines to phase out HCFCs. For instance, the European Union barred production and consumption of HCFC refrigerant in new equipment in 2001 and set a 2015 deadline to entirely halt HCFC usage, whereas the U.S. Environmental Protection Agency prohibited the production or import of HCFC-142b (monochlorodifluoroethane) and

HCFC-22 (monochlorodifluoromethane) for new equipment by 2010. (Each have among the highest global warming potential ratings of HCFCs.)

Note that although the Montreal Protocol bans the production of halon, use of recycled halon or halon manufactured prior to the ban (either 1994 or 2010) is still permitted. It's inadvisable to construct a new Data Center with halon fire suppression because of environmental considerations and presumed future price volatility as halon becomes rarer, but if you have halon fire protection installed in a legacy Data Center, you are not mandated to remove and replace it.

Note Aware of the potential for environmental regulations to impact the future use of their products, some fire suppression system vendors now offer warranties to either replace an agent or refund its original purchase price if it is later prohibited for use.

DuPont and Fike Corporation offer a "sustainability warranty" for any Fike suppression system that uses DuPont's FE-25 or FE-227 (HFC-125 or HFC-227) products, agreeing to either replace the material or refund the original purchase price, at their discretion. Similarly, 3M offers a "Blue Sky" warranty for its Novec 1230 product, committing to refund the original purchase price. Each warranty is for 20 years.

Fire in the Data Center

While designing a new Data Center, you might find yourself contemplating skipping the installation of a fire suppression system beyond what is minimally required by local building code or your insurance provider. The cost and environmental impact of such infrastructure can be high while odds of a fire are low, so why not do without it?

It's a valid approach, but be sure to fully consider the impact that a fire would have on your server environment.

Note Even if you've worked in the Data Center industry for decades, you probably haven't had firsthand experience with a major fire in a Data Center or even spoken with someone who has. Not only are they rare but if a business does suffer a Data Center fire, company officials also can be hesitant to discuss the event because they don't want to publicize that their facility incurred downtime or was somehow vulnerable.

While conducting research for this book, I learned of a fire that occurred within a Data Center owned and operated by Camera Corner/Connecting Point, a combination web hosting provider, computer reseller, and retail electronics store based in Green Bay, Wisconsin. Shawn Massey, the company's Data Center director, graciously agreed to discuss the fire, the lessons his company learned from the event, and the ultimate fate of the server environment.

Tucked within the 26,000-square foot (2415-square meter) building where Camera Corner/Connecting Point conducts its retail operations, including a Digital Photo Café space where customers edit and print digital photos, was a 500-square foot (46.5-square meter) Data Center containing approximately 70 servers—a mix of hardware used for its own computing needs and to support hundreds of websites.

The server room, built in 2000, had an 11-inch (28 -centimeter) raised floor with electrical conduits and patch cords routed below providing power and connectivity to its hardware. An air-conditioning unit mounted above the false ceiling cooled the room, and each server cabinet was equipped with a portable UPS to provide standby power. A gaseous fire suppression system was considered but passed over because of its price tag of approximately $40,000.

By March 19, 2008, plans had been made to modernize the Data Center's operations by virtualizing many of the servers and leasing a second hosting space to grow into. Massey had received a service-level agreement from a colocation facility just the week before and was awaiting Camera Corner/Connecting Point's owner to return from vacation to sign off on which facility to contract with.

At approximately 7 p.m. that evening, flames smoldered within one of the Data Center's server cabinets and then spread. Massey's first hint that something was amiss came when a client called him, reporting that it had lost communication with its hardware; an automated page from one of the servers arrived shortly after.

Massey, assuming it to be a minor problem, drove to the store and was surprised to find fire trucks in front of the building. He entered to check on the servers, stopping short of entering the Data Center when he found its door hot to the touch. The crew from the local fire department was already on the scene, having been alerted by automated smoke alarms.

Heat and smoke from the fire devastated the Data Center's contents—only one of the 70 servers in the room could be rebooted. A fire investigator spent 3 days inspecting the site, even summoning representatives from each manufacturer whose hardware was in the cabinet in which the fire began. Faulty wiring or electronic equipment are suspected, but no definitive cause was ever determined.

Equipment was offline for 8 days, impacting not only Camera Corner/Connecting Point's operations, but also an estimated 500 websites of clients they hosted.

"With our application hosting customers, if you think about it, it wasn't just our company that had a fire," said Massey. "It was dozens of companies that had a fire."

Initial estimates suggested that the fire would cost Camera Corner/Connecting Point approximately $3 million. Including the initial recovery effort, fixing smoke damage, reconstructing the Data Center, and purchasing replacement hardware, the actual figure was about half that.

The timing of the blaze was both maddening and fortuitous. Maddening because if it had happened a few weeks later, the additional colocation facility would have been online, providing a fully functional hosting space to operate from and allowing some servers to have avoided the fire. Fortuitous because several pieces of Data Center equipment had already been purchased and were on site in preparation for the intended expansion, including a standby generator, room-sized UPS, and call manager hardware. Also, Massey already had a plan for how he wanted Camera Corner/Connecting Point's Data Center to look in the future.

In the wake of the fire, the company opted to rebuild and completely redesign the Data Center, both in terms of physical infrastructure and hardware. The renovated Data Center features new servers and networking devices (including a high ratio of virtualized servers), prewired structured cabling to all cabinets, an 18-inch (46-centimeter) raised floor, cabinets arranged in a hot- and cold-aisle configuration, a single UPS for the entire room, a standby generator, and an FM-200 gaseous fire suppression system.

Along with the physical changes to the room, Massey says that his approach has changed in the aftermath of the fire.

"Like most people, I always thought it (a disaster) wouldn't happen to us," said Massey. "Now I will forever for the rest of my life be expecting that next disaster. And that next time will be ready."

Summary

Fire suppressants and refrigerant substances contribute to the destruction of the ozone layer, causing greater exposure to ultraviolet radiation that can, in turn, cause skin damage, immunosuppression issues, and eye problems.

Refrigerants used in chillers have evolved over the years from chlorofluorocarbons (CFCs) containing chlorine, fluorine, and carbon to hydrochlorofluorocarbons (HCFCs) containing hydrogen, chlorine, fluorine, and carbon to hydrofluorocarbons (HFCs) containing hydrogen, fluorine, and carbon. Each compound has had less ozone depletion potential than what came before yet are still significant contributors to global warming.

Data Centers have been equipped with halon 1301 (bromotrifluoromethane) for roomwide fire suppression and halon 1211 (bromochlorodifluoromethane) for portable fire extinguishers since the 1960s, due to their relatively low toxicity and the ability to use them safely around electronic equipment. HFCs are more commonly installed in Data Centers now, due to their less ozone depletion potential.

You can help mitigate the damage potential of refrigerants to the environment by choosing efficient chillers that are less likely to leak refrigerant, employing high-efficiency purge systems, rapidly identifying and fixing leaks, developing a comprehensive refrigerant management plan, and regularly inspecting and maintaining chiller equipment.

You can make your Data Center fire suppression system greener by forgoing conventional gaseous suppressant in favor of traditional water-based sprinklers, a mist system, inert gas suppressants, potassium-based aerosol spray, or fluoroketones.

The Montreal Protocol on Substances That Deplete the Ozone Layer was signed into law in 1987 and called for eliminating CFCs. Provisions of the treaty have been steadily expanded since then and now include provisions for eliminating halons and HCFCs.

Eliminating a fire suppression system from the design of your Data Center can reduce the construction costs and environmental impact of your Data Center, but if a fire does occur, the effects can be devastating.

Chapter 8

Choosing Greener Gear

This chapter offers strategies for making a Data Center greener through IT hardware choices, outlines server energy efficiency standards and metrics, and discusses both hardware utilization and how to reduce hardware power consumption.

Environmental Impact of IT Hardware

In and among greening the facilities-related technologies of your Data Center—power, cooling, and fire suppression—don't overlook opportunities to green the systems that drive your Data Center power consumption in the first place—your IT hardware. Because servers, networking devices, and storage units are the final destination of your Data Center's power and cooling delivery chains, anything you do to reduce their power consumption and heat generation has a cumulative benefit.

As mentioned in Chapter 4, "Powering Your Way to a Greener Data Center," every watt of power conserved at the server level actually saves nearly three. Although energy consumption is the most obvious green factor of Data Center hardware, other elements such as what materials are consumed to manufacture a device and their footprint—smaller systems use fewer materials than larger ones—are also valid to consider.

Aside from the environmental benefits of choosing energy-efficient hardware are the cost savings. Exactly how much money is saved depends upon the cost of power where your Data Center is located, but in the mid-2000s, several Data Center industry groups began predicting that energy costs over a server's lifetime would soon exceed the initial price tag of the device.

Note   Electrical costs associated with IT hardware have become so significant that a British manufacturer of energy-efficient servers now offers to provide its machines to companies at no capital cost in exchange for a portion of the Data Center utility savings its hardware provides over other models.

Under VeryPC's Free Green Server Initiative, customers can trade in more than 135 types of servers—a variety of Dell, Fujitsu, Hewlett Packard, and Sun systems—in exchange for leasing the company's GreenServer Janus 2 hardware. A customer's monthly lease payments are calculated based upon anticipated electrical cost savings from replacing the old hardware with the new servers.

You can find more information about the Free Green Server Initiative at http://www.freegreenservers.co.uk/.

When evaluating IT equipment for your Data Center, keep in mind that your overall goals are to obtain hardware that can meet your processing needs for a long time and are efficient not just as individual machines, but as a complete system. That means rather than simply defaulting to whatever hardware draws less power, focus on processing per kilowatt. Strategically choose more powerful devices that have greater capabilities and can perhaps enable other systems to be consolidated. For example, a small economy car consumes much less fuel than a large school bus, yet the greater seating capacity of the bus makes it more efficient for transporting a large number of people. The bus, in essence, takes the place of multiple small cars.

If your Data Center is equipped with servers that draw less electricity than other models yet don't provide adequate performance, it will only be a matter of time before you feel compelled to add more hardware or upgrade.

Note   I've encountered some businesses over the years that learned the impact of hardware choices upon their Data Center resources the hard way. Having run critically low on electrical capacity in their Data Center, they were forced to ration what little power capacity remained until a new server environment could be brought online. New hardware purchases and installations were heavily scrutinized for their power consumption, and the default policy was that no additional hardware could be installed until other systems were removed that accounted for at least as much power usage.

Not surprisingly, the experience left a lasting impression, causing the companies to focus on power consumption when choosing new hardware long after they had resolved the capacity shortage.

Hardware Energy Efficiency Targets

As the role of power has increased in importance in the Data Center—power is both the defining factor of a server environment's true capacity and its greatest operational expense these days—so too has interest grown concerning the energy efficiency of IT hardware. Understanding power-efficiency targets for servers and networking devices that have been set by various agencies and choosing hardware that meet them can help make your Data Center greener.

Energy Star Specifications

The U.S. Environmental Protection Agency is issuing a series of specifications for Data Center-related hardware to receive its Energy Star label.

The first standard, issued in 2009, applies to individual servers that include one to four processing slots. A second tier of the standard, scheduled to come out in 2010, is to encompass systems with more than four sockets, blade servers, fully fault tolerant servers, server appliances, and multinode servers.

Additional Energy Star specification are intended to be developed in the future for storage devices and networking hardware. Initial work on the storage specification began shortly before publication of this book.

To qualify for the Energy Star designation, servers are required to meet several criteria, including

- **Efficiency standards for power supplies:** Server power supplies are required to meet minimum efficiency and power factor requirements under various loads. Distinct performance minimums are called out for a variety of power supplies: AC-DC and DC-DC, varying wattages, and multiple and single output power supplies.

- **Idle power limits:** Servers must not exceed certain power thresholds while idle. The maximums vary based upon the configuration of the server, including the quantities of processors, installed memory, and hard drives.

- **Reporting requirements:** Manufacturers are to provide data sheets on their website detailing the Energy Star-qualified hardware model, including maximum, minimum, and typical configurations for the hardware.

- **Data measurements:** Most of the server configurations eligible for the Energy Star designation must additionally be capable of providing input power consumption, inlet air temperature, and processor utilization data during normal operation.

Table 8.1 shows the minimum power supply energy-efficiency requirements for servers to qualify for the Energy Star designation.

Server power supplies are additionally required to meet the minimum power factor thresholds outlined in Table 8.2.

Table 8.1 *Energy Star Efficiency Requirements for Computer Server Power Supplies (Tier 1)*

Power Supply Type	Rated Output Power	10-Percent Load	20-Percent Load	50-Percent Load	100-Percent Load
Multi-Output (AC-DC and DC-DC)	All Output Levels	N/A	82 percent	85 percent	82 percent
Single-Output (AC-DC and DC-DC)	500 watts	70 percent	82 percent	89 percent	85 percent
	>500 to 1,000 watts	75 percent	85 percent	89 percent	85 percent
	>1,000 watts	80 percent	88 percent	92 percent	88 percent

Various governments, energy agencies, and public utility companies provided comments during the 2 1/2-year development period of the specification as did hardware manufacturers including Dell, EMC, Fujitsu, HP, IBM, Intel, NetApp, Sun Microsystems, and VMware. The agency estimates that servers with the Energy Star label are 30 percent more efficient than conventional systems.

The Energy Star Computer Server Specification is available online at http://tinyurl.com/qwxc8a.

Table 8.2 *Energy Star Power Factor Requirements for Computer Server Power Supplies (Tier 1)*

Power Supply Type	Rated Output Power	10-Percent Load	20-Percent Load	50-Percent Load	100-Percent Load
DC-DC (All)	All Output Levels	—	—	—	—
AC-DC Multi-Output	All Output Levels	—	0.80	0.90	0.95
AC-DC Single-Output	500 watts	N/A	0.80	0.90	0.95
	>500 to 1,000 watts	0.65	0.80	0.90	0.95
	>1,000 watts	0.80	0.90	0.90	0.95

Power factor requirements do not apply where output power is less than 75 watts.

Note   Energy efficiency and power factor are common benchmarks for defining power supply efficiency, but what do they mean?

An energy-efficiency rating equals how much power a power supply provides divided by how much energy is input into it. So, a server with a power supply that is 80 percent efficient uses 8 watts of every 10 watts drawn from the power source to which it is connected (8 watts / 10 watts = 80 percent). To put it another way, a computing device that requires 400 watts to function that has a power supply that is 80 percent efficient actually draws 500 watts. The less efficient a power supply is, the more power wasted—that same device equipped with a 60-percent efficient power supply would draw 667 watts to reach its needed 400 watts.

Power factor, meanwhile, is the ratio of active power to apparent power of an alternating current circuit. Expressed as a value between zero and one, it indicates how closely current and voltage are in phase with one another. A score of one indicates they are in phase; the nearer a score is to zero, the closer to 90 degrees that the current leads or lags the voltage. The lower the power factor, then, the more amperage required to provide a given amount of useful power.

Climate Savers Computing Initiative

In 2007, Google and Intel began the Climate Savers Computing Initiative, inviting makers and users of personal computers (PCs) and servers to commit to manufacture and purchase, respectively, systems that meet energy-efficiency standards of 80 percent and higher at various power load levels. More than 300 companies and organizations are, as of this writing, members of the initiative.

Organizers projected that by 2010 the program could, with sufficient participation, reduce the energy use of computers shipped that year more than 50 percent compared to 2007 and over that 3-year period save 62 billion kWh of energy and avoid 54 million tons (49 million metric tons) of carbon dioxide emissions. At 8.85 cents per kWh, that totals more than $5.5 billion in avoided energy costs.

The Climate Savers Computing Initiative introduces higher efficiency targets year over year, reaching their highest mark—deemed gold—in 2010. Table 8.3 shows efficiency targets for single-output power supply units typically used in Data Center hardware. Table 8.4 shows efficiency targets for multi-output units typically used in desktop PCs and workstations.

The Climate Savers Computing Initiative additionally calls for participating members to include an increasing proportion of energy-efficient servers and desktops among their hardware purchases and commit to using power management features on their computers.

An online database of hardware that meets the Climate Saver Server Initiative standards is available at http://tinyurl.com/56eenh.

Table 8.3 *Climate Savers Computing Initiative Power Efficiency Targets for Single-Output Power Supply Units (Servers)*

Power Load Condition	Bronze (2007)		Silver (2008)		Gold (2010)	
	Efficiency	Power Factor	Efficiency	Power Factor	Efficiency	Power Factor
20 percent	81 percent	—	85 percent	—	88 percent	—
50 percent	85 percent	—	89 percent	0.9	92 percent	0.9
100 percent	81 percent	0.9	85 percent	—	88 percent	—

Note The desktop computer efficiency levels named by both the Climate Savers Computing Initiative and the U.S. Environmental Protection Agency's Energy Star program are based upon those of the 80 Plus Program, which was launched in 2004 in the wake of a study of power supply energy efficiency and called for computer systems to be at least 80-percent efficient at various load levels.

Table 8.4 *Climate Savers Computing Initiative Power Efficiency Targets for Multi-Output Power Supply Units (Desktop Computers)*

Power Load Condition	Base (2007)		Bronze (2008)		Silver (2009)		Gold (2010)	
	Efficiency	Power Factor	Efficiency	Power Factor	Efficiency	Power Factor	Efficiency	Power Factor
20 percent	80 percent	—	82 percent	—	85 percent	—	87 percent	—
50 percent	80 percent	—	85 percent	0.9	88 percent	0.9	90 percent	0.9
100 percent	80 percent	0.9	82 percent	—	85 percent	—	87 percent	—

Efficiency Metrics for Hardware

As discussed in Chapter 2, "Measuring Green Data Centers," there are several metrics used in varying degrees across the Data Center industry to gauge energy efficiency and environmental impact of server environments. As valuable as those metrics are, however, they give only a partial view into how efficiently a Data Center's resources are used and, consequently, how green the facility is functioning.

For further insight, it's useful to also determine the relative efficiency of the specific hardware deployed in the Data Center. This is especially relevant considering that Data Center metrics universally include IT energy consumption as a factor. If you know precisely the ratio of power consumed in your Data Center by IT hardware versus facilities equipment (that is, Power Usage Effectiveness [PUE] or Data Center Infrastructure Efficiency [DCIE]), for instance) yet have no idea what sort of performance is accomplished by that IT hardware energy consumption, it's hard to draw complete conclusions about the efficiency of your company's computing activities.

A handful of metrics have been suggested to assess the energy efficiency of Data Center hardware. Although none have reached the level of discussion and usage as PUE and DCIE, consider whether they can provide insight into your Data Center's computing activities.

Energy Consumption Rating (ECR)

One proposed metric, Energy Consumption Rating (ECR), tallies the amount of energy required to move data across a networking device; specifically, the energy consumed to move one gigabit worth of line-level data per second:

$$\text{Energy Consumption Rating (ECR)} = \frac{E \text{ (Energy Consumption)}}{T \text{ (System Throughput)}}$$

Normally expressed in watts/gigabits per second, ECR can be calculated at a networking device's peak load or weighted to include a device's energy-saving idle mode as well.

Because networking hardware models can vary considerably, various product classes are suggested to be used in conjunction with ECR, including

- **Class 1:** Routers. These include core, edge, and multipurpose routing platforms.

- **Class 2:** WAN/Broadband aggregation devices.

- **Class 3:** Ethernet Layer 2/Layer 3 switches. Carrier-grade Ethernet switching platforms, including Data Center/large enterprise switches and desktop/generic Ethernet platforms.

- **Class 4:** Experimental. (This class is a placeholder for equipment that does not fit another class.)

- **Class 5:** Security appliances. Various security platforms including deep packet inspection (DPI), firewalls, virtual private network (VPN) gateways, and more.

- **Class 6:** Application gateways. Variable application platforms including load balancers, accelerators, and compressors.

Energy Efficiency Rating (EER)

Just as the factors used to calculate PUE can be flipped to provide the inverse DCIE metric, so too can the factors of ECR be flipped to provide the inverse known as Energy Efficiency Rating (EER):

$$\text{Energy Efficiency Rating (EER)} = \frac{T \text{ (System Throughput)}}{E \text{ (Energy Consumption)}}$$

ECR and EER were developed by IP performance test system provider Ixia, Juniper Networks, and Lawrence Berkeley National Laboratory and introduced in 2008.

You can find more information about ECR and EER at http://www.ecrinitiative.org/.

Space, Watts, and Performance (SWaP)

Another metric, known as Space, Watts, and Performance (SWaP), evaluates server efficiency by juxtaposing the computing performance of the hardware against its physical footprint and energy consumption. The higher a machine's SWaP rating, the greater productivity it presumably provides relative to your Data Center resources:

$$\text{Space, Watts and Performance (SWaP)} = \frac{\text{Performance}}{\text{Space} \times \text{Power Consumption}}$$

For example, if one server in your Data Center is 2U high and performs 250 operations during a given period of time while consuming 200 watts, while another server is 4U high, performs 350 operations, and consumes 400 watts, which machine is more efficient? According to SWaP, the first machine is about three times as efficient, achieving a score of 0.63 (250 / (2 × 200) = 0.63) compared to the second machine's score of 0.22 (350 / (4 × 400) = 0.22).

SWaP was developed by Sun Microsystems and introduced in 2005. The company offers an online calculator to compare SWaP ratings between servers, which you can find at http://www.sun.com/servers/coolthreads/swap/index.jsp#how.

Note   SWaP can be an effective tool for making Data Center users think about how servers with various physical characteristics provide computing capability versus consume Data Center resources. Looking at the formula does make me wonder, though, if the relative weights of power consumption and physical footprint should be adjustable in certain circumstances.

For example, if two servers provide the same performance and one is twice the height, yet consumes half of the power of a second system, both receive the same SWaP score. Because more Data Centers these days seem to have power constraints rather than space limitations—plus power usage impacts operational costs—I consider power savings more valuable than space savings. Given the choice of the two sample machines, I would rather have the bigger, more energy-efficient server every time. Anyone managing a Data Center where cabinet space is limited but ample power is available thinks the opposite.

Applying a small multiplier to either the power consumption or space value would increase its importance in the calculation in favor of whichever resource that you consider most valuable within your Data Center.

Hardware Utilization

Just as important as choosing energy-efficient hardware to make your Data Center green is using them efficiently after they are installed. The more of a hardware device's capacity that you use, known as its *utilization*, the better. Having the most energy-efficient servers and storage devices available on the market provides little green value if each of those systems are lightly utilized, and you end up operating—and therefore powering and cooling—several of them.

Think of utilization and capacity in terms of a motor vehicle. The more seats that are filled with passengers the fewer trips you have to make, the less gas that you consume, and ultimately the fewer automobiles you need to provide the necessary transportation. As with Data Center hardware, the most fuel-efficient passenger car isn't particularly green if it is used only to transport one person and its several other seats are vacant.

Industry approximations of average Data Center server and storage utilization vary significantly—optimistic estimates suggest 40 percent utilization, others estimate as low as just 5 percent. Chapter 9, "Greening Your Data Center Through Consolidation, Virtualization, and Automation," offers methods to improve the utilization rates of your server and storage devices, potentially to as high as 80 percent.

Beyond Energy Consumption and Utilization

Although energy efficiency is arguably the most important factor for evaluating how green a server, networking device, or storage unit is, it's not the only one. Other elements contribute to the environmental impact of Data Center hardware and are relevant to consider when making purchasing decisions:

- **Cooling efficiency:** Aside from the power that they consume directly, Data Center machines indirectly use additional energy due to their need to be kept cool. Servers that are optimized for cooling—generating less heat and oriented with their air intake in the front and exhaust venting in the back, thereby matching the hot- and cold-aisle designs prevalent in modern Data Centers—reduce that secondary energy consumption.

- **Materials:** Limit buying hardware made of materials that are bad for the environment or require large quantities of resources to produce. The European Union has restricted the use of six materials—lead, cadmium, mercury, hexavalent chromium, and flame retardants polybrominated biphenals and polybrominated diphenyl ether—in electrical and electronic equipment since mid-2006 and it's likely that similar regulations will ultimately be adopted in other countries in the future. The Restriction of Hazardous Substances [RoHS] Directive does allow lead-based solders through 2010 for servers and storage arrays and indefinitely for networking infrastructure equipment.

Note Material Declaration Data Sheets (MDDS) that outline what substances a product is made of—and often what hazardous materials the item does not include—can be obtained from hardware manufacturers. Many offer them online on their company website.

- **Capability to upgrade:** What happens when your Data Center hardware ages? Systems that enable you to replace key components with new ones are greener because you can extend their useful life using fewer materials than if you fully decommissioned and replaced them.

- **Capability to recycle:** The more components that can be kept out of the landfill when a piece of Data Center hardware does reach the end of its useful life, the better. Some manufacturers facilitate this process by promoting the return of their old systems. (Chapter 10, "Greening Other Business Practices," discusses green considerations and strategies for dealing with e-waste.)

- **Small form factor:** Smaller hardware involves fewer manufacturing materials and requires less Data Center supporting infrastructure. If your company's processing needs can be supported by a given number of 1U servers instead of the same number of 4U servers, for instance, your Data Center could theoretically be built at one fourth the size, reducing everything from the quantities of server cabinets to the lengths of structured cabling to the overall amount of building materials. This assumes your Data Center has sufficient power and cooling capacity to support significant equipment density and, therefore, take advantage of the small form factor, of course. Be sure to consider this in the context of groups of hardware as well—a larger machine can be a greener choice when it takes the place of multiple smaller devices that, taken together, have a larger footprint (and perhaps consume more energy).

Data Centers typically house hundreds or even thousands of pieces of hardware, and many of those machines come from a relatively small number of vendors. If you are going to purchase multiple systems from a manufacturer within a short period of time, ask whether it can consolidate how the items are packaged. If everyone did this, manufacturers would consume fewer resources (and spend less money) for packaging and accessories, and customers would end up with fewer materials that are often discarded.

If you order 10 of a given server model, it's doubtful that you need more than one copy of its installation manual, for instance. Cables and adapters that are packed with many hardware models are also superfluous if those items are already stocked in your server environment—a common practice in rooms where color-coding schemes are used.

Note It's also a good idea to ask manufacturers of the consumable items used in your Data Center for consolidated packaging options. I once placed a bulk order for a few hundred patch cords and when they arrived, I was startled to discover each cable had been individually wrapped in plastic—a complete waste of material, not to mention of my time to open every wrapping.

The most wasteful packaging of Data Center items I have ever seen involved shelving for server cabinets. During my first week working for Cisco, I was asked to help clean up and organize a caged portion of a receiving dock that contained a jumble of Data Center items and miscellaneous items that were more suitable for an office supply closet. The biggest objects in the cage were a dozen or so boxes, each about the size of a kitchen refrigerator and extremely heavy, that contained shelves for use with four-post server cabinets.

To my surprise, each box contained only about 15 shelves. Despite being made of sturdy steel, each shelf was thoroughly wrapped in packing foam, capped on all four corners with cardboard, nestled within an individual box and then all those boxes were in turn stacked inside an outer box. The shelves seemed quite damage resistant, yet had been wrapped as if constructed of flimsy, breakable material. After I removed all the packaging, the shelves occupied maybe one-third of the space of the outer box, freeing up considerable room in the cage.

How Budget Process Impacts Hardware Choices

Although it might not be obvious, the manner in which funds are budgeted at your company could be hindering how green your Data Center is.

In many businesses, the IT department has a defined budget for the purchase of computing hardware. The funding is typically available for a finite period of time, such as a fiscal quarter or perhaps an entire year. For a large company, smaller groups within the IT organization might each have their own budget, but otherwise the conditions are the same. Because one of IT's main measures of success is how well it provides computing services for the company and because IT personnel know their funding will go away if they don't spend it—and perhaps even resulting in a smaller budget allocation next period—there is a natural tendency to buy the highest-performing machines possible. This approach can seem harmless. If some of the hardware capabilities exceed what is needed, who cares?

Hardware performance does come with a price, though. The faster processing a server can do, typically the more power it consumes and more heat it generates. If your company continuously buys more powerful servers than it requires, it's putting excess power and cooling demand upon the Data Center. It's much like buying a high-performance sports car even though you need to drive only in town where speed limits are low. You rarely see the benefit of the car's excellent acceleration (the server's greater processing) over that of an average vehicle, but you suffer with its poorer gas mileage (excess power consumption) every day.

The ongoing cost of higher-performing hardware can be more difficult to detect at companies where utility bills are paid by the facilities organization. With no view into those costs, the IT department has no idea of how much impact it has upon Data Center power consumption and no incentive to change its buying habits.

Communication between the IT and facilities departments can improve this situation. At minimum, have IT management see the monthly power bills associated with the Data Center. Give them visibility into the energy consumption associated with their hardware choices and an understanding of the finite resources of your server environment.

The ultimate extension of this is to establish a chargeback model for Data Center resources. Under this approach, you operate your server environment much like a colocation facility, charging clients for using Data Center capacity. Although you're not looking to make a profit off of the chargeback model the way that an external colocation business does, by assigning a monetary value to your Data Center resources and requiring departmental groups to pay when they use them can influence behavior. Groups are less likely to overstate their capacity needs "just in case" they need it, and with a chargeback policy in place, they even have a direct incentive to consume fewer Data Center resources.

Note   I vividly recall the year that Cisco began to charge a small fee to internal groups for the building floor space they occupied. Managers who had absolutely required storerooms and to own various functional work areas suddenly didn't feel they needed the space so badly anymore. Whereas my team had once had to compete to obtain sufficient space in which to keep Data Center-related equipment, plenty became available.

Years ago Data Center chargeback models involved rack units or floor space because physical dimensions, and available cabinets were a server environment's leading finite capacity. Today, chargeback models focus on different critical Data Center resources. For Data Centers housing conventional servers, it's power. For Data Centers in which systems are virtualized, they're increments of CPU usage, RAM, and storage (see Chapter 9 for details).

Consider the user behavior that is promoted by the different models. Charging based upon cabinet space encourages Data Center clients to buy hardware with the smallest footprint and to install those systems as tightly as possible. Such high-density machine installations can lead to hot spots and exceed the power budget of cabinet locations. Charging based upon power usage puts the value on maximizing the use of energy, leading to reduced consumption and emphasizing greater processing efficiency per amp. Charging based upon processing and storage encourages clients to maximize the use of those resources.

During the 2000s, many colocation facilities changed their pricing structure so that customers began to be charged for energy usage rather than cabinet space. Some continue to charge for overall floor space but also have a hard cap on how much power is provided to the floor space that a client leases. In that case, obtaining more power requires leasing more space.

Note   I worked at Syracuse University before coming to Cisco, and for several months some of the on-campus cafeterias had a salad bar in which patrons could buy a salad for a set price based upon the size of the bowl. I became very good at constructing a tall, heaping salad—not unlike a Data Center manager occupying every rack unit of cabinet space with hardware.

One day when I went to pay for a salad that I had so carefully constructed, the cashier weighed it and charged me on a cost-per-ounce basis. Now calculated based upon the resources that I was consuming, the price doubled!

I still ate salads at the cafeteria, but nowhere near as frequently, and when I did I focused more on which ingredients I truly wanted.

Idling Servers

Data Centers are massive consumers of electricity, not just because they power and cool thousands of pieces of high-performing computing hardware, but also because they power and cool those systems constantly—24 hours a day, 7 days a week, 365 days a year, year after year. Imagine how much higher the power bills for your home would be if you kept all your electronic appliances and lights on around the clock.

Even when Data Center machines are idle, they draw a significant amount of energy—various estimates place that consumption as 30 percent, 50 percent, or nearly 70 percent of when a system is at peak load. Because hardware serves no useful purpose while idling, how about turning them off and avoiding that energy usage?

Several studies have been conducted to demonstrate the feasibility and energy savings of deactivating idle Data Center hardware and then reactivating them when demand warrants:

- Microsoft tracked usage patterns such as login rates, connection counts, and connection failures on its instant messaging service, Windows Live Messenger, over a 45-day period along with server performance data such as CPU usage, memory usage, and power consumption. The company then developed server provisioning and load dispatching algorithms, adjusting parameters such as how many logins are routed to various servers, in hopes to find a balance point where energy usage could be reduced without notable impact upon connection services for users. The study, *Energy-Aware Server Provisioning and Load Dispatching for Connection-Intensive Internet Services*, published in 2008, reported energy savings of 20 percent to 30 percent with only minor impacts to user experience.

- In a separate study, Microsoft determined that spinning down storage disks when they are idle can save 28 percent to 36 percent in energy consumption. By redirecting blocks normally written to one volume to other storage systems, a technique Microsoft calls *write off-loading*, idle time can be increased and raise energy saving to 45 percent to 60 percent. The study, *Write Off-Loading: Practical Power Management for Enterprise Storage*, published in 2008, analyzed 36 volumes containing 179 disks on 13 servers during a 1-week period and then conducted write off-loading techniques on a test bed of 56 disks on four servers.

- A company that sold software that can automatically power servers off or on according to various preset conditions, performed a 6-week study in which 89 servers were power-cycled a cumulative 3,500 times, simulating 6.3 hours per day of idle time. Having the systems offline saved approximately 26 percent of the power typically used by those system, a total about 2,400 kWh, according the documented study, *Resource Optimization through Active Power Management*. The study was performed by Cassatt, whose assets have since been purchased by IT software firm CA.

Despite the obvious potential to reduce energy consumption by powering down hardware, many Data Center managers are hesitant to do so because they are concerned about possible system malfunctions due to repeated power-cycling. Energy savings are desirable for a Data Center but not as important as reliable uptime. The study was performed by Cassatt, whose assets have since been purchased by IT software firm CA.

Note I attended the Data Center Energy Summit sponsored by the Silicon Valley Leadership Group in 2008, at which the results of the aforementioned Cassatt case study were first presented. Although audience interest in the results was strong, there were some skeptical comments based on the relatively limited times that machines were powered off and on—3,500 cycles of 89 machines equals about 40 times apiece.

Although not documented in a published paper, former Cassatt vice president of product engineering Vinay Pai blogged in 2007 about a study performed in one of the company's engineering labs in which 123 servers were each power-cycled about once a day for a 5-month period—for a total of 18,826 times—without a single power supply or disk drive failure in the ensuing 2 years.

More than half of the servers were HP machines, and the remainder were a mix of Dell, IBM, and Sun systems according to Pai's blog entry, titled "Yes It's Still Safe to Power Off and Power On That Server."

"So if you're still afraid to power down that server, don't worry!" Pai wrote. "Power supplies and hard drives are very reliable these days. From several different studies we've seen that power supplies hold up quite well from (and are even designed for) power cycling."

Eliminating Less Efficient Hardware

As you focus on purchasing new, greener hardware, don't overlook the systems already in your Data Center. Companies often have ample processes in place concerning obtaining and installing new servers, but few concerning the decommissioning or replacement of older ones. Avoid allowing outdated hardware that is poorly utilized and not energy-efficient to consume your Data Center's valuable resources.

It's a good idea to regularly check the machines in your server environment, especially legacy machines, to determine their utilization. If a piece of equipment isn't used, turn it off, and remove it. If the equipment is used but only lightly, determine whether the machine can and should be upgraded to a newer configuration that is more energy-efficient.

Newer systems are generally more energy-efficient, so it can sometimes make financial and environmental sense to upgrade to new models—much like trading in an old vehicle for an economy car when fuel prices are high.

Cisco Product Efficiency Calculator   Don't be shy about asking hardware manufac-turers for information about how energy-efficient their models are that you use (or are considering using) in your Data Center. This can help you choose greener systems that won't need to be upgraded for an extended period of time.

As part of its Efficiency Assurance Program, Cisco offers an online tool that enables you to determine the power usage, electrical efficiency, and energy costs of its devices. You can even set certain variables in the tool to reflect specific conditions within your particu-lar Data Center.

Users enter local electric rates (per kWh), the type and quantity of various networking devices, an estimate of how many watts are consumed cooling the Data Center relative to those consumed by IT hardware, and an estimate of the network devices' overall utiliza-tion. In return, the Product Efficiency Calculator shows the nominal power draw of the networking gear, typical thermal energy loss, and the total annual electrical costs. The tool also provides a chart of the electrical efficiency of the specified networking device at vari-ous power loads.

Figure 8.1 shows the Cisco Product Efficiency Calculator, profiling a single Nexus 7000 model.

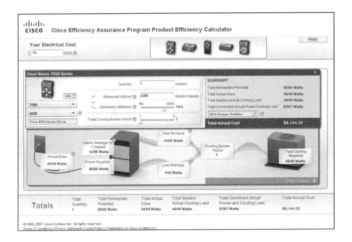

Figure 8.1   *Cisco Product Efficiency Calculator*

Figure 8.2 shows the power efficiency of a Nexus 7000 power supply, at various load lev-els, according to the Cisco online Product Efficiency Calculator.

The Cisco Efficiency Assurance Program is located at www.cisco.com/go/efficiency.

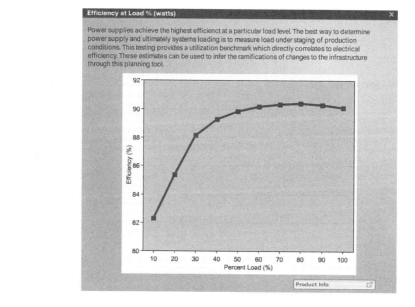

Figure 8.2   *Power Efficiency of a Cisco Nexus 7000 Power Supply*

Summary

Hardware within your Data Center impacts how green your facility is as well its operational costs. When considering equipment purchases, look for an overall configuration that meets your computing needs, today and in the foreseeable future, and provides the most processing per kilowatt.

The U.S. Environmental Protection Agency's Energy Star Specification for Servers calls for hardware to meet minimum energy-efficiency ratings with their power supplies, to stay within certain power consumption limits when idle, and to facilitate data gathering about operational conditions such as power usage, inlet air temperature, and processor utilization.

The Climate Savers Computing Initiative, which calls for energy-efficiency standards of 80 percent and higher for desktop PCs and servers, has the goal to cut energy usage of new computing equipment in half between 2007 and 2010, saving 62 billion kWh of energy, 54 million tons (49 million metric tons) of carbon dioxide, and more than $5.5 million in energy costs.

Various metrics have been proposed to capture IT hardware efficiency, including ECR (dividing energy consumption by system throughput), EER (dividing system throughput by energy consumption), and SWaP (dividing performance by space times power consumption).

Utilization, that is how much of a server's, networking device's, or storage unit's capacity is used, is another indicator of efficiency within your server environment.

Other factors to consider when determining how green a piece of Data Center hardware is include cooling efficiency, what materials the machine is made of, how easy it is upgrade with new components, how easy it is to recycle the machine, and the machine's size. Further limit the environmental impact of your Data Center hardware by requesting that packaging and other associated materials be consolidated by the manufacturer.

The budget cycle used by many businesses in which the IT department is given money for Data Center hardware on a quarterly, use-or-lose basis promotes the acquisition of more powerful machines that consume more energy than other models. This is especially problematic in businesses where IT has no visibility into company power bills whereas facilities, which pays those bills, has no input into hardware selection. Implementing a chargeback model based upon power consumption provides visibility for IT and rewards energy reduction and efficiency within the Data Center.

Idle servers consume 30 percent to nearly 70 percent of what they do at peak load. Various software applications can shut down Data Center hardware when not in operation, reactivating them at a later time. This practice can provide significant power savings if you are comfortable with regularly power-cycling such equipment.

Remove old Data Center hardware that is less energy-efficient and poorly utilized to optimize energy consumption.

Chapter 9

Greening Your Data Center Through Consolidation, Virtualization, and Automation

This chapter explores the energy-saving opportunities you can realize by transforming the way IT infrastructure provides, allocates, and operates Data Center resources. This transformation is loosely sequenced in three steps:

Step 1. Consolidation

Step 2. Virtualization

Step 3. Automation

These three steps are applicable to multiple resource and service types, including networking, storage, servers, databases, applications, and even entire facilities. The benefits from this transformation are not limited to reducing the environmental impact of your Data Center but also include lowering the total cost of ownership, increasing agility, and simplifying business continuity.

Vision: The Service-Oriented Data Center

Your Data Center offers your company the opportunity to be greener not only through its physical infrastructure elements but also because of its role offering IT resources and services.

An organization meets its top-level objectives—generating revenue growth, profit, and shareholder value, or supporting and engaging in activities of public or private interest—through its prime business processes. These business processes are composed of integrated applications and data stores, which leverage Data Center resources as part of their ongoing operations. The Data Center resources consume environmental resources such as power and raw materials throughout their lifecycle.

Even if you adopt all the green opportunities covered in the earlier chapters, there is no guarantee that you are realizing the lowest environmental impact for the given top-level objective of your organization. For example, your company's top-level objective could be to grow revenue by 5 percent in the next year. To do so, your chief information officer decides to introduce 20 new applications. As a result of organizational silos, each application runs on its own dedicated and underutilized hardware. Simplified, the IT organization installs 20 new servers, instead of perhaps the 5 or 10 that would be required if servers could host multiple applications. As a result, the IT resources consume more power than they need to, accelerating the need for Data Center expansion. Although you might have managed to achieve an excellent Power Usage Effectiveness (PUE) rating in your Data Center, the average utilization of IT infrastructure might still be very low, leading to power and material waste. Many opportunities exist to enable you to optimize the IT infrastructure and green the Data Center.

Transforming the way IT services (such as applications) consume IT resources (such as compute resources) enables you to execute on these optimization opportunities. Figure 9.1 illustrates the problem statement and the optimization opportunity.

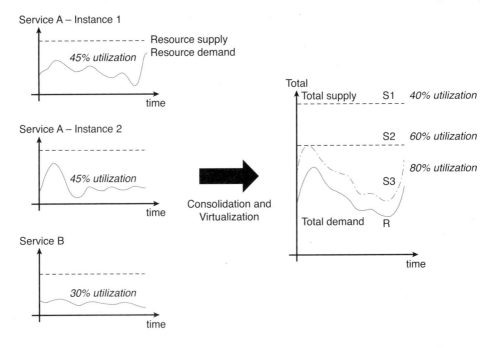

Figure 9.1 *Optimization at the IT Services Layers*

The diagrams on the left in Figure 9.1 illustrate the Data Center resource demand and supply for two services A and B, one of which (A) has two instances. In this terminology, the term *resource* equates to server and storage hardware; *service* is an application; and *instance* refers to separate installations of the same application. The supply is constant in time and exceeds the peak demand by a predefined supply cushion. Service A has an 80-percent peak utilization and a 45-percent average utilization. Service B represents a service in which the supply has a fixed minimum size that is too large for the demand, resulting in only 30-percent average utilization. The connection with the natural environment takes place through the IT resources, which consume environmental resources to operate.

The diagram on the right represents the total resource demand and a number of total supply curves. The first supply curve S1 is the total supply taken by adding the respective supply curves on the left. The space between S1 and R represents wasted resources and is a measure for the environmental inefficiencies. Achieving only 40-percent average utilization, the inefficiencies for S1 are excessive. If the IT architecture supports resource sharing through consolidation and virtualization, supply curves S2 and S3 become feasible. Curve S2 achieves 60-percent average utilization. Like S1, it still assumes a static model, in which the resource supply is flat in time. Curve S3 achieves additional efficiencies by dynamically varying the resource supply over time, yielding 80-percent average utilization. The supply cushion is reduced to its absolute minimum. The joint efficiency is optimal, within the operational boundaries needed to account for anticipated peak demand, change, and failure.

This brings us to the IT vision for greening the Data Center—the service-oriented Data Center. This architecture treats compute and storage resources as a consolidated shared utility and includes virtualization technology and an automation system to manage the flexible provisioning, change, and decommissioning of the resources. Efficiencies are high as a result of the resource-sharing benefits—resources are supplied on a just-enough and just-in-time basis. This architecture further extends into the application layer, where reuse is one of the key principles of a service-oriented architecture (SOA). The benefits from increased efficiencies are cumulative: Saving one kilowatt of power demand in the server or storage layer results in similar savings in cooling, and might result in new facility construction avoidance or delay when extrapolated to a larger scale. This is also known as the *cascade* effect, and it is substantial. Recall the whitepaper, "Energy Logic: Reducing Data Center Energy Consumption by Creating Savings that Cascade Across Systems," published by Emerson Network Power, that states every 1 Watt of power savings realized at the server results in 2.84 Watt of total power savings.

From Dedicated to Service-Oriented: a Paradigm Shift

The service-oriented model is reflective of a paradigm shift in the Data Center operating model. Resources are now shared across your entire organization and show similarities to a standard supply chain model, in which resources are treated as shared utilities or resource pools, and supply is determined by demand. Figure 9.2 illustrates how this paradigm shift manifests itself in multiple phases.

Before diving into the details of this paradigm shift, you need to understand the following terms:

- **Resource:** The entity used to achieve an objective. As an example, IT resources enable information to be stored and processed. IT resources include compute resources (CPU), memory, storage, and network resources. Natural resources include power, cooling, and raw materials. Within the context of a Data Center, an application is not considered a resource.

- **Resource type:** Resources differ in what capability they provide and how they provide it. A resource type represents all resources providing the same capability, although they might differ in how they provide it. Specific resource types in the Data Center include compute resources, memory resources, data storage resources, and network resources. Subtypes exist; for example, the data storage resource subtypes include disk storage, tape storage, and solid-state device storage.

- **Service:** A function that is provided when requested; for example, an application service returns a response when invoked. Services have multiple attributes defining their use, lifecycle, and management, such as a definition for how to request the service or an agreement on the service level. By defining these attributes for resources, the resources become service-oriented.

- **Instance:** Resources or services are not provided as one single, standalone occurrence. Instead, there will be multiple, which are called *instances*. One individual physical server and one individual installation of an application package are called instances of compute resources and the application service, respectively.

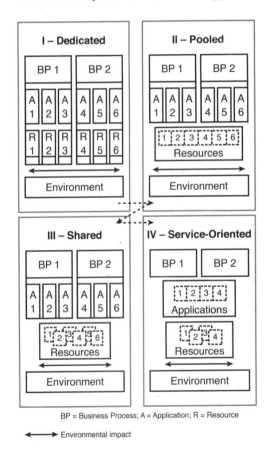

BP = Business Process; A = Application; R = Resource

◄─────► Environmental impact

Figure 9.2 *Paradigm Shift in the Data Center Service Model*

The four phases of the paradigm shift from a dedicated to a service-oriented Data Center are as follows:

- **Phase I: Dedicated:** Historically, most Data Center environments started with a dedicated model where applications and resources are dedicated to a given business process. Although there are benefits in terms of fault domain isolation and simplicity, the model is cost-prohibitive and has a larger-than-needed impact on the environment because many foundational services are duplicated and resources underutilized.

- **Phase II: Pooled:** As a first transformational step, the resources are pooled: Multiple discrete resource units are grouped into a larger continuous and consistently managed pool, from which only the needed capacity amount is carved out and provided to the consuming entity. The environments are shared, but the effective resource is still dedicated, albeit at a more granular level. Pooling requires the introduction of new technology and changes to the operational process. Provisioning is still a manual process. The transformation from Direct Attached Storage (DAS) to Networked Storage (Network Attached Storage [NAS] and Storage Area Network [SAN]) represents a good example of how storage resources such as disks are provided from a central pool on an as-needed basis. Hard partitioning of mainframe resources presents another example.

- **Phase III: Shared:** As a next transformational step, the variation of resource demand over time is exploited to realize additional savings. In addition to sharing the environment, the actual resources are now shared—any given smallest resource unit might be allocated to different clients at different points in time. Like pooling, sharing requires the introduction of new technology and impacts operational processes. Resource reallocation over time requires automation and scheduling as part of the solution. The management capabilities are local to the resource. The introduction of server virtualization technologies presents a good example of this phase. Multiple virtual hosts consume the same compute resources (CPU) at different points in time. Multiple applications or data traffic types sharing a single network present another example.

- **Phase IV: Service-Oriented:** In the final transformational step, the way in which shared resources and applications are developed, provisioned, and managed evolves and increasingly focuses on integration and reuse. Infrastructure resources, application logic, and data are now considered services, by augmenting their functionality with service-level attributes and capabilities. Coordinating the lifecycle management of disparate services is called orchestration. These services act as building blocks, which connect to build the applications enabling the business processes. The building blocks follow the following service-oriented principles:

  - **Encapsulation:** The process of enclosing the functionality of the service and exposing only what is required for consuming the service.

  - **Abstraction:** Services hide the internal logic, complexity, and platform beyond what is contracted.

- **Modularity:** The concept of breaking up one large function into multiple, independent, smaller functions.

- **Reusability:** The capability to consume the same service for different use cases without making modifications to the service.

- **Standardization:** The process of establishing and conforming to standards.

- **Composability:** The capability to create higher-level functionality through assembling services.

- **Interoperability:** The capability of services to exchange information and work together.

- **Loose coupling through well-defined interfaces:** The internal mechanics of a service can change transparently to its consumers if the interface does not change from its definition.

- **Discoverability from a service repository:** A common location lists all services and their attributes relevant for consumption so that they can be easily found and assembled.

- **Contracting:** The notion of agreeing upfront on the service levels of the service.

- **Automated provisioning and delivery:** The process of preparing, initiating, and delivering a service for use without manual intervention.

- **Monitoring:** The process of testing if and how the consumers can use the service.

- **Tracking:** Measuring the consumption of services.

As an example of this paradigm shift at the application level, your IT organization might decide to replace multiple custom data mining applications each requiring their own copy of the data with a single reusable service relying on a single data copy. As an example of this paradigm shift at the resource level, the capability to provision a virtual server and revoke it when no longer needed transforms a resource into a service.

Table 9.1 lists the attributes of the various phases.

The phases do not have a distinct start and stop point, but overlap in time. Many enterprise and nonprofit organizations are in Phase II and III of this transformation. The pace at which you realize this paradigm shift varies from one resource type to another. As an example, sharing of storage pools tends to happen prior to compute capacity virtualization, and integrated automated provisioning and scheduling requires sharing to be realized across all resource types. It is imperative for your Data Center strategy that you accompany the incremental execution of this paradigm shift with corresponding changes in the people area, process area, and governance models, up to and including organizational changes.

Table 9.1   *Analysis of Phased Paradigm Shift to Service-Oriented Data Center*

	Phase I (Dedicated)	Phase II (Pooled)	Phase III (Shared)	Phase IV (Service-Oriented)
Resource sharing	None	Partitioned from shared environment	Environment and resource sharing over time	Environment and resource sharing over time
Application and data reuse	None	Limited, ad hoc	Limited, ad hoc	Extensive, pervasive, and well-architected
Enabling technologies and principles	None	Network, standardization, consolidation	Virtualization	Automation, orchestration, integrated management and service-oriented architecture
Management	Inconsistent, not integrated	Consistent, not integrated	Consistent, not integrated	Consistent, integrated
Resource Provisioning	Manual through physical resource supply	Manual soft configuration from pool; manual physical resource pool supply	Manual soft configuration from pool; manual physical resource pool supply	Automated soft configuration from pool; semi-automated physical resource pool supply
Resource reallocation	Not Applicable	Manual	Automated, locally managed	Automated, locally and from integrated management system
Environmental impact optimization opportunity	None	Increased utilization (across the pool), economies of scale, tiering opportunity	Additional increase in utilization (over time), economies of scale, tiering opportunity	Cross-layer optimization through integration
Green value	Very low	Medium	High	Very high

For example, consider the evolution of an email application:

- During Phase I, email servers store the e-mail data on physical disks residing inside or directly attached to the server chassis. Overall utilization is low, because disk sizes come in finite increments, and servers are dedicated to processing email.

- In Phase II, the storage demand is supplied from a shared storage frame over a SAN. Because there is only one storage pool shared for the entire Data Center, storage allocation can be managed much more carefully and utilization increases. In addition, storage tiers are introduced, including larger disks with lower power consumption per storage unit. The e-mail service owner determines that these provide adequate performance for the e-mail archival solution. The overall environmental impact decreases.

- In Phase III, the Data Center team goes an extra step and introduces server virtualization. The e-mail servers now run on virtualized hosts, which share memory and compute resources with other virtualized hosts. The server virtualization technology takes care of scheduling access to compute resources. As the average compute capacity utilization increases, fewer physical servers are required and the overall environmental impact decreases again.

- Finally, in Phase IV, the fact that the system load reduces during weekends and overnight represents another optimization opportunity. The load shifts to a smaller number of active servers, while the remaining servers go into an idle state with minimum power consumption. Rather than overprovisioning capacity to deal with employee and e-mail store growth, the increased supply is provided on demand. Reusing the e-mail data store services to enable voicemail and unified communication services requires less environmental resources than replicating the raw data stores. The environmental impact further decreases.

The green savings realized in every phase can vary but add up to potentially significant end-to-end savings. The whitepaper, "Reducing Data Center TCO through Network and Storage Consolidation," published by Cisco Systems and EMC in 2009, illustrates how some real-world enterprise data center transformation programs delivered a reduction in Data Center power and cooling of more than 70 percent.

Optimization Opportunities

The layered approach of the Data Center as an integrated system provides a holistic framework for identifying all opportunities to minimize the environmental impact of your Data Center.

Optimizing layered services in the Data Center has a multiplicative effect on the efficiency—the total efficiency is the product of the efficiencies of each layer. For example, the IT infrastructure is layered on top of the Data Center facility infrastructure. A 30-percent average IT utilization in combination with 50-percent power efficiency for the Data Center physical components (a PUE of 2) results in 15-percent total efficiency. Optimizing parallel services, on the other hand, has an averaging effect on the efficiency; the total efficiency becomes a weighted average of the respective service efficiencies. For example, 40-percent server utilization in combination with 60-percent storage utilization results in a net average efficiency between 40 percent and 60 percent, depending on the relative power draw of server and storage. These rules are important when you plan to green your Data Center. You might gain more overall by investing moderately in multiple opportunities than you would by being overly aggressive in just one opportunity.

Specific attention should go to

- **Governance:** A successful green Data Center strategy does not stop at the physical layers. It is imperative that a centralized governance body oversees the various activities. This includes endorsement at the CxO level and identification of accountable parties, for example, a green czar or power manager. The governance model also enables the required people, process, and potentially organizational changes associated with your Data Center transformation to take place without a negative impact to the business.

- **Consolidation and standardization:** Within each layer, multiple resource types exist. Furthermore, each resource type is materialized through multiple instances. Standardization reduces the number of resource types—for example, you might choose to standardize on a single storage technology and vendor. Consolidation reduces the number of instances by sharing the resources—for example, you might decide to consolidate the engineering and finance storage pools into a single shared pool. Together, these enable higher efficiencies and thus reduce the overall impact to the environment. The capability to leverage economies of scale further increases the achievable efficiency. As an example, a single Data Center with standardized server equipment placed in a location in which power from a reusable energy source is available can require less raw materials and have a smaller environmental impact than an equivalent set of distributed ad hoc server rooms, in which each server room has varying types of server hardware.

- **Virtualization:** Inserting an additional abstraction layer in the IT resource layer substantially increases the attainable level of resource sharing. Virtualization results in the raw resources being aggregated into resource pools, shared with multiple clients. In addition, it enables resources to be treated as services. As an example, server virtualization enables multiple applications to operate concurrently on a single physical server. This eliminates dedicating server hardware to applications with low processing demand and reduces the overall server hardware and power demand.

- **Integrated automation:** Automation enables optimized resource use in space and time, and flexible reuse of resources. These enable additional opportunities for optimization, not limited to the boundaries of a Data Center zone, hall, or facility. Integration of automation capabilities across the layers enables joint optimization, further increasing the achievable efficiencies. As an example, automation might rebalance the server workload distribution, place unused servers in a power-saving mode, reduce the overall cooling supply, and migrate the workload to a different part of the Data Center or a different Data Center altogether should that result in an environmental impact reduction.

- **Alternative hosting models:** A myriad of hosting models exist today, and newer ones keep hitting the market. Although these are not guaranteed to have a lower environmental impact, they create opportunities for optimization and increased efficiencies by leveraging economies of scale and resource sharing with external parties. For example, cloud computing enables multiple tenants to share an aggregate pool of IT infrastructure not limited to a single Data Center facility location or even a single provider.

The sections that follow further explain all but the first item in the preceding list. Combining consolidation, standardization, virtualization, automation, and integration enables you to realize the vision of the service-oriented virtualized Data Center, managed as an integrated system.

Consolidation and Standardization

In the days when networks were unreliable and of limited capacity, many application services were distributed and running on or in close proximity of the client endpoint. This resulted in many more replicas of application and data stores than were strictly needed for resiliency purposes. In addition, each instance was typically underutilized and of limited size and, therefore, less efficient. With the advent of cost-effective and reliable networks comes the opportunity to host these services in a centralized location.

As a result of this centralization, there is a need for more powerful systems. Merging the load of multiple small systems into one virtual or physical larger system is defined as *physical consolidation* or *consolidation* in general. Reducing the number of geographical places where the units are deployed is a special case of *physical consolidation* called *geographical consolidation*.

In addition to the grouping of multiple units into a single unit, the "many-to-one" principle can be applied to the number of unique unit types. In this context, consolidation refers to the reduction of number of variations to a single, more flexible type, also known as *functional consolidation*, *logical consolidation*, or *standardization*. It makes sense to jointly execute on logical consolidation and physical consolidation.

Although there are few direct environmental benefits, standardization is a prerequisite to consolidation in the traditional sense. Standardization brings a lot of long-term operational and financial benefits because it makes the environment simpler and more manageable. The perceived downside of standardization is that application developers have fewer foundational capabilities to leverage and must account for more limitations during the application development cycle. This calls for a fair balance between standardization and the acceptation of one-off features, which might have a significant long-term support cost.

Consolidation and virtualization are related. In many cases, virtualization acts as a technical enabler for consolidation. As an example, Virtual Storage Area Networks (VSAN) enable multiple logical SANs to share the same underlying physical infrastructure, thus reducing the number of physical SANs from multiple to one.

This section describes how the principle of consolidation is applicable to multiple resource and service types, and how it results in a greener Data Center.

Consolidation comes in the following two forms:

- **Backward consolidation:** A proactive effort takes a look at what is out there *today* and combines the number of units to one or fewer. This aggressive approach can be successful only if the organizational culture supports it.

- **Forward consolidation:** Whatever is out there today is left as is, but a new consolidated environment is initiated, and all *new* services leverage the consolidated environment. Eventually, the lifecycle results in the retirement of the legacy environments and consolidation is complete. This might take an extended time.

Often, a hybrid approach is the approach of choice. Consolidation starts as forward consolidation. Over time, the technology, people, and processes mature whereas the number of legacy environments naturally decreases. At some point, the decision is made to change the strategy to backward consolidation.

As the consolidated environment serves a larger number of clients than the nonconsolidated environments, its scalability attributes are critical. Scalability comes in two forms:

- **Vertical scalability:** Vertical scaling of systems leverages units of larger size and is typically associated with physical consolidation.

- **Horizontal scalability:** Horizontal scaling of systems follows a farm or pool model in which the overall capacity is increased by deploying additional units to the farm or pool. Technology enables the farm or pool to be treated as one logical unit. This type of scalability is typically associated with logical consolidation.

Horizontal scalability is fundamentally less constrained in capacity than vertical scalability but is not always transparent to the consuming entity. Client-side changes or the introduction of virtualization technologies as described in the next section are required to leverage the full capacity in the farm or pool. When this is achieved, horizontally scaling systems scale better in principle, tend to depend less on proprietary technology, and are, therefore, architecturally preferable as a general rule.

Less Is More

So how does consolidation contribute to a greener Data Center? There are a few levers that play into this, all of which are cumulative.

The first lever comes from reuse and elimination of unnecessary replicas. Every unit might require a specific component. Prior to consolidation, this component exists as many times as there are units out there. After the consolidation, this component exists only once, or a much smaller number of times. For example, the storage environment might consist of multiple SAN islands prior to consolidation. Every SAN island has dedicated SAN switches and dedicated storage controllers. After consolidation, a single pool remains with fewer SAN switches and controllers. This eliminates unnecessary equipment and reduces the environmental impact. The impact to complexity is mixed; although reducing the number of variations to manage reduces complexity, consolidation might introduce new technology and break down natural fault isolation between systems, which negatively impacts the operational complexity. The net result can vary from one environment to another one.

The second lever comes from the increased utilization opportunity. In a fragmented and distributed environment, it is hard to tweak the supplied compute and storage capacity on an ongoing basis. The time and effort to do so often outweighs the potential benefits. In a centralized and consolidated environment, however, the optimization reward is much higher whereas the effort is lower. This leads to increased utilization, which subsequently results in the supply of less raw capacity to meet the demand. Pooling and resource sharing technologies are essential to realize this benefit. Although average compute resource utilization typically is in the 5-percent to 15-percent range, consolidation—enabled by virtualization—increases this to the 60-percent to 80-percent range in a well-managed consolidated environment, according to "Virtualization Overview," a whitepaper published by VMWare in 2006. The average storage utilization in a nonvirtualized environment varies from 30 percent to 50 percent for disk, and from 20 percent to 40 percent for tape, according to the *Storage Virtualization Technical Tutorial* published by the Storage Networking Industry Association. In a virtualized and shared environment, utilization rates of 60 to 80 percent for disk should be feasible. Note that increased utilization in a shared resource environment might broaden the impact of a capacity shortage—for example, when a burst in demand hits your infrastructure, or your supplier cannot deliver the anticipated growth in a timely manner. This results in increased risk, and you should account for this in your plans.

The third lever comes from the fact that size matters when it comes to efficiencies, also known as *right sizing*. In many cases, larger is better, known as the *economies of scale* argument. For example, a large purpose-built Data Center can operate much more efficiently than a small server room inside an existing building, when compared on a relative basis. A multicore blade server chassis provides more compute capacity per unit of power than a single-core appliance. In other cases, the industry has settled on specific standard unit sizes and invested heavily in optimizing around this unit size, leading to *breakpoint optimization*. For example, industry-standard batteries integrated into server hardware might yield higher efficiencies than centralized UPS systems. In addition, many resources have a minimum unit size as well, which might supply significantly more capacity than is needed. As an example, the smallest server on the market might provide too much compute capacity for one distributed application serving only a handful of users in a remote office.

The fourth lever comes from the creation of opportunities to leverage other green techniques. Especially in the case of geographical consolidation, the network tolerance creates the opportunity to build or lease a special-purpose Data Center facility located in an area where power is available from a renewable source or has a greener electrical mix, where the loss from power transport is minimized, and where cold weather is available to deploy economizers, thus improving the power utilization effectiveness of the facility.

A hypothetical e-mail service transformation example demonstrates the potential impact of these four levers. A large enterprise has one campus with 5,000 employees and 100 distributed sales offices with an average of 50 employees each. The total employee count is 10,000. The average e-mail quota on the server is 200 MB per user, and a standard CPU core provides compute resources for 500 users. Prior to consolidation, the e-mail architecture is distributed and uses standard 1 RU servers with internal storage up to 100 GB available for storing e-mail, enough to store the e-mail from 500 users. After consolidation, the e-mail architecture is centralized and uses a multicore blade server chassis and a SAN. The consolidated environment is hosted in a purpose-built facility off-campus where efficient energy cooling is used. Table 9.2 calculates the total power demand before and after consolidation using a number of assumptions.

As Table 9.2 indicates, this optimistic example illustrates how consolidation can lead to an 80-percent reduction in total power demand and complete elimination of nonrenewable power demand for e-mail services. If there were no opportunity to go to a new Data Center with the lower PUE, the reduction would still be 75 percent. The example is simplified because it does not account for a capacity cushion for growth and peak demand, backup, disaster recovery, records retention, and network requirements. It is also on the extreme side of the spectrum because many applications are not distributed prior to any consolidation effort. In addition to the environmental benefits, the re-architecture has

Table 9.2   *Consolidation Example: Power Demand Savings from Consolidation*

	Prior to Consolidation	**After Consolidation**
Campus infrastructure	10x 1RU server (includes storage)	—
Remote office Infrastructure	50x 1RU server (includes storage)	—
Purpose-built Data Center	—	2 blade chassis with 5x dual-core blade servers each; 2 Tbyte storage from SAN
Power assumption	0.25 kW per 1RU server including storage	0.3 kW per blade (includes chassis average); 1 kW per TB (including SAN)
IT net power demand	Campus: 2.5 kW Remote office: 12.5 kW	Server: 3 kW Storage: 2 kW
PUE	Campus: 1.8 Remote office: 2.5	Data Center Facility: 1.4
Power consumption form provider	Campus: 4.5 kW Remote office: 31.3 kW	Server: 4.2 kW Storage: 2.8 kW
Total power consumption	Total: 35.8 kW	Total: 7 kW
Power source	60% renewable, 40% nonrenewable	100% renewable

transformed traditional e-mail services into a platform for mobile applications and unified communications. This enables further service reuse and application-layer efficiencies throughout its lifecycle.

How much consolidation can do for your Data Center efficiency depends on how efficient it is today and how aggressive you are with the transformation. Case studies publish optimistic results of more than 70-percent reduction in power consumption, although a range of 20 percent to 40 percent not including any Data Center PUE improvements should be considered more realistic.

The *Report to Congress on Server and Data Center Energy Efficiency Public Law 109-431* published by the U.S. Environmental Protection Agency (EPA) in 2007 proposes three sets of assumptions for analyses of alternative efficiency Data Center transformation scenarios: an "improved operation" scenario resulting in a 30-percent improvement in combined IT and facility infrastructure energy efficiency, a "best practice" scenario resulting in up to 70-percent improvement, and a "state-of-the-art" scenario resulting in up to 80-percent improvement.

According to *Capital Goes Green*, a case study published by Dell in 2009, the Municipality of Copenhagen expects to reduce power consumption and carbon emissions by approximately 77 percent through its Data Center transformation program, which included a mix of consolidation, virtualization, and technology upgrades.

Consolidation Areas

The principle of consolidation is applicable to multiple resource types, for example, compute resources in the server platform area. As part of the development of your green Data Center strategy, it is important to assess the current and future environmental impact of your Data Center infrastructure, broken down by resource. For each resource type, you must weigh the benefits against the cost and risk.

The relative power consumption and overall environmental impact varies by resource type. As a rule of thumb for the typical Data Center environment, the power consumption is 20 percent for network equipment and services, 20 percent for storage, and 60 percent for compute resources, according to *Green Storage I: Economics, Environment, Energy, and Engineering*, published by the Storage Networking Industry Association Green Storage Track. The *Report to Congress on Server and Data Center Energy Efficiency Public Law 109-431*, published by the U.S. Environmental Protection Agency (EPA) in 2007, documents different estimates: 10 percent for network equipment, 10 percent for storage, and 80 percent for servers. These numbers might differ for your Data Center. The relative storage portion is trending upward.

Network

Network consolidation comes in the form of both physical and logical consolidation. As a result of network consolidation, all network traffic shares a single underlying network, consisting of shared network switching equipment and transport links. In some cases, the solution requires a logical form of segmentation, which virtualization technology can deliver.

Inside your Data Center network environment, a number of consolidation opportunities exist. You might have both an IP and a storage network, and you might even have more than one of each. Let us first discuss the consolidation of different network protocols or I/O consolidation, followed by the consolidation of the same network types for different functions or functional consolidation, and close with the elimination of having multiple links purely for capacity reasons:

- **I/O consolidation:** Most traditional Data Centers have three networks—a standard IP network, which runs on top of Ethernet and copper or fiber; a Fiber Channel (FC) fabric, which runs on fiber but uses a different protocol stack; and an out-of-band IP network. Some Data Centers even use a fourth one—Infiniband, which is an interconnect technology providing high throughput and low latency required in high-performance computing environments. I/O consolidation replaces some or all of these networks with one unified fabric, also known as Unified I/O. With a unified fabric, a single, redundant fabric consolidates multiple traffic types—IP-based client-to-server traffic, IP-based server-to-server traffic, and FC-based server-to-storage traffic.

  A unified Ethernet fabric solution relies on innovation at both the network protocol and product level. New protocols such as Fiber Channel over Ethernet (FCoE) address the encapsulation requirements, enabling Fiber Channel traffic to be transported over Ethernet. The Ethernet network must be able to guarantee delivery of packets, transforming it into a lossless fabric. This requires extensions to the Ethernet protocol as well as new product capabilities. Finally, a new host adapter called Converged Network Adapter (CNA) is required. This adapter replaces the Ethernet Network Interface Card (NIC) and Fiber Channel Host Bus Adapter (HBA). Recent cabling developments leverage Twinax Small Format Pluggable plus (SFP+) technology to deliver the CNA functionality at very low-power consumption per port.

  Figure 9.3 illustrates the effect of I/O consolidation.

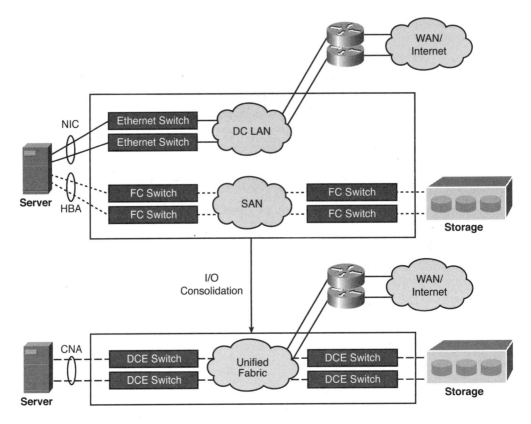

Figure 9.3　*I/O consolidation Reduces the Total Amount of Networking Equipment*

As Figure 9.3 illustrates, prior to consolidation, each server has both NICs and Host Bus Adapters (HBA). After I/O consolidation, these are replaced with CNAs. Although only 4 and 2 interfaces are shown respectively, there can be as many as 5 or even 7 interfaces prior to consolidation in a real-world scenario, depending on the operational and security requirements. After I/O consolidation, this number typically reduces to 3, which results in a significant reduction in the environmental impact of the network switching hardware and the cabling infrastructure.

Additional server access network consolidation is feasible with the latest generation of blade server architecture: The number of cables can be further reduced through uplink aggregation based on multiplexing and through the consolidation of out-of-band traffic.

In a 2009 webcast discussing the internal deployment of the Cisco Unified Computing System, Cisco IT presented a case study concerning a 1 MW greenfield Data Center, where I/O consolidation down to the server access layer leads to a reduction of over 5,000 cables from a total of nearly 6,500 cables to less than 1,500 cables.

■　**Functional consolidation:** Your Data Center environments might have multiple separate networks for historical, operational, or security reasons. These networks are "functional" in that they support a specific function. The advent of high-capacity networks and increasingly mature network virtualization technologies such as Virtual LANs (VLAN) and Virtual SANs (VSAN) enable consolidation of these functional networks. This includes backup networks, networks owned by separate organizations, networks separated for security reasons, and such. VLANs also provide a logical segmentation capability: Different Layer 3 (IP) segments can be allocated to different clients who prefer to be isolated, without having to introduce dedicated hardware.

- **Capacity as an enabler:** High-capacity links based on 10 Gigabit Ethernet or higher (40 / 100 Gigabit Ethernet) present opportunities for reducing the number of links in the Data Center fabric, effectively consolidating the transport links. In addition, they remove a barrier to consolidation in other areas, such as the server or storage area. As a result of server virtualization and consolidation, the I/O demand grows beyond what is feasible with legacy technologies.

Networks also connect Data Centers with each other and provide connectivity to the end clients. This leads to additional consolidation opportunities:

- **Wide-area network (WAN) consolidation:** Some organizations have multiple WANs, which might be the result of a number of scenarios. It can come as a result of mergers and acquisitions, where each of the respective prior companies had their own WAN. It can also be the result of organizational barriers, where one division does not want to leverage a network service from another division. It could also be the result of a legacy architecture in combination with a risk avoiding culture, where multiple WAN backbones are used for different networked services—internal IP traffic, communications traffic such as voice or video, or specific applications. Multiple advances in networking technology lead to higher throughput capacities at lower unit cost thus increasing scalability and enable various forms of network sharing with varying degrees of service level guarantee, resiliency, and scalability. These technologies include QoS, IP-based virtual private networks (VPN), Coarse and Dense Wavelength Division Multiplexing (CWDM and DWDM respectively), Fiber Channel over IP (FCIP), and MetroEthernet. Leveraging these technologies through a myriad of architectures and business models enables reduction of the total wide-area infrastructure environmental impact. As an example, consider a large global enterprise recently acquiring another global company. The respective global WAN backbones can be consolidated into one WAN backbone, reducing the equipment on a ratio of nearly 2 to 1.

- **Enabling Data Center consolidation:** In addition to its direct consolidation opportunity, the WAN is in a position to enable an often much larger environmental impact reduction by enabling consolidation of Data Center facilities, optimized site selection, and centralization of applications. As the WAN provides increasingly more bandwidth at lower latency and with QoS, the distance between the server and the client can increase. This enables consolidation of Data Center facilities. There is often no requirement anymore for the consolidated Data Center facility to be in close proximity to the client base; locating the facility in an area in which power from renewable energy sources is available, and in which cold weather can be used to provide natural cooling further contributes to the green performance of the facility. Alternatively, the facility can be located to enable reuse of the heat generated by the Data Center for specific use cases, such as heating a greenhouse or a swimming pool.

Compute Resources

The most efficient use of compute resources in your Data Center is achieved when the server CPU technology delivers the highest performance per unit of power consumed; when the memory capacity matches the CPU capacity to ensure a balanced configuration; when all CPUs are maxed out under peak load situations; and when CPUs consume only as much power as their workload requires during periods when the load is not at its peak. For simplicity, this statement takes no notion of service continuity and disaster recovery requirements. These would make the analyses more complicated, but the core principles remain intact.

In the real world, many Data Centers have deployed server hardware with the highest performance CPU technology rather than the most power-efficient technology. The average utilization of all CPUs in a typical Data Center is substantially lower than the ideal state, even under peak load. According to *Virtualization Overview*, a 2006 VMWare whitepaper, average CPU utilization figures prior to virtualization are typically in the 5-percent to 15-percent range. Because server CPUs consume significantly more than 5 percent to 15 percent of their full load consumption at these utilization levels, the servers waste a lot of power.

The concept of server consolidation is to replace an existing set of servers of varying characteristics and load profiles with a smaller set of usually more powerful servers, which deliver the required compute capacity at lower power consumption. This results in higher utilization and can be achieved through a number of approaches:

- **Server sharing:** The most straightforward way to increase utilization is to install more applications on fewer servers. Unfortunately, without additional resource protection mechanisms, this leads to an environment lacking resilience and maintainability. It might also result in a complex configuration, which is hard to support and has numerous security challenges. Identifying a common service window is a major obstacle in many environments. These risks limit the adoption of this approach.

- **Server partitioning—OS virtualization:** Server partitioning takes a larger physical system and breaks it down into smaller segments called partitions, each with its own manually allocated resources. Although only one kernel is running, each partition runs its own copy of the OS image and presents itself as a small standalone system to the application. Each system operates at the efficiency of a large system. As such, the efficiency benefits from the economies of scale from large systems are inherited, even when the resource demand is low. The requirement for a single OS version might be a limitation in the real world. Partitioning can come in a number of forms: physical or logical. With physical partitioning, each segment follows the physical boundaries of the resource components (CPUs, memory, or disks). With logical partitioning, segments no longer need to align with physical boundaries. This leads to a much higher degree of flexibility and efficiency, but might come at the cost of performance and overall system robustness compared with physical segmentation. The performance impact is limited and much smaller than the resource sharing efficiency opportunity assuming a 5-percent to 15-percent average server utilization. In both forms of partitioning, resources can be reallocated dynamically, often without system downtime. Server partitioning is not a new concept. It gained a lot of ground in the mainframe space and is being reapplied in the space of distributed server computing. A more recent example is described in *Solaris Zones: Operating System Support for Consolidating Commercial Workloads*, published in the Proceedings of the 18th Large Installation Systems Administration Conference (USENIX LISA '04). Zones or containers refer to logical server partitions isolated from each other. The multiple containers share an OS, but each container has its own name, network interfaces, and storage.

- **Server virtualization—Hardware emulation:** Similar benefits can be achieved by inserting a server operating system (OS) abstraction layer following a host/guest paradigm. The physical resources such as CPU, memory, and disks are controlled by the host operating system. This host system also runs hardware emulation software, which supports multiple virtual machines, each running its own independent version of the guest operating system. Unlike server partitioning, operating systems might differ, but this flexibility comes at the price of higher performance impact. More details on server virtualization technology are provided in the "Virtualization" section. The utilization benefits are the same; by sharing physical resources, the utilization increases and fewer servers are needed to support the same application workload.

- **Application platform virtualization:** The same principle of resource sharing can be applied at higher layers of the application stack. The next layer above the operating system is the application foundation layer or middleware layer. This layer includes software platforms for running applications, enabling application developers to reuse functionality and develop applications more effectively. A notable example is the Java Platform, Enterprise Edition architecture, which hosts a large number of web-based portable applications on a consolidated shared server environment without the explicit need for OS or hardware virtualization. Microsoft .NET represents another such example.

- **Functional consolidation:** The perceived barriers to server consolidation are not all technical or operational. For example, in larger commercial enterprises or nonprofit institutions, consolidation of server environments dedicated to specific business functions can lead to additional efficiencies.

Adoption of server consolidation—often enabled by virtualization technologies—results in a paradigm shift of how compute resources are employed to run applications. In the new model, computing resources are treated as a utility and are consumed much like electricity is consumed from the utility provider. All compute resources are pooled and treated as one continuous and scalable resource type rather than a discrete and step-wise incremental resource type. The term *utility* implies that consumption of compute services is metered, which might not be the case in the initial phases of a server virtualization and consolidation adoption strategy.

Following the adoption of this model, the active server footprint can be compacted under nonpeak situations to deliver additional gains. This puts a number of servers into an idle CPU state, and a control system can subsequently turn these off or put them into a sleep mode or hibernation state in which the power consumption is close to zero. Depending on the load variation, aggressiveness of compute demand resumption, technical maturity of server technology, and your willingness to accept risk, this dynamic form of server consolidation might further reduce the total power consumption for the compute resource pool. The risk is limited and can be mitigated by ensuring a supply cushion and early adoption in nonproduction or lab environments. According to *Energy-Aware Server Provisioning and Load Dispatching for Connection-Intensive Internet Services* published by Microsoft Research, energy savings in a range of 20 percent to 30 percent can be realized for a specific workload type.

Storage

Inside your Data Center, the storage resources store the information the organization produces, processes, and consumes. This includes but is not limited to business data, digital media, and personal information. It also includes data required to operate the entire set of IT services, such as the Data Center, applications, and IT infrastructure. Disk is the most common media type, but tape, optical, and solid-state devices are also in use.

Figure 9.4 illustrates the three distinct architectures that are commonly used in the storage area prior to consolidation.

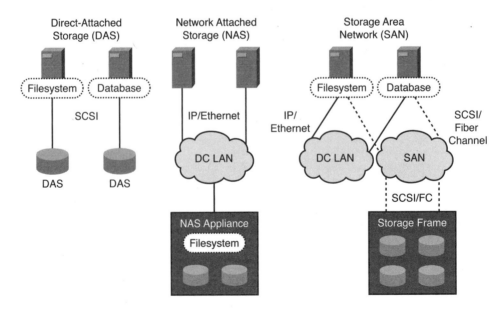

Figure 9.4 *Overview of Storage Architectures Inside the Data Center*

The three architectures shown in Figure 9.4 are as follows:

- **Direct-Attached Storage (DAS):** Disk drives are enclosed or directly attached to the server. Direct attachment refers to a physical connection that is not shared with any other equipment and solely under the control of the server equipment. The only way for other servers to access the data is through the server that controls the storage.

- **Network Attached Storage (NAS):** Disk drives are enclosed in standalone devices, also known as NAS appliances or filers. These appliances store the data on disks inside the physical enclosure and are directly connected to the IP network. Information is accessed at a file level, and file metadata controls access, security, and locking. This architecture enables information sharing between multiple servers without the need for a separate network. The most common network protocols include Common Internet File System (CIFS) and Network File System (NFS).

- **Storage Area Network (SAN):** High-end requirements are met through the introduction of a dedicated SCSI Fiber Channel (FC) network, assuming no I/O consolidation has taken place. An additional dedicated fault-tolerant storage fabric in combination with high-end frames provides increased reliability at the expense of higher complexity and cost. Information is accessed at the block level, which is a lower level than the file level. High-end database servers for mission-critical systems are a good example of a server environment with high-end requirements justifying a SAN investment. In some cases, there are multiple smaller standalone SAN networks, called SAN islands.

Consolidation in the storage space refers to the transformation from a dedicated storage architecture to a shared storage architecture. This transformation leads to higher utilization, by eliminating fragmentation and overprovisioning. Higher storage resource utilization and reuse of the storage infrastructure leads to a smaller footprint, reducing the power and cooling demand, consequently lowering the environmental impact. At the same time, this improves the agility to grow or provide new storage and reduces the total operating cost. In the end state, storage is managed as a shared pool and provisioned as a utility.

The following commonly observed consolidation efforts might apply to your Data Center environment:

- **Storage networking:** In the DAS architecture, disks are dedicated to a server. To avoid the operational impact and downtime of adding disks, storage is often overprovisioned. Storage networking technologies such as SAN, on the other hand, provide shared storage, and the allocated storage can grow with significantly less impact. This enables a higher degree of utilization.

- **SAN island consolidation:** First-generation SAN deployments consist of multiple standalone nonintegrated SAN networks called islands. Connecting these networks together enables consolidation of their respective storage pools. This reduces the total SAN infrastructure.

- **NAS/SAN convergence:** Many Data Centers have both large-scale NAS and SAN environments. The SAN will have its own pool of storage resources, whereas the

NAS environment consists of multiple NAS appliances each with limited scalability. These can be consolidated into a single pool through the introduction of NAS gateways, also known as NAS heads. A NAS gateway presents itself as a NAS appliance to the clients but leverages the SAN on the back-end instead of using built-in disks. Not only does this provide scalability, it also enables a higher degree of utilization and sharing.

- **Storage tiering:** Storage tiering or hierarchical storage management (HSM) is the solution to the "no one-size-fits-all" problem. Instead of a single storage pool with uniform performance, cost, and power characteristics, multiple pools called tiers are maintained. Tiers might vary from highly expensive solid state drive technology, over spinning disks of varying speed, capacity and RAID levels, to optical and tape-based archival solutions. Each tier has its own cost, performance, reliability, and electrical characteristics. Storage tiering enables an optimal balance between lowering cost and environmental impact on the one hand and meeting performance and functional requirements on the other hand. Storage virtualization can enable automated data lifecycle management from one tier to another one. This automated transparency accelerates the effects and provides additional gains. This concept is mostly relevant in large-scale enterprise and service provider class environments.

- **Thin provisioning:** Traditionally, storage teams allocate a lot more storage to application servers than what is used to account for growth, and the unused storage cannot be reused for another purpose. This is called *fat provisioning*. In an alternative approach, storage is allocated on a just-enough and just-in-time basis from a shared pool of unused storage. This is called *thin provisioning*. The servers are fooled into believing that a large amount of storage is available to them, but physically the storage is not allocated until needed. This model further increases the utilization but is exposed to the risks associated with oversubscription. For instance, an unexpected peak in demand or delay in supply might result in all storage clients participating in the pool experiencing storage issues at the same time.

- **Diskless servers:** Applying the principle of storage consolidation to the server footprint at the extreme level leads to server configurations that have no disks inside the chassis or blade at all. Because the typical utilization of internal disks is low, this approach leads to higher utilization. This configuration requires specific OS boot capabilities to function.

- **Massive Array of Idle Disks (MAID):** In a traditional high-end SAN environment, disks are always spinning and therefore consuming power. This provides a level of responsiveness that is not always needed. Some application profiles access data less frequently. Powering off the disks when they are not needed reduces the power demand. A MAID leverages this principle to provide storage with a lower average power consumption. Additional advances in power management further mature this model. According to *MAID for Green* published by Fujitsu in 2007, MAID technology can realize energy consumption savings of 20 percent or more.

- **WAFS/WAAS-enabled NAS Consolidation:** Looking beyond the confines of the Data Center, NAS appliances are often found in branch offices. Performance issues, the cost of bandwidth capacity, and the limited delay tolerance are the main driver for this distributed deployment. Deploying Wide-Area File Services (WAFS) devices in the branch office and in the Data Center enables consolidation of NAS appliances into the Data Center in a centralized site. Intelligent proxy and optimization technologies for file access at both sides of the WAN link are at the heart of this technology. The Wide-Area Application Services (WAAS) architecture is an extension of WAFS, providing network optimization and acceleration for other protocols than CIFS or NFS. The net effect on the storage requirements is twofold: Fewer distributed copies are maintained in addition to realizing the advantages of storage consolidation.

In addition to consolidation at the storage resource and infrastructure layer, consolidation can take place at the data or information layer:

- **Data reduction:** Most data is redundant and often in multiple ways. For example, a database might have similar names and records, and at the same time multiple copies of the database might exist within the storage environment. In another example, multiple copies of the same e-mail attachment are stored on the e-mail server storage environment. Compression reduces the amount of storage required by eliminating redundant information inside a given file, block, or object. Data deduplication applies the same principle at a broader scale, often relying on intelligence at the application layer. Effectively, duplicate data is detected and represented through references to the original data. In the e-mail example, only one copy of the attachment is stored, and other mailboxes have an index to the one copy. The net effect is increased utilization, at the cost of additional complexity, or a small decrease in reliability.

- **Lifecycle stage consolidation:** If not managed properly, data copies might proliferate throughout the storage environment. In one enterprise example, a critical production database has more than ten copies used for nonproduction application lifecycle stages, such as development, performance testing, and staging. Each of these copies is subsequently backed up. As the primary production database grows, so do all copies. The capacity impact can be huge, which leads to both a high financial and environmental impact. Reducing the number of size of the lifecycle stage environments through resource reuse can result in major savings.

- **Long-term archive and purge:** Long-term archive onto storage media with minimal environmental impact such as tape or optical drives remains a sustainable solution from an environmental perspective. Although the future of tape might be questioned, the principle of archive and purge remains intact for the foreseeable future, and only the underlying media technology will evolve. Purge refers to deleting the data that is no longer wanted.

The storage and data consolidation opportunities are numerous. Careful analysis of risk and reward is imperative to the formulation of your green Data Center strategy.

Note The whitepaper, "Reducing Data Center TCO through Network and Storage Consolidation," published by Cisco Systems and EMC in 2009, references a case study

continues

continued

from the Cisco Systems IT department, demonstrating the potential from storage consolidation. Cisco IT's storage demand is growing at 50 percent year over year and passed the 10-PB (petabyte) mark in 2008. Prior to the rollout of the Data Center wide storage pool, the storage resource utilization was approximately 20 percent. After the transformation, the utilization increased to approximately 68 percent. Additional consolidation and virtualization opportunities are expected to further improve the efficiencies. The consolidation resulted in more than $70-million cost avoidance over a 4-year period.

Note that the storage resource utilization metric does not reflect some of the optimization opportunities. A good example is consolidation of lifecycle stages. This reduces the storage capacity demand in absolute terms but does not lead to higher utilization of existing storage resources. You should consider this when defining the set of metrics to measure and manage your green Data Center strategy.

Application and Database

The scale of the IT infrastructure to be supplied and refreshed on a regular basis is determined by the application and data demand. Optimizing the demand at these layers of the stack reduces the needed supply and also reduces the environmental impact.

Application consolidation can mean multiple things. At the one end, it means rationalizing the number of applications needed to support the business. Effectively, following a thorough analysis of value versus cost, consolidation results in either decommissioning a number of applications or replacing them with a suite-based vendor offering that provides the aggregate functionality on a smaller application footprint.

At the other end, it means keeping the applications in their current shape and form but running them on top of a consolidated footprint. This is equivalent to the compute resource and storage consolidation opportunities previously described.

In many cases, it ends up being a combination of both; some applications get decommissioned or replaced, whereas others are deployed in a more efficient manner.

Transforming the application architecture to become service-oriented further augments this approach. In a SOA, applications are composed by integrating services. This enables a higher degree of reuse, which is another method to increase overall efficiencies. Transforming to a SOA is more involved than the aforementioned approaches of rationalizing applications and consolidating compute resources.

Another opportunity to green your IT stack is to tune the performance of your applications. Especially if one or a few applications dominate the server infrastructure, tuning the code or the application configuration for efficiency not only increases the performance, but it also reduces the infrastructure resource demand.

Consolidation of databases is similar to the consolidation approach for applications, compute resources, and storage. Prior to consolidation, many organizations have multiple database instances associated with different business processes, business units, and lifecycle stages. In many cases, the different instances use different technologies, often from different vendors. As part of database consolidation, the number of database instances is reduced by storing all data from multiple instances onto one or a few database instances with multiple schemas. In addition to the reduction of the number of instances, consolidation opportunities span earlier opportunities, such as geographical consolidation, technology standardization, lifecycle stage reduction, and leveraging compute resource and storage consolidation.

Facilities

Having increasingly more network capacity available at ever-decreasing cost enables the consolidation of Data Center facilities. Reducing the latency intolerance of applications through network optimization, application transformation, and acceleration technologies further enables this consolidation.

In the most aggressive scenario, this includes construction of new purpose-built facilities and consolidation of all existing facilities into the new ones. In many real-world scenarios however, Data Center facility consolidation can take place without new facilities—older, outdated facilities are consolidated into existing facilities.

Facility consolidation should be accompanied with transformation of the IT infrastructure to realize the full optimization potential. Without IT infrastructure transformation, the benefits are limited to leveraging economies of scale and realizing other green building opportunities such as increased cooling efficiencies and consuming renewable energy if the consolidation involves new facilities. When combined with IT infrastructure transformation, the multiplicative effect kicks in as a result of the additional optimization. The opportunity to remove facility consolidation barriers is another benefit.

Facility consolidation comes in two forms:

- **Data Center facility consolidation:** A small number of new, renewed, expanded or existing Data Center facilities replace a more distributed and fragmented Data Center facility footprint. As an example, a global company replaces a global fragmented set of more than 50 Data Centers worldwide with a reduced footprint of two Data Centers in each continent. The new facilities are purpose-built with expansion opportunities and located in strategic places. As a real-world example, HP estimated savings of $1 billion from consolidating 85 Data Centers down to 6, cutting the total energy consumption in its Data Centers by 60 percent as the result of a combined consolidation and technology transformation program.

- **Branch office consolidation:** As part of the consolidation effort, the IT department reduces the IT infrastructure deployed at every branch office to a bare minimum and centralizes all server-side infrastructure into the consolidated Data Center facilities.

Make sure your facility consolidation plans are aligned with your business continuity plans, your overall resiliency strategy, and your user experience requirements that might impact latency. A challenge associated with pure facility consolidation lies in the scarcity of opportunities and the extended lead times.

Note   The principle of consolidation is also applicable to business functions, organizational roles and responsibilities, and processes. The environmental benefits are not straightforward, but like any other change, consolidation at these layers presents both a direct and indirect opportunity for reducing the Data Center environmental impact.

At the business layer, you should consider merging business unit responsibilities; pursuing or accelerating the IT integration from mergers and acquisitions; and merging IT organizational roles and responsibilities. The concept of sharing and reuse is at the heart of many optimization efforts. For some organizations, this results in building out an internal service provider organization operating the Data Center, subject to similar fundamental business governance models as any external service provider would do. This includes cost-recovery mechanisms, service-level management, streamlined engagement processes, and management tools.

Additional Benefits and Challenges

It is clear that the principle of consolidation applies to multiple areas. As you embark on the consolidation journey, the environmental benefits are not the only benefits. In many cases, economic incentives will be the primary driver for consolidation. The result is the same though, and a holistic cost-benefit analysis is key to any strategy. This not only covers the spectrum of benefits, but you should also consider the challenges, costs, and risks that go with any consolidation effort. The result of this analysis can influence how you prioritize the multiple opportunities and what risk mitigation efforts need to be included in your plans.

The additional benefits from consolidation are similar in nature but differ in their value dimension. You can realize benefits in the following areas:

- **Simplicity:** Having fewer technology variations leads to a more consistent environment, which is easier and, therefore, cheaper to sustain and maintain. Through standardization and consolidation, simplicity extends in the area of automation; consolidated, standard environments are much easier to build automation around than disparate designs and architectures. The skills and collaborative behaviors required to develop and maintain the environment will evolve.

- **Manageability:** If executed well, a consolidated environment will have fewer instances and fewer variations to manage. This requires fewer management tools and increases the overall manageability of the environment.

- **Total cost of ownership:** Consolidated environments result in a smaller overall infrastructure at reduced complexity. This reduces the total cost of ownership compared to an equivalent scenario in which no consolidation is pursued. In addition, the cost distribution might shift. The classic example is that the network cost might go up, while the cost for Data Center infrastructure decreases.

- **Data protection:** A significant benefit from consolidation is the streamlining of data protection services, also known as backup. Increased control of the data, which often includes the core of the intellectual property of an organization, is an additional benefit.

The challenges and risks to account for in the consolidation plans can differ and be unique for your organization. Consolidation efforts impact the following areas. Note that the impact often contains both positive and negative elements, and the net of this mix is determined by the specifics of your consolidation plans.

- **Performance:** The impact on application performance can work both ways. On the one hand, locating all interoperable services in a close geographic proximity can improve performance of the integrated environment. On the other hand, increasing the latency between the server side and the client side can decrease the performance. Careful technology selection can mitigate the latter, by a combination of robust application development practices that can tolerate latency and acceleration technologies.

- **Security and legal compliance:** Similar to performance, security, and legal compliance, requirements might be impacted by consolidation, and this impact can work in two ways. These requirements translate to segmentation techniques (both physical and logical), architectural updates, and operational process innovation.

- **Complexity:** Some aspects of consolidation, especially the ones resulting in shared resources, might increase the configuration and troubleshooting complexity. This is a result of the fact that hard boundaries have disappeared.

One particular area that any Data Center transformation can impact is the overall resiliency, flexibility, and agility of the new environment. Resiliency is defined as the ability of an organization to absorb the impact of a business interruption, and continue to provide a minimum acceptable level of service. If executed to extreme levels, consolidation compromises the overall robustness of the IT infrastructure, which negatively impacts the resiliency, flexibility, and agility. For example, one Data Center with one giant shared server is hard to change over time without extensive downtime; it cannot withstand any serious component failure or a disaster.

As a result, you should never execute consolidation to an extreme level, but balance it with segmentation capabilities instead. Segmentation assures resources, limits the fault domain, and helps meet security requirements.

Virtualization

Virtualization within the context of your Data Center and IT infrastructure is the introduction of an abstraction layer that enables physical resources to be consumed at a logical level. This enables resource pooling, leading to a higher degree of utilization in alignment with the overall optimization objective characterizing the greener Data Center.

Virtualization and consolidation go hand in hand by mutually enabling each other. Virtualization provides logical segmentation capabilities, which addresses some of the consolidation challenges. Consolidation results in fewer but larger environments, which provides opportunities to accelerate the realization of the virtualization benefits.

Abstraction Layer

The abstraction capability called virtualization is typically realized through a technical capability. This technical capability comes in the form of software, hardware, or a combination of both. As a simple example, hardware emulation software enables server virtualization, or network software and hardware technology enable VPN.

Virtualization applies to two different models:

- **Resource virtualization:** The abstraction technology repackages the physical resources into logical resources, which can be smaller or larger than the original physical resource. Figure 9.5 illustrates this concept. A number of resource virtualization approaches exist:

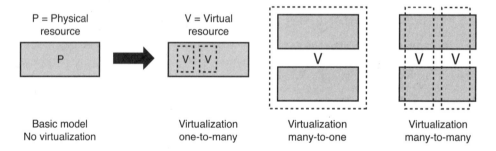

Figure 9.5 *Resource Virtualization*

- **One-to-many:** The virtualization technology carves up a single physical resource unit into multiple smaller virtual resource subunits. For example, a single physical server supports multiple guest virtual server instances. This approach has the largest contribution to the optimization principle.

- **Many-to-one:** The virtualization technology combines a number of physical resource units to act as one larger and more resilient virtual resource. For example, multiple physical disks act as one larger, logical storage unit.

- **Many-to-many:** The virtualization technology carves up and recombines multiple subunits from different physical resource units to create one virtual but resilient resource.

- **Service virtualization:** Service consumers connect to a virtual endpoint instead of a physical endpoint. The virtual endpoint subsequently maps the connection to a physical endpoint. Load balancing servers in a server farm is a good example. Figure 9.6 illustrates this concept.

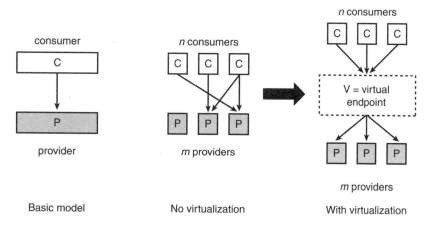

Figure 9.6 *Service Virtualization*

Virtualization Areas

Like consolidation, the concept of virtualization applies to all resource and service types—network, compute resources, storage, applications, and so on. There are additional benefits beyond increased utilization, but there are also some challenges to the adoption.

Whereas consolidation is enabled through the commitment of a functional organization, virtualization is predominantly enabled by technological advances. A high-level overview of these technologies by area follows, with an emphasis on those that reduce the environmental impact of your Data Center.

Network Virtualization

Although the network is not the biggest source of power consumption in the Data Center, its relative consumption is increasing as a result of increasing compute power density and compute resource virtualization. To avoid the spiraling effect of this trend, you must pursue an integrated approach that includes adoption of high-density networking equipment and network virtualization. Fortunately, multiple opportunities exist.

The generic principle of network virtualization follows the resource-oriented model. The one-to-many approach provides the functionality of multiple networks at the environmental impact of a single shared physical network. Effectively, the virtualization technology enables consolidation. This approach enables the largest reduction to the environmental impact. Figure 9.7 illustrates this concept and a number of technical implementations.

Specific technologies that enable network virtualization and, therefore, act as the abstraction layer include the following:

■   **Virtual LAN (VLAN):** The local-area network (LAN) connects multiple devices residing in close geographical proximity. Security, scalability, and operational requirements demand some form of segmentation between sets of devices with similar functionality. Traditionally, segmentation was physical and required separate network equipment and cabling. VLANs provide this form of segmentation on top of a single shared physical network, thus reducing the total size of the network infrastructure.

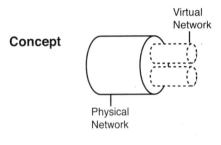

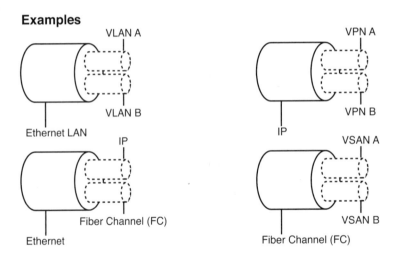

Figure 9.7 *Network Virtualization: Concept (Top) and Technology Examples (Bottom)*

- **Virtual SAN (VSAN):** The same principle applies to the storage-area network (SAN). Through VSANs, a single physical storage network delivers functional separation.

- **Virtual private network (VPN):** Extending the network virtualization concept to the wide-area network (WAN) and the Internet enables further network optimization. Through VPN technologies, which can operate at Layer 2 (as is the case for Frame Relay) and at Layer 3 (as is the case for Multi-Protocol Label Switching VPN [MPLS-VPN] and IP Security VPNs [IPSec VPN]), multiple logical networks can run on top of a single physical network infrastructure. Layer 2 and Layer 3 represent the data link and the network layers in the Open Systems Interconnect (OSI) stack. The Internet Protocol (IP) is one of the best-known network protocols residing at Layer 3 and provides end-to-end connectivity to logical network endpoints across multiple physical networks. The data link layer enables network connectivity between physical endpoints inside a single physical network. Some of these technologies are tunneling technologies, referring to their overlay nature. Use cases are numerous and include remote access, home network connectivity, remote office connectivity, guest networking, and WAN segmentation. The latter connects multiple subsidiaries over a single organization-wide network backbone operated by an internal service provider.

- **Unified I/O:** As described in the network consolidation section, transporting both IP and storage traffic on top of a single Ethernet fabric significantly reduces the total amount of network switches, network cards, and cabling. Fiber Channel over Ethernet (FCoE) and Data Center Ethernet (DCE) are at the core of this technical capability.

- **Out-of-band network:** Traditionally, physical separation was considered a must-have for an out-of-band network. With the advent of unified fabrics and unified computing, the out-of-band network has become virtualized and shares the same physical transport medium as the IP and storage traffic.

There are additional network virtualization opportunities that do not map crisply to the aforementioned conceptual model. Although their environmental savings might not be as significant, they are worth mentioning because they enable virtualization in other areas:

- **Internal virtual networking:** With the increased adoption of virtual servers, software-based network functionality inside a single physical host provides the functionality needed to meet security requirements.

- **Network-attached services:** The concept of pooling resources is not limited to generic compute and network resources. Pooling specific processing capabilities and attaching them to the network realizes additional efficiencies. These processing capabilities include Secure Socket Layer (SSL), firewall functionality, and Intrusion Detection System (IDS) functionality. A high-performance shared appliance or network module physically implements this functionality.

Virtualizing the network and network-attached services platforms enables optimization opportunities that are relevant in a multitenant scenario. As an example, instead of having a pair of load balancers dedicated to each client, all clients can share a single scalable hardware platform but only access a pre-allocated subset of the resources (throughput, memory).

Network virtualization in the many-to-one and many-to-many approaches also exists, but the environmental value is not as prominent. Examples include port channel or port aggregation protocols. These enable multiple physical network links to be aggregated to one virtual link of higher capacity.

Compute Resource Virtualization

As compute resources represent the largest relative power consumption in the Data Center at often low average utilization levels, it is most likely the area in which you can realize the largest utilization benefits. For some organizations, this does not only lead to a significant reduction or avoidance in power consumption, but it also eliminates or postpones the need to bring a new Data Center facility online.

As discussed in the consolidation section, the concept of sharing compute resources across multiple applications is not new. The mainframe world embraced this concept well in advance of the recent attention in the industry. However, the ability to adopt these technologies on a large range of commodity-based platforms and the resulting scale of the adoption makes compute resource virtualization the flagship technology to greening many Data Centers. Figure 9.8 illustrates the conceptual architecture of a typical server virtualization technology.

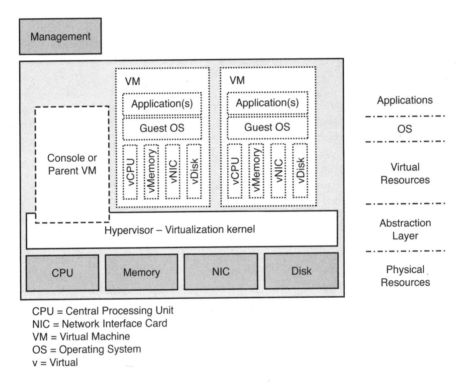

CPU = Central Processing Unit
NIC = Network Interface Card
VM = Virtual Machine
OS = Operating System
v = Virtual

Figure 9.8   *Compute Resource Virtualization: Server Virtualization (Hardware Emulation)*

The architecture in Figure 9.8 shows how a purpose-built kernel takes control of the physical server resources such as compute resources (CPU), memory (Random Access Memory [RAM]), network connectivity (NIC), local disks, and possibly storage connectivity (Host Bus Adapter [HBA]). This kernel, also called the hypervisor, presents these resources to virtual partitions called *virtual machines* and provides them fair access in a shared way. The kernel is similar to a traditional OS kernel, but with new resource control capabilities and stripped from unneeded features. The new capabilities include resource management, scheduling, a virtual network switch, and a virtual filesystem. A console provides access to the hypervisor to enable administrative control.

Each virtual machine runs its own standalone operating system (OS), called the guest OS. This OS leverages the virtual resources that have been assigned to it and enables the applications to make use of them. A physical server can run multiple virtual machines. All these virtual machines run independently from each other, and each virtual machine can run a different OS version. The resource requirements and load profiles for the applications determine the number of virtual machines that can be run on a single physical server. Running tens of virtual machines on a fairly inexpensive 1RU (one rack unit height) or blade server platform is not uncommon. The virtualization software schedules access to the physical resources and translates instructions. This abstracts the physical details from the upper-layer OS and applications. Abstraction not only enables sharing, but it also eliminates a number of real-world shortcomings of any physical solution, such as provisioning lead times, geographical migration of systems, component failure, and so on.

Variations of this architecture exist. In an alternate approach, the hypervisor has less functionality, and the effective resource virtualization is done by a special-purpose virtual machine called the parent virtual machine. It is also possible to operate the virtualization software as an application on top of a traditional OS. And finally, as described in the consolidation section, virtualizing the OS by partitioning it also abstracts the application from the underlying physical resources.

One of the challenges associated with virtualization technologies is the overhead associated with the abstraction, more specifically the translation of instructions. There are three approaches to mitigate this performance impact:

- **Approach 1:** The guest OS takes care of the incompabilities, which avoids translation at the lower layers. The downside associated with this approach, called *paravirtualization*, is that it is not transparent to existing physical machines. This impacts the ability to migrate from a physical server to a virtual server.

- **Approach 2:** The virtualization software takes care of the translation. The downside now becomes that the translation is always required and is executed in software. This results in reduced performance—not only does virtualization not increase the total compute power, but it also effectively decreases it.

- **Approach 3:** Resource vendors build special-purpose capabilities into their components (CPUs, NICs) to take care of the mismatch. This approach is the most promising from a performance perspective, but requires the latest physical equipment, which might not be available or have a significant lead time for large-scale adoption.

As illustrated in Figure 9.8, server virtualization is broader than pure virtualization of compute resources. It spans all resources included in a physical server chassis. And it does not stop there—extending the virtualization concept further to the interface between the physical servers and the physical network leads to an area called *server edge virtualization* or *server access virtualization*. Two opportunities arise:

- **Virtual I/O:** As described in the network consolidation section, IP traffic and Fiber Channel traffic can be transported on top of a shared physical network if that network has the appropriate capabilities.

■ **Virtual connectivity:** A virtual connectivity architecture, typically delivered through technology integrated into a bladeserver chassis, consolidates the multiple network interfaces into fewer. On top of the infrastructure reduction, this enables seamless migration and rebalancing of virtual servers across a compute resource pool that is no longer limited to an individual server chassis. This form of virtualized server access leads to the concept of *stateless computing*, whereby the workload can move transparently between physical machines.

The virtualization vision entails more advanced virtualization models, by altering the compute resource access boundaries across physical and virtual machines. As an example, virtual CPUs in one machine could have access to memory in another machine. Technology advancements are required to make this vision a reality on a large scale.

Note   An internal case study from the Cisco IT department demonstrates the potential from compute virtualization. Prior to the adoption of server virtualization, the average server utilization was approximately 10 percent, based on a sample of more than 100 servers.

So far, the server virtualization program results in 50 percent of the servers being virtualized, with an average of ten virtual servers per physical server. Assuming that servers represent 60 percent of the power consumption inside the Data Center prior to consolidation, and ignoring the power differences between server types, the server virtualization effort would reduce the power consumption by 27 percent.

At the same time, this transformation reduces the server provisioning time from approximately 90 days to approximately three days, by eliminating the product order and lead time from the provisioning process. The three days represent a change process limitation and are the result of a self-imposed SLA to clients. Technically, Cisco IT can provision a virtual machine in approximately 30 minutes.

Storage Virtualization

Storage accounts for less power demand than servers in a typical Data Center. According to *Green Storage I: Economics, Environment, Energy and Engineering*, a Tutorial published by the Storage Networking Industry Association, the IT equipment power demand consumed by the storage infrastructure varies from under 10 percent to more than 40 percent, with 20 percent as a fair industrywide estimate. This portion is likely to increase if no action is taken; as the amount of data grows, the need to store historical data increases for compliance reasons, and server virtualization disrupts the compute resource demand trend.

Whereas virtualization in the server space directly results in environmental benefits, this is less evident in the case of storage. Instead, in storage, virtualization technology acts as a foundational enabler to realizing the environmental benefits that come from new storage technologies and the increasingly intelligent storage services.

The storage technology domain was one of the first to adopt virtualization technologies. Virtualization enables the detail and complexity to be hidden, which subsequently enables storage services to become resilient, scale, and remain manageable. The functionality of virtualization technologies varies from the individual component level to the complete storage pool of a large organization. Multiple storage virtualization technologies interoperate transparently in large-scale environments. Figure 9.9 illustrates the simplified conceptual storage access model following a stack view.

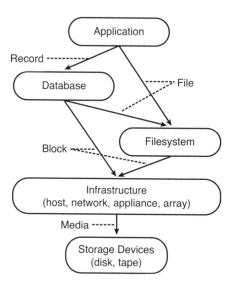

Figure 9.9   *Stack View of the Storage Access Model*

The stack view in Figure 9.9 provides a high-level view of what the opportunities for virtualization are, which leads to the following classification:

- **Block-based virtualization:** Blocks represent the smallest logical data unit that is accessible on a storage device such as a hard disk, typically 512 bytes or 1,024 bytes. Block-based virtualization includes the following capabilities:

    - Logical block addressing (LBA) maps each such logical unit to a physical space and address on a disk (often described as cylinder, head, and sector [CHS]).

    - Block aggregation or Redundant Array of Inexpensive Disks (RAID) technology creates virtual disks by combining two or more physical disks. RAID can have varying levels of data protection, capacity, and performance. As an example, RAID level 0 virtually concatenates disks to act as a larger one, and the controller stripes the data evenly over the set of disks. As a more advanced example, RAID level 6 adds two parity disks to a set of disks, which enables recovery from double disk failures.

    - Partitioning and volume management enables the creation of virtual disks or volumes that are no longer multiples of equal-sized physical disks: Virtual disks can be smaller than the underlying physical disks or can be larger. The underlying physical disks can have varying geometry and performance characteristics.

- **File-based virtualization:** An abstraction technology that decouples logical file objects, systems, and names from the underlying physical components. File-based virtualization includes the following:

  - **File virtualization:** A single file or directory represents a set of files or directories, or represents a single file or directory on a different system. As an example of the first use case, the guest OS in server virtualization sees an entire filesystem, but technically this is only a single file on the parent OS. As an example of the second use case, hierarchical storage management (HSM) migrates infrequently accessed files to a lower tier. File virtualization enables this migration to be transparent to the client. The lower tier will be more cost-effective and also have a lower environmental impact.

  - **Filesystem virtualization:** A single logical filesystem maps files to physical files that can be on different physical filesystems. As an example, an appliance takes on the role of a localized or globalized fileserver but connects to multiple physical fileservers to execute file operations. Globalized fileservers require a new namespace to identify each file globally without relying on the physical server name; this is called a *global namespace.*

- **Media virtualization:** An abstraction technology presents one physical medium as a different one, without requiring the storage client to change hardware, software, or processes. For example, a virtual tape library (VTL) leverages disk drive media to present a backup system that has the same attributes as a physical system.

The abundance and adoption of virtualization technology in the storage space makes it the resource type that has progressed the furthest toward a true utility model. By pooling the assets, you can build logical storage units with the capacity, performance, and protection that matches your needs.

Storage virtualization technologies enable a more efficient Data Center through the following use cases, some of which are described previously in the consolidation section:

- **Utilization:** Virtualization eliminates the fragmentation inefficiencies by decoupling logical capacity from physical capacities. This leads to higher overall utilization.

- **Abstraction from heterogeneous assets:** By abstracting the physical technology details, virtualization enables aggregation of physical storage assets from different vendors and geometries. This leads to higher utilization and increased efficiencies. It also enables you to select the vendor that demonstrates the highest commitment to preserving the natural environment.

- **Economies of scale:** The introduction of storage tiering in combination with the use of larger disk drives lowers the overall physical resource supply for a given logical storage demand.

- **Thin provisioning and resizable volumes:** The capability to transparently change the mapping of logical volumes to physical resource allocation eliminates some of the efficiencies associated with the traditional over-provisioning practices. This enables the storage utility to follow a just-in-time supply model.

- **Data reduction and de-duplication:** Virtualization enables transparent implementation and operation of data reduction and de-duplication mechanisms.

- **Snapshots and virtual cloning:** Many organizations require multiple point-in-time copies to protect them from data corruption issues. In addition, the application development lifecycle requires multiple environments in which the application is developed, tested, and staged before it goes into production. Without any virtualization capabilities, each of these copies would equal the original dataset. With virtualization, virtual copies can be generated. These differ from only the original or each other in those blocks that have been changed since the last synchronization point.

- **RAID optimization:** The introduction of newer, more advanced RAID levels deliver higher protection levels at often lower resource requirements. For example, RAID 10 provides both striping and mirroring, which doubles the storage resources and might be impacted by double disk failures. RAID 6 on the other hand needs only two extra disks for each base set and protects against any double disk failure scenario. If a base set consists of five disks, the overhead is 40 percent, as opposed to 100 percent with RAID 10.

Implementing any virtualization technology requires a change to the way the data is exchanged between the application and the disk devices. There are three places to insert this technology: at the host level, in the network, or at the storage array. The reference model on the left in Figure 9.10 shows these places.

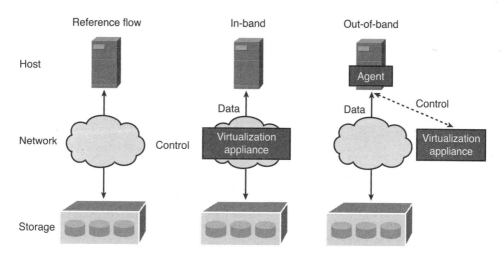

Figure 9.10 *Virtualization Technology Insertion Places: Reference Model (Left) and Two Suboptions for Network-Based Insertion (Right).*

The two suboptions on the right in Figure 9.10 illustrate two suboptions for inserting virtualization in a network-based model. The first one uses in-band virtualization, in which either an appliance or a switch module intercepts and changes all data as it traverses the network. The second uses out-of-band virtualization, in which an agent installed on the host communicates control traffic with a virtualization appliance, and subsequently makes the appropriate changes to the data flows to deliver the virtualization capability.

Application and Database Virtualization

Defining virtualization of applications is not as straightforward as defining virtualization of the IT infrastructure resources. In addition, the net benefits to the environmental impact are less evident, or might not be positive in certain cases. As an example of the latter, moving the virtual desktop into the Data Center without eliminating the local physical desktop increases the total environmental impact. In theory, application virtualization is a more lightweight method than server virtualization because it does not require similar overhead as multiple OS instances. On the other hand, as it makes explicit assumptions about the applications, it is less transparent and cannot be adopted unconditionally.

At the core lies the same concept: Decouple the logical execution of application functionality from the physical underlying layers, including OS and IT infrastructure resources. Multiple types exist:

- **Dynamic application service distribution:** By applying the principles of grid computing to application execution, the functional logic of applications is decomposed into smaller tasks, and each task is distributed over a dynamically expanding or shrinking set of machines. This type achieves similar utilization, sharing, and environmental benefits as server virtualization but requires the applications to become grid-enabled. Applications that follow an SOA are well-suited for this approach. This approach also applies to applications developed from the ground up to operate on top of a distributed compute grid infrastructure.

- **Application virtual machines:** Executing each application in a contained runtime environment on top of a shared application execution environment follows the same concept as server virtualization, but at a higher layer. Java virtual machines (JVM) present a classic example of this use case. This type applies to both the server-side Data Center server infrastructure and the client-side desktop but also imposes certain constraints on the application code. Because the virtualization takes place higher in the stack, more resources are shared resulting in a higher environmental benefit. Unlike server virtualization, there is no need to keep a hypervisor and multiple guest OSs running.

- **Application streaming:** This type moves away from the traditional application installation model on a client machine. Instead, an abstraction layer running on the client machine requests the application code on demand and intercepts all OS calls and underlying resource requests. An application streaming server streams the packaged application to the client on demand. The abstraction layer fools the application into believing it directly interfaces with OS resources such as files, environment variables, and registries. This type delivers application portability across machines, but has limited environmental benefits.

- **Virtual desktop:** By executing an application on remote infrastructure and only delivering the terminal output to the client, the application execution is abstracted from the client machine. The environmental impact might decrease or increase as a result of this approach, depending on the balance of increased server infrastructure in the Data Center and decreased client infrastructure. The green value lies in the removal of a Data Center facility consolidation barrier. Security and licensing costs are the primary drivers for this type of virtualization.

The same abstraction principle applies to databases. Database virtualization creates a logical instance of a database that is decoupled from the underlying physical database instances. The system utilization and associated environmental impact change as a result of this but is not as outspoken as in the other virtualization areas. The primary drivers for database virtualization include performance, resiliency, high availability, and creating an opportunity to leverage low-cost commodity components through a horizontally scaling architecture.

Facilities Virtualization

The virtualization of a Data Center facility is conceptual in nature. Two approaches are at the basis:

- **Logical segmentation:** Today's multitenant Data Center facilities rely on physical segmentation, such as walls or cages. Although this provides the highest perceived level of security, it also equates to a hard allocation of physical resources such as space, and to some extent power, and cooling, for instance UPS systems and chillers. Any hard allocation of physical capacity means that it cannot be reused for other tenants, even when the primary tenant no longer needs all the capacity that has been allocated to him. This results in fragmentation and impacts utilization. By moving to a shared physical platform and relying on logical segmentation capabilities built into the virtualization technologies, the Data Center provider can limit or even completely eliminate the fragmentation impact. Many variations exist between the extremes of purely physical and purely logical segmentation. As an example of physical segmentation, a Data Center service provider decides to physically segment a 10-MW facility into ten 1-MW halls. Each hall has a dedicated power distribution system and a fixed amount of cooling capacity and is allocated to a potentially different tenant. At some point, some halls are full, but other halls might still be empty or half full. The unused power and cooling capacity cannot be reused because capacity allocation took place at the hall level, which is equivalent to a 1-MW unit size. By adopting logical segmentation, the entire floor space is allocated to tenants based on cabinets or even smaller unit sizes and bundled with a physical operations shared service. All clients share the same total power, UPS and cooling budget, and it is relatively straightforward to assign the remaining unused capacity to the clients who are in need of expansion. The segmentation requirements are met through the virtualization technologies described earlier.

■ **Virtual Data Center aggregation:** In this model, two or more physical Data Centers are virtually united by building upon multiple virtualization technologies following an integrated and managed architecture. The operational model assumes only one Data Center, but under the hood, the infrastructure ensures transparent distribution, movement, availability, and recovery of IT services across multiple physical Data Centers to deliver a highly resilient single virtual Data Center. Following this principle, two Tier III Data Centers could deliver the resiliency of a single Tier IV Data Center, or even better. There are severe latency-related constraints that limit either the applications or the location of the physical Data Centers. Wide-area application services or careful use of latency tolerant protocols and application architectures might reduce the impact of these constraints.

The net result of these two concepts is that the virtual Data Center facility is decoupled from the physical Data Center facilities through a pervasive adoption of virtualization technologies operating in an integrated way.

Additional Benefits and Challenges

In addition to increased efficiencies, virtualization brings benefits that result from eliminating the shortcomings associated with physical resources and components.

Virtualization abstracts the detail and hides internal complexity from the consumer of the service or resource. For instance, storage virtualization enables provisioning of an arbitrarily sized virtual disk, and the client is not aware of the vendor type, the physical disk characteristics, or the built-in parity features to protect the data from single-disk or dual-disk failures. To the client, the virtual disk meets the size, performance, and protection requirements. This simplifies the consumption of services and resources, leading to a more scalable and easier to operate Data Center architecture. It also enables heterogeneous resources to be presented as a single homogeneous utility.

The fact that physical components might fail, require replacement over time, and take manual effort to provision, limits the overall availability, agility, and flexibility. Virtualization creates an opportunity to mitigate these shortcomings and deliver increased availability, dynamic provisioning, and a transparent technology refresh path. If performance is not an issue, virtualization can span geographic areas, which increases the overall resiliency of the system. For instance, physically operating websites from multiple locations but making them appear as one logical website with automated failover virtualizes the website and makes it more resilient.

The way the client connects to the resource or service also changes. If the client is a person, a more straightforward logical naming standard for virtualized entities improves the user experience.

The relationship with management is twofold. On the one hand, consuming the resources is greatly simplified, which reduces the management overhead. On the other hand, the management overhead increases because it now needs to account for the mapping of virtual to physical resources. To mitigate the latter, you should never adopt a virtualization technology on a large scale without the supporting investment in management capabilities. For instance, virtual server technology comes with a management solution to manage the physical resource pool, the provisioning process of new virtual machines, and the mapping of virtual to physical machines. In addition, as the scope of virtualization expands to cover the entire Data Center space, there is an opportunity to adopt orchestration, which coordinates management activities in various resource areas to deliver the solutions with minimal manual effort.

Challenges to adoption of virtualization technology include the overhead from inserting another function in the path. This overhead manifests itself as performance degradation, especially when executed in software. Like any other technology, virtualization technology can fail and require additional architecture, design, testing, and operational efforts. In some cases, the overhead can become a barrier to adoption in the near term, until alternate architectures are devised or the technology matures.

As virtualization changes the capacity dynamics of the Data Center, you should revalidate and update the Data Center designs. Existing assumptions on fan-out, load, and throughput no longer hold. As an example, aggressive server virtualization depletes your IP address resources more rapidly than anticipated and might trigger the need for a Data Center network capacity upgrade.

The inherent sharing nature of virtualization is a point of concern to many security departments. Evolving from a physical segmentation to a logical segmentation model makes it harder to validate the boundaries between the segments. Maturing products in combination with in-depth security principles mitigate some of these concerns. Your adoption plans and engineering processes should account for this.

Two specific challenges associated with virtualization are not technology-oriented. The first one is vendor support and certification. There are many examples in the server virtualization domain in which independent software vendors refuse support when their software packages run on virtualized platforms. The other challenge is related to licensing. Many licensing models make explicit physical hosting platform assumptions, and a virtual platform might not be conducive until the licensing model changes.

Integrated Automation

The increasing proliferation of resources—now both physical and virtual, and increasingly more dense—increases the need for an integrated management system. Virtualization also creates the opportunity, as changes can be executed by logical reconfiguration rather than a physical activity executed by a person.

The management system automates the underlying tasks that enable the resource or service lifecycle, which starts with ordering, includes provisioning and operations, and ends with decommissioning of the resource or service. With automation comes cost reduction, faster execution time, and increased reliability.

The integration of multiple disparate management systems creates automation opportunities at a higher level. As a visionary example, codifying the specification of an entire business processes enables the business process to be built or restored by the push of a button if the underlying physical resources are available. Integrated management of all resources inside the Data Center is called *Data Center orchestration*.

Automation in itself does not directly save energy. The relevance of integrated automation within the context of greening your Data Center comes from its creation of new optimization opportunities that help you keep driving your Data Center efficiencies. This section describes a few, but many more exist.

Like any other technology, automation is a product of human beings and is subject to failure. A robust architecture, design, and operational process augmented with the appropriate people skills need to be in place to mitigate the risks associated with automation. Specific examples of mitigation strategies include thorough integrated testing, limiting access to the automation system, containment of failure domains, and passive-safe designs.

Dynamic Cooling

Traditional Data Center systems have their cooling set at a level that is fixed in time and consistent across the entire Data Center place. However, the amount of heat generated usually varies from one place to another inside the Data Center. In addition, the allowed temperature range varies from one hardware type to another. The varying cooling demand with the fixed supply results in more energy spent on cooling than strictly needed. The overall power efficiency of the Data Center is impacted.

Dynamic cooling optimizes the energy spent on cooling by cooling only as much as is needed for the specific space and time.

Dynamic cooling *in space* supports the real-world scenario that Data Centers are filled gradually over time. It also enables localized inlet temperatures because some resources are designed to operate at a higher inlet temperature than others. The higher the inlet temperature, the lower the cooling cost.

Dynamic cooling *in time* supports the same real-world scenario of filling the Data Center over time. In addition, with energy-efficient components, cooling follows the IT load. As the processing load is lower, less cooling is needed. Virtualization accelerates this trend.

Idling Servers

Similar to dynamic cooling, dynamically changing the state of compute resources to match the compute demand enables power consumption savings. As the processing load decreases, a control system puts the servers into some form of low-power, sleep, or hibernation mode and reactivates them when the demand for resources goes up. Virtualization in combination with new technical capabilities provide the opportunity. The automation becomes truly integrated, as application processing load is integrated into the server state and the overall cooling system settings.

Follow-the-Moon

Traditional power generating systems are best operated at a consistent level over time. Unfortunately, the power demand follows the rhythm of people and the business, matching a day-and-night schedule. Storing energy for later use or transporting the generated electricity around the world is an unrealistic approach. But shifting the workload in place or time is a feasible approach in a number of use cases. As the processing load now aligns with a nightly schedule, this is called the "follow-the-moon" approach. Because electricity providers incentivize their clients through their pricing models, there is an economic benefit to this approach if the supporting systems can adapt to the workload.

Alternative Data Center Operating Models

So far, the assumptions for this chapter imply that you are the owner or operator of the Data Center, and that you or your organization is directly accountable for the environmental impact. That will not always be the case. Alternative operating models allow for content, applications, or even entire business processes to be delivered from a shared platform that is often optimized for the specific service at hand. This shifts the environmental impact to another party and results in a reduced overall environmental impact, if executed well.

Content and Application Delivery Networks

Performance of content and applications delivery in a global environment is a nontrivial matter. Unless the latency tolerance is high or the user interface is lightweight, some form of global distribution is required.

One approach is to completely replicate the entire Data Center services stack around the world. If resiliency requirements are also accounted for, this results in a significant environmental impact. In an alternate approach, the delivery architecture leverages a shared external content distribution network (CDN) or application distribution network (ADN). The performance acceleration opportunity is limited, but there is a double impact to the overall infrastructure need. Firstly, the global infrastructure is reduced to the presentation layer of the application, reducing the amount of compute and storage capacity needed in each of the distributed nodes. Secondly, the CDN or ADN provider will deliver the content or applications from a shared infrastructure. Because these providers assume that not all their clients reach peak at the same time, they can oversubscribe the installed capacity, which leads to increased utilization. In addition, the unit size of a remote distribution node is often too large to get significant utilization in remote locations. By sharing the infrastructure, that constraint goes away.

Everything-as-a-Service

As the network becomes increasingly more powerful and reliable, and as businesses become more collaborative with rapidly changing partnerships, the application delivery model is shifting from an install-and-maintain model based on ownership to a pay-as-you-go model based on usage. This new delivery model is called Software-as-a-Service (SaaS) but can be extended beyond software, creating the Everything-as-a-Service (XaaS) model. It is more advanced than the Application Service Provider (ASP) model, which merely hosts the server-side of the architecture as-is in an external Data Center.

Application services that enable collaborative business operations, that have a high degree of commonality between customers and communication systems are some of the first adopters of this model. There are a lot of architectural commonalities between this delivery model and the often free Internet-scalable Web 2.0 services, such as e-mail, photo sharing, and instant messaging: They both need to scale, are delivered over the Internet, and have unique multitenant architectures.

Although SaaS or XaaS is not guaranteed to be more environmentally friendly, it creates a lot of opportunities. Their application and data services are almost always virtualized and have their code optimized to enable the needed scalability. The multitenancy aspects enable a high degree of resource sharing by assuming that not all clients will see their demand reach peak levels at the same time. The economies of scale enable additional efficiencies. The fact that the hosting costs are absorbed by the provider is a strong incentive to optimize the environment. As an example, it is possible to run a Human Resource application from a centralized Data Center facility on hundreds of servers for thousands of customers. In contrast, the traditional model would require at least one server for each customer. It would take an extreme degree of virtualization technologies and optimization efforts to deliver the same functionality.

The application acquisition and deployment model for SaaS differs substantially from the traditional approach based on purchased software, and you should consider this in your Data Center planning and your negotiations with the provider. In summary, although there might not be a formal guarantee for being greener, the hyperscaling, resource sharing, and multitenancy principles align with increased utilization and efficiencies.

Cloud Computing

The concept of SaaS can be abstracted away from specific applications to generic Data Center compute and storage resources. Providers offer these resources as a virtualized service to their customers, delivered over the network, and make it possible to rent a farm of well-specified compute and storage capacity. The term cloud computing refers to the computing activity executed somewhere in the network (the cloud). Clouds are also elastic and create the perception of infinite capacity: they are able to expand and shrink the resource supply in alignment with the demand. Challenges related to security, stability, performance, network dependency, and trust exist and need to be overcome.

The concept of cloud computing is not limited to external offerings. Large organizations recognize the flexibility and efficiencies associated with this model and are adopting a similar model to offer to their internal clients. Many of the challenges previously identified naturally disappear when you consider building an internal cloud.

Like XaaS, there is no guarantee that cloud computing will be more environmentally friendly than the traditional computing model. Its multitenant and elastic nature expands the resource sharing opportunity, and its virtual-only nature enforces virtualization. Together, these lead toward the opportunity to increase the average resource utilization. Because it is based on the same green principles discussed earlier, it aligns well with a green strategy, and you should focus on this point for both your internal Data Center strategy and the eventual selection of an external provider.

Summary

Supply of the physical components in your Data Center is determined by the IT resource demand. Minimizing the resource demand through the principle of reuse reduces the environmental impact of your Data Center. The paradigm shift from dedicated platforms to service-oriented architectures embodies this principle.

The first enabler for reuse is consolidation, which reduces the number of physical instances (physical consolidation) or variations (logical consolidation or standardization). Consolidation applies to network resources, compute resources, storage, applications, databases, Data Center facilities, people, and processes.

The second enabler for reuse is virtualization, an abstraction technology layer enabling logical consumption of physical resources and services. This provides the capability to pool and share resources, creating the opportunity to increase utilization and efficiencies. Like consolidation, virtualization applies to multiple resource and service types. Virtualization of compute resources yields the most direct improvements, followed by networking. Virtualization of storage services acts as an enabler for other optimization opportunities.

There are additional benefits and challenges associated with consolidation and virtualization, and the environmental benefits might not be the primary driver for these initiatives. Benefits include simplification, manageability, total cost, data protection, end-user experience, and transparency. Challenges include performance, organizational impact, security risks, compliance, vendor support, new complexity, and licensing. This classification into benefits and challenges is not always binary. Comprehensive analyses and staggered adoption are imperative to your Data Center strategy.

The third enabler is integrated automation, which couples the various layers of the Data Center services stack. This enables execution of joint optimization opportunities. Specific examples include dynamic cooling, idling servers, and having the workload follow the moon.

Alternative operating models revisit the ownership of the services and the Data Center and might shift and optimize the overall environmental impact. Alternative models include content and application delivery networks, Everything-as-a-Service, and cloud computing.

The vision of the green Data Center implies a highly optimized state in place and time, where only as much power and resources are consumed as is strictly needed to operate the business processes.

Chapter 10

Greening Other Business Practices

This chapter discusses additional green measures that a company with a Data Center can pursue to make its facility and operations greener.

Prior portions of this book focus on green strategies directly associated with the design, construction, and operation of a Data Center or with the evaluation and purchase of hardware hosted in such a facility. A final set of green considerations are those that are relevant to companies that have a server environment, although not as Data Center-specific as strategies for optimizing airflow and high-efficiency power distribution units.

Data-Center Consumables

Several consumable items are typically employed in the operation of a Data Center, and where there are consumables, there are often opportunities to reduce waste and, therefore, be greener. Consider the following items used regularly in your facility:

- **Patch cords:** Many server models are shipped to customers with their own patch cords. If you employ a color-coding scheme for cables in your Data Center—a good practice to clarify connection paths and simplify troubleshooting—it's likely that the cables that arrive with the hardware won't fit that scheme.

- **Connectors:** As with patch cords, adapters and connectors are often included by default with several hardware models yet are not used.

- **Power cables:** Although power cables included with Data Center hardware are used during installation, they're often sized to enable a machine to be installed in a cabinet and then plugged into an electrical receptacle located above the cabinet or under a raised floor. In actual practice, many of those installed systems are plugged into the outlet of a cabinet's vertical power strip close to the machine. A Data Center containing thousands of servers likely has dozens of miles (kilometers) worth of surplus power cord length. That's not only a waste of materials involved in the manufacture of the over-long cable, but also the excess length can potentially inhibit airflow and, therefore, cooling efficiency.

- **Server cabinets:** Ideally, your Data Center is designed in such a way as to isolate hot and cold airflow, likely with fully enclosed server cabinets to take advantage of the cooling and energy-efficiency benefits. If you have an older server environment where airflow isn't isolated and channeled in a specific pattern, there's little to no efficiency value to the doors and side panels on the cabinets.

- **Mounting rails:** Rack-mount kits are sometimes ordered for hardware yet not used, with the machines instead placed on server cabinet shelves.

Fortunately, several approaches can reduce waste associated with these Data Center consumables. For one, talk with the manufacturer to see whether unneeded items can be eliminated from your order. Many hardware makers try to be greener these days, so they might welcome the opportunity to leave out the cables and connectors normally packed with hardware. Also, ask whether items can be made available that are appropriate to your needs, such as a cable that matches your Data Center's color-coding scheme or a power cord that is of a more suitable length.

If you still receive consumables that you have little use for in the Data Center, see whether any of the other work areas in your company can make use of them. Labs need many of the same components as Data Centers, for instance, and even standard offices and cubicles need patch cords to connect desktop or laptop computers. Sharing or repurposing Data Center materials is both green and can reduce costs.

Finally, if you can't make use of surplus consumable items within your company, check whether any schools in the region can use them. Your business might not see a direct green or monetary benefit from donating patch cords to a local high school computer lab, but it is good for the community and is better for the environment than just discarding the items.

Note   Whatever measures you take to be more efficient with your Data Center consumable items, keep track of how much you save or donate over time—say each quarter or year. You might be surprised at the totals, and the information can make a good data point as you communicate your green practices to both upper-management and customers.

E-Waste

A sometimes overlooked aspect of a Data Center's environmental impact is what happens to the hardware that it houses when those systems reach the end of their useful lives.

The United Nations' Solving the E-waste Problem (StEP) initiative estimates that there are 40 million tons (36.3 million metric tons) of so-called e-waste generated globally per year. Although that figure includes much more than just computing hardware—cellular phones, stereo equipment, electronic toys, and practically any office or household appliance that contains circuitry or a power supply are considered e-waste—servers and desktop computers can contribute significantly to the total if not disposed of properly. As with other electronic items, the decreasing costs and increasing performance of new computing hardware can make older systems obsolete faster, increasing how rapidly additional e-waste is generated.

Make your Data Center greener by ensuring that your old hardware doesn't end up in a landfill. Several major manufacturers including Cisco, Dell, EMC, Hewlett-Packard, and IBM offer programs for dealing with outdated equipment in ways that are environmentally responsible. Some programs facilitate the donation of older systems to schools or developing countries, for instance. Others employ vendors that break down hardware into their component materials, recycle as many elements as possible, and safely dispose of the rest.

Such programs are optional in many parts of the world, although in the European Union are mandated by the Waste Electrical and Electronic Equipment (WEEE) Directive. The directive requires the makers of electrical and electronic equipment to be responsible for financing, arranging take-back, and reusing or recycling their products placed on the EU market. As with the EU's Restriction of Hazardous Substances Directive, it's a model likely to be followed in the future by other countries.

Non-Data Center Consumables

Aside from Data Center supplies and hardware, there are other more generic items used at your facility that, in keeping with being green, shouldn't be discarded as conventional trash. These items include the following:

- **Batteries:** Cellular phones, laptop computers, and pagers used by Data Center personnel all use batteries that should be recycled rather than discarded.

- **Lightbulbs:** Fluorescent lightbulbs contain mercury that, if not disposed of properly, can be introduced into bodies of water and then converted into methylmercury that accumulates within fish or shellfish. This is harmful both to sea life and to any people or animals that, in turn, eat them.

Note   Keeping fluorescent lightbulbs out of landfills is mandated by law in some regions. Within the United States, for instance, the states of California, Minnesota, Ohio, Illinois, Indiana, Michigan, and Wisconsin all prohibit disposing of fluorescent lightbulbs as you would regular trash.

- **Packaging material:** Data Center hardware and consumable items are almost universally packaged in cardboard boxes and transported on wooden pallets, both of which are readily recyclable. Packing material—whether consisting of polyurethane (soft foam), polystyrene (foam peanuts), or polyethylene (bubble wrap)—can either be recycled or in many instances reused for future shipping needs.

- **Inkjet and toner cartridges:** Ink- and toner-containing cartridges used in office photocopiers and printers can be cleaned and refilled by manufacturers. Several major office supply store chains accept cartridges for recycling and even offer a small amount of money for cartridge brands that they sell. (Some schools and charities additionally collect ink or toner cartridges as a fund-raising activity.)

■ **Paper:** Most Data Center items come with printed documents, be it the installation manuals and warranty forms of a server or the invoices of a shipment of patch cords. Use of the aforementioned photocopiers and printers also inevitably generates wasted documents. Fortunately, paper recycling programs are among the most prevalent worldwide.

■ **Glass, plastic, and aluminum:** If the facility housing your Data Center also includes a traditional office environment with work cubicles and a meeting area, it's likely that there are drink containers on the premises. As with paper, these items can be readily collected and recycled rather than thrown out with other trash.

If your company doesn't already have recycling programs in place for these items, consider starting them as a step to make your overall facility greener.

Power Efficiency Outside the Data Center

If your Data Center is housed in a mixed-use facility, be sure to design and manage the infrastructure for the spaces outside of your server environment to be energy-efficient as well. Although your Data Center consumes power on a much greater scale than conference rooms, employee cubicles, or other general office work areas, it's still worth conserving Watts wherever you can. Options to consider for non-Data Center spaces include the following:

■ **Building power management:** Although the operational functions of a Data Center's physical infrastructure—namely cooling and power delivery—can be optimized for efficiency, such functions can be managed more aggressively in other building spaces that aren't required to remain fully operational 24 hours a day, 7 days a week. Networking technologies now enable you to govern multiple workplace appliances and climate control systems. Imagine the energy savings and avoided carbon emissions of automatically turning on lights, desktop computers, and telephones in specific building spaces only when an employee who needs the items arrives at work and then automatically powering down those items when that employee leaves.

Note   The Cisco EnergyWise software platform, available on its Catalyst switches, is an example of a building power management tool that enables users to control what building elements are provided with power, how much power they receive, and when they can receive it.

The software can govern systems including IP-based telephones, video surveillance cameras, and wireless access points; desktop computers, laptops, and printers; and (as of 2010) HVAC, elevators, lights, badge access systems, fire alarm systems, and security systems.

You can find more information on the Cisco EnergyWise software platform, including a calculator that can illustrate the potential savings from using a power management tool, at http://www.cisco.com/web/go/energywise.

- **Expanding operating temperatures:** Just as higher operational temperatures for your Data Center reduce the demand upon its cooling system, thereby reducing energy consumption, so too can a broader temperature range in your general office area reap energy savings. You obviously don't want to make building users uncomfortable, but a minor temperature adjustment can often be made with no detrimental effect or perhaps even an improvement in comfort.

Note   An analysis of temperatures of air-conditioned office buildings in the United States, completed in 2008, actually suggests that many buildings are overly cooled in the summer and overly warmed in the winter, causing occupants to suffer more frequently from headaches, fatigue, and other symptoms.

The analysis, "Indoor Thermal Factors and Symptoms in Office Workers: Findings from the U.S. EPA BASE Study," was conducted by researchers at Lawrence Berkeley National Laboratory. It draws upon a study of internal air quality factors of 100 office buildings in 37 cities and surveys of more than 4,100 occupants in those buildings, conducted by the U.S. Environmental Protection Agency between 1994 and 1998.

In the EPA study, building temperature and humidity conditions were assessed for one week during the summer or winter, and occupants filled out written surveys pertaining to building-related symptoms—those experienced in the building that lessened when they were elsewhere—including shortness of breath, cough, nose or throat irritation, eye irritation, dry or irritated skin, headaches, fatigue, and difficulty concentrating.

LBNL researchers analyzed the data to look for connections between building-related symptoms and indoor temperature and humidity. They found that symptoms including headache, fatigue, and difficulty concentrating increased more than 50 percent for occupants in office buildings kept below 73.4 degrees Fahrenheit (23 degrees Celsius) in the summer, and that half of the buildings measured were maintained below that mark. They also found that symptoms including headache, eye irritation, nose irritation, and skin irritation increase 30 percent to 80 percent in office buildings kept above 73.4 degrees Fahrenheit (23 degrees Celsius) in the winter.

In short, it's possible that adopting less restrictive temperature ranges for the office areas within your Data Center building won't just reduce energy consumption and save money for your business but might also improve the comfort of your workers.

- **Raising operating temperatures for refrigeration equipment:** If your building has employee break rooms that contain refrigerated beverage coolers or general-purpose refrigerators, you can also slightly raise the temperature at which drinks and food are kept in them. The U.S. Department of Agriculture's Food Safety and Inspection Service recommends that refrigerators maintain a minimum temperature of 40 degrees Fahrenheit or below (4.4 degrees Celsius or below). Higher temperatures allow for the rapid growth of bacteria, which can cause illness.

- **Efficient fixtures and appliances:** Strategies for lighting, office electronics, desktop power strips, kitchen appliances, and even plumbing fixtures are outlined in Chapter 3, "Green Design and Build Strategies."

Energy-saving green strategies already mentioned for the exterior of your building obviously provide benefits for all interior work spaces, not just the Data Center. A cool roof lessens how hard your cooling system needs to work to regulate any interior space, for instance.

Alternative Transportation

Among the Data Center site selection considerations mentioned in Chapter 3 is proximity of the property to your work force. The greater the distance that employees, vendors, and other personnel must travel to reach the facility, the more carbon dioxide that is emitted during their transport.

A gallon of gasoline produces 19.4 pounds (8.8 kilograms) of carbon dioxide, according to the U.S. Environmental Protection Agency. Therefore, if a worker uses just half a gallon (1.9 liters) of gas more or less per day when traveling to and from a Data Center site, that's a difference of 2,522 pounds (1,142 kilograms) per year in carbon dioxide emissions:

.5 gallons × 19.4 pounds × 5 days a week × 52 weeks a year = 2522 pounds or 1142 kilograms

Multiply that times the number of people who regularly work at the facility, and the quantity easily adds up to a difference of hundreds of thousands of pounds (kilograms) of emissions, depending upon a small potential shift in the location of the Data Center.

If your Data Center isn't located close to its workers, your company can help reduce travel-related carbon emissions by encouraging employees to use alternative transportation. Options to promote this include

- **Bike storage lockers:** Providing a secure place for employees to store bicycles during the workday makes it more practical for them to commute by bicycle.

- **Locker rooms and showers:** You don't want an employee to have to choose between appearing neat and professional for the day or commuting by bicycle.

- **Subsidized passes for the local bus or train system:** Providing free or discounted passes to employees can be a significant financial incentive, allowing them to save the money that would otherwise be spent on gasoline and automobile maintenance. Extended-term passes, such as monthly or annual, can typically be obtained at a discount from the local operator when purchased in bulk.

- **Carpool programs:** Carpool incentives can be as simple as reserving a few parking spaces close to each company building for carpoolers or as extensive as operating a program that helps coordinate rides among interested employees. Carpool programs can be especially popular around major cities where high-occupancy vehicle lanes exist on major highways to help deal with busy rush-hour traffic.

■ **Emergency rides:** A stumbling block for some people to take alternative transportation is the concern that they would be unable to depart work quickly in an emergency—bicycling or local transit often takes longer than driving a car, and it can be difficult for a carpooler to get an emergency ride home from a traveling companion. Offering a program to drive an employee home in an emergency—when the employee falls ill or is contacted to pick up a sick child, for instance—provides a safeguard for employees against unforeseen circumstances.

■ **On-campus lunch options:** People can also be reluctant to take alternative transportation if they feel they need a personal vehicle during their lunch hour. The presence of an on-site cafeteria and awareness of nearby restaurants that either deliver or are within walking distance can help mitigate this. Some large companies go so far as to provide free or deeply discounted lunches to employees, further encouraging them to remain on campus.

■ **Incentive and recognition programs:** Acknowledging and rewarding employees who use alternative transportation encourages the behavior in others. Recognition can be accomplished through prizes (that is, gift cards, framed certificates, or T-shirts), articles in a company newsletter or on an internal website, or other creative rewards (such as lunch with a high-ranking company official). Setting competitive goals among departments or even with other nearby companies can also be effective. (Which group logs the most carpool trips in a month? Which group bikes the most commute miles in a week?)

Some of these measures—bike storage lockers and showers, for example—might not be compatible with your server environment if it's located within a dedicated, Data Center-only building rather than in a mixed-used facility. If other, general-purpose buildings are within walking distance to your Data Center, consider installing the items at one of those nearby locations.

Note Cisco offers several incentive programs to promote the use of alternative transportation. At the company's main campus in San Jose, California, that includes providing a free annual pass to employees for the light rail system operated by the local Santa Clara Valley Transportation Authority.

During the first six months of researching and writing this book, I made a point to take light rail to and from work at least twice a week. I have a 20-mile (32.2 kilometer) one-way commute to Cisco headquarters, so during that time I avoided 2,080 miles (3,347 kilometers) of driving (20 miles × 4 trips per week × 26 weeks = 2080 miles or 3347 kilometers). My car gets about 27 miles per gallon (11.5 kilometers per liter), which equates to 77 gallons (291 liters) of conserved gasoline from my use of light rail. Using the EPA estimate of how much carbon dioxide is produced by gasoline—19.4 pounds (8.8 kilograms) per gallon—I saved 1,494 pounds (678 kilograms) of carbon dioxide emissions (77 gallons × 19.4 pounds = 1494 pounds or 678 kilograms).

continues

continued

It's practically impossible to spend some 20 hours a week delving into green topics like energy consumption and carbon emissions and not start considering your own activities and how to be greener. Fortunately for me, riding light rail not only had an environmental benefit but also provided some isolated time to write some of the book's content!

Summary

You can implement additional design and operational strategies beyond your server environment to make your overall facility greener.

Avoid wasting Data Center consumables such as patch cords, connectors, power cables, equipment cabinets, and hardware mounting kits by asking hardware manufacturers to eliminate accessory items that are delivered with equipment by default but that you won't use. Share unused items with other company work areas such as labs or perhaps donate them to local schools.

Properly dispose of obsolete Data Center hardware so that it does not enter the landfill as e-waste. Many equipment manufacturers have take-back programs for systems, ultimately donating them to schools or developing countries or recycling their component materials.

Pursue recycling programs for general office consumables including batteries, lightbulbs, packaging material, inkjet and toner cartridges, paper, glass, plastic, and aluminum.

Optimize electrical efficiency in non-Data Center spaces through networked building power management, broadening the operational temperatures of office areas, raising the cooling temperature for refrigeration equipment, and employing efficient fixtures and appliances.

Further reduce carbon emissions associated with your Data Center site by promoting employee use of alternative transportation. Supportive activities can include offering bike storage lockers and shower facilities on-site, subsidizing passes for area bus and train systems, hosting a carpool program, offering emergency rides, providing on-site lunch options, and operating recognition programs that reward employees who do take alternative transportation.

Appendix

Sources of Data Center Green Information

The entities and organizations cited in this appendix can be valuable sources of information on topics relevant to the design or operation of a green Data Center. Some are developing or have developed key green standards or metrics; others promote various green best practices; and others still are conducting or have conducted case studies that form the basis of effective strategies for green Data Center design.

Organizations are arranged alphabetically within general topic areas: the building industry (Table 1), the Data Center industry (Table 2), Data Center-related technologies (Table 3), and energy efficiency (Table 4). Several agencies have offices worldwide. Contact information is generally provided for their primary headquarters. Check their respective websites for additional contact information.

Table 1 *Building Industry*

Organization	Contact Information	Description
The American Institute of Architects (AIA)	Committee on the Environment 1735 New York Avenue NW Washington, DC 20006-5292 Phone: 800 242-3837 E-mail: infocentral@aia.org Website: http://www.aia.org/cote	AIA's Committee on the Environment works to advance, disseminate, and advocate—to the professions, the building industry, the academy, and the public—design practices that integrate built and natural systems and enhance both the design quality and environmental performance of the built environment.
Building Green, Inc.	122 Birge Street, Suite 30 Brattleboro, VT 05301 Phone: 800 861-0954 E-mail: info@buildinggreen.com Website: http://www.buildinggreen.com	Building Green is an independent publishing company committed to providing accurate, unbiased, and timely information designed to help building-industry professionals and policy makers improve the environmental performance and reduce the adverse impacts of buildings. The company also maintains GreenSpec®, an online directory of green building products.
Building Research Establishment Ltd. (BRE)	Bucknalls Lane Watford WD25 9XX Phone: 44 0 1923 664000 E-mail: enquiries@bre.co.uk Website: http://www.bre.co.uk	The BRE Trust Companies, BRE and BRE Global, are world-leading research, consultancy, training, testing, and certification organizations delivering sustainability and innovation across the built environment and beyond. BRE oversees the BREEAM environmental building assessment system.

Table 1 *Building Industry*

Organization	Contact Information	Description
Green Building Initiative	2104 SE Morrison Portland, OR 97214 Phone: 877 424-4241 E-mail: info@thegbi.org Website: http://www.thegbi.org/	The Green Building Initiative is a not-for-profit organization whose mission is to accelerate the adoption of building practices that result in energy-efficient, healthier, and environmentally sustainable buildings by promoting credible and practical green building approaches for residential and commercial construction. The Green Building Initiative oversees the Green Globes environmental building assessment system within the United States.
International Initiative for Sustainable Built Environment (iiSBE)	40 The Driveway, Suite 100 Ottawa, Ontario K2P 2C9, Canada E-mail: larsson@iisbe.org Websites: http://www.iiSBE.org and http://www.sbis.info	The iiSBE hosts the Sustainable Building Information System database that contains information regarding sustainable building in several languages.
National Institute of Building Sciences (NIBS): Whole Building Design Guide	1090 Vermont Avenue NW, Suite 700 Washington, DC 20005 Phone: 202 289-7800 Website: http://www.wbdg.org	NIBS provides the Whole Building Design Guide (WBDG), a web-based portal with information on a wide range of building-related guidance, criteria, and technology from a whole buildings-perspective. The WBDG is a collaborative effort among federal agencies, private sector companies, nonprofit organizations, and educational institutions.
Sustainable Buildings Industry Council (SBIC)	1112 16th Street NW, Suite 240 Washington, DC 20036 Phone: 202 628-7400 E-mail: sbic@sbicouncil.org Website: http://www.sbicouncil.org	SBIC is an independent, nonprofit trade association that seeks to dramatically improve the long-term performance and value of buildings through outreach, advocacy, and education programs.

continues

Table 1 *Building Industry   (continued)*

Organization	Contact Information	Description
United States Green Building Council (USGBC)	1800 Massachusetts Avenue NW, Suite 300 Washington, DC 20036 Phone: 800 795-1747 E-mail: info@usgbc.org Website: http://www.usgbc.org	The USGBC is a nonprofit organization committed to a prosperous and sustainable future for the United States through cost-efficient and energy-saving green buildings. USGBC oversees the Leadership in Energy and Environmental Design (LEED) Green Building Rating System.
World Business Council for Sustainable Development (WBCSD)	4, chemin de Conches 1231 Conches-Geneva Switzerland Phone: 41 22 839-3100 E-mail: info@wbcsd.org Website: http://www.wbcsd.org	The WBCSD is a CEO-led, global association of 200 companies dealing exclusively with business and sustainable development. WBCSD provides a platform for companies to explore sustainable development; share knowledge, experiences, and best practices; and advocate business positions on these issues in a variety of forums, working with governments and nongovernmental and intergovernmental organizations.
World Green Building Council (WorldGBC)	Toronto Secretariat 9520 Pine Valley Drive Woodbridge, ON L4L 1A6 Phone: 289 268-3900 E-mail: info_council@worldgbc.org Website: http://www.worldgbc.org/home	WorldGBC is a union of national councils whose mission is to accelerate the transformation of the built environment toward sustainability.

Table 2 *Data Center Industry*

Organization	Contact Information	Description
*7 x 24 Exchange	322 Eighth Avenue, Suite 501 New York, NY 10001 Phone: 646 486-3818 E-mail: info@7x24exchange.org Website: http://www.7x24exchange.org	7 x 24 Exchange is the leading knowledge exchange for those who design, build, use, and maintain mission-critical enterprise information infrastructure. 7 x 24 Exchange's goal is to improve end-to-end reliability by promoting dialogue among these groups.
*AFCOM	742 E. Chapman Avenue Orange, CA 92866 Phone: 714 997-7966 E-mail: afcom@afcom.com Website: http://www.afcom.com	AFCOM is a leading association supporting the educational and business development needs of Data Center management, executives, and vendors around the world.
*Critical Facilities Round Table	Website: http://www.cfroundtable.org	The Critical Facilities Round Table is dedicated to the discussion and resolution of industry issues regarding mission-critical facilities, their engineering and design, and their maintenance.
*DatacenterDynamics	70 Clifton Street London EC2A 4HB Phone: 44 0207 377 1907 E-mail: info@datacenterdynamics.com Website: http://www.datacenterdynamics.com	DatacenterDynamics is a full-service business-to-business information provider at the core of which is a unique series of events tailored specifically to deliver enhanced knowledge and networking opportunities to professionals that design, build, and operate Data Centers.
*Data Center Pulse	E-mail: users@datacenterpulse.com Website: http://www.datacenterpulse.com	Data Center Pulse is a nonprofit global organization of experienced individuals who face similar challenges and share common interests around the purchase and consumption of products and services in the Data Center.

continues

Table 2 *Data Center Industry* *(continued)*

Organization	Contact Information	Description
The Green Grid	3855 SW 153rd Drive Beaverton, OR 97006 Phone: 503 619-0653 E-mail: admin@lists.thegreengrid.org Website: http://www.thegreengrid.org	The Green Grid is a global consortium dedicated to advancing energy efficiency in Data Centers and business computing environments.
*Uptime Institute	2904 Rodeo Park Drive East, Building 100 Santa Fe, NM 87505-6316 Phone: 505 986-3900 E-mail: admin@uptimeinstitute.org Website: http://www.uptimeinstitute.org	The Uptime Institute is a leading independent think tank, corporate advisor, knowledge exchange, and education and professional-services provider serving the owners and operators of the world's largest enterprise Data Centers.

*Organizations within the Data Center industry that, although they don't have an exclusive focus on green, often include green Data Center topics as part of the conferences they host.

Table 3 *Data Center-Related Technologies*

Organization	Contact Information	Description
American Society of Heating, Refrigeration and Air Conditioning Engineers (ASHRAE)	1791 Tullie Circle, NE Atlanta, GA 30329 Phone: 800 527-4723 E-mail: ashrae@ashrae.org Website: http://www.ashrae.org	ASHRAE advances technology to the arts and sciences of heating, ventilation, air conditioning, and refrigeration to serve humanity and promote a sustainable world.
Standard Performance Evaluation Corporation (SPEC)	6585 Merchant Place, Suite 100 Warrenton, VA 20187 Atlanta, GA 30329 Phone: 540 349-7878 E-mail: info@spec.org Website: http://www.spec.org	SPEC is a nonprofit corporation formed to establish, maintain, and endorse a standardized set of relevant benchmarks that can be applied to the newest generation of high-performance computers.
Storage Networking Industry Association (SNIA)	425 Market Street, Suite 1020 San Francisco, CA 94105 Phone: 415 402-0006 E-mail: larsson@iisbe.org Websites: http://www.snia.org	SNIA is a nonprofit trade association whose members are dedicated to developing and promoting standards, technologies, and educational services to empower organizations in the management of information.

Table 4 *Energy Efficiency*

Organization	Contact Information	Description
American Council for an Energy-Efficient Economy (ACE3)	529 14th Street NW, Suite 600 Washington, DC 20045-1000 Phone: 202 507-4000 E-mail: info@aceee.org Website: http://www.aceee.org	ACEEE is a nonprofit organization dedicated to advancing energy efficiency as a means of promoting economic prosperity, energy security, and environmental protection.
Consortium for Energy Efficiency (CEE)	98 N. Washington Street, Suite 101 Boston, MA 02114-1918 Phone: 617 589-3949 Website: http://www.cee1.org	CEE is a nonprofit public benefits corporation that develops initiatives for its North American members to promote the manufacture and purchase of energy-efficient products and services.
Electric Power Research Institute (EPRI)	3420 Hillview Avenue Palo Alto, CA 94304 Phone: 800 313-3774 or 650 855-2121 E-mail: askepri@epri.com Website: http://www.epri.com	EPRI is an independent, nonprofit organization that conducts research and development relating to the generation, delivery, and use of electricity for the benefit of the public.
European Commission	Joint Research Centre Institute for Energy Renewable Energies Unit TP450 21020 ISPRA Italy Website: http://www.ec.europa.eu	The European Commission embodies and upholds the general interest of the European Union and is the driving force in the EU's institutional system. Its main roles are to propose legislation to Parliament and the European Council, to administer and implement Community policies, to enforce Community law, and to negotiate international agreements. Energy-efficiency activities by the European Commission include the Data Centre Code of Conduct, the GreenBuilding Programme, the EU Standby Initiative, and the Code of Conduct on AC Uninterruptible Power Supplies.

continues

Table 4 *Energy Efficiency*   *(continued)*

Organization	Contact Information	Description
Lawrence Berkeley National Laboratory (LBNL) (Berkeley Lab)	1 Cyclotron Road Berkeley, CA 94720 Phone: 510 486-4000 General Website: http://www.lbl.gov/ Data Center energy efficiency Website: http://hightech.lbl.gov/htindex.html	LBNL has been a leader in science and engineering research for more than 70 years. Berkeley Lab is a U.S. Department of Energy National Laboratory managed by the University of California.
United States Department of Energy	Office of Energy Efficiency and Renewable Energy Mail Stop EE-1 Washington, DC 20585 Phone: 877 337-3463 E-mail: high_performance@nrel.gov Website: http://www.eere.energy.gov/buildings/highperformance	The U.S. Department of Energy through its High Performance Buildings Initiative supports the development of commercial buildings that are energy-efficient, healthy, and comfortable places to learn, work, and play.
United States Environmental Protection Agency (EPA)	Ariel Rios Building 1200 Pennsylvania Avenue, NW Washington, DC 20460 Phone: 202 272-0167 General website: http://www.epa.gov/ Energy Star website: http://www.energystar.gov	The U.S. EPA leads the nation's environmental science, research, education, and assessment efforts. Among EPA activities is the Energy Star program, which includes energy-efficiency benchmarks for various commercial and residential electronics items. Ratings criteria have been developed for both enterprise servers and for Data Centers under the Energy Star label.

Glossary

AC (alternating current) An electric current that changes direction in a circuit. For conventional Data Centers, power is delivered from the utility power in alternating current and converted multiple times between AC and DC (direct current) formats.

ADN (Application Delivery Network) A network of distributed application nodes, often operated by a third party, to optimize the delivery of application traffic to a distributed client base.

affinity laws Laws illustrating relative variables in pump or fan performance, such as airflow, pressure, speed, and power.

air changes per hour The movement of a volume of air in a certain period of time.

automation The use of management systems to reduce the need for human intervention. This increases the sophistication, reliability, speed, and complexity of the targeted controls.

biofuel Fuels made from biomass materials. Alcohol-based ethanol and biodiesel made with used vegetable oil are the most common.

blow-down Water drained from a cooling tower to remove sediment.

BREEAM (Building Research Establishment Environmental Assessment Method) The first environmental building assessment system created to rate building performance. Used in the United Kingdom and the basis of several other building assessment systems.

Brownfield Abandoned property believed or thought to contain contaminants. In some regions, any previously developed building.

building commissioning A systematic review of building equipment to ensure all components work according to their specifications and that interactions between equipment happen properly.

CADE (Corporate Average Data Center Efficiency) Data Center efficiency metric calculated by multiplying facility efficiency (facility energy efficiency times facility utilization) by asset efficiency (server energy efficiency times server utilization).

carbon footprint The amount of carbon dioxide produced by a person, business, or activity.

carbon offset A project or measure that reduces carbon dioxide or other greenhouse gas emissions.

CASBEE (Comprehensive Assessment System for Building Environmental Efficiency) An environmental building assessment system used in Japan.

CDN (Content Delivery Network) A network of distributed content delivery nodes, often operated by a third party, to optimize the delivery of content to a distributed client base.

cellulose insulation Building insulation made from plant fiber. Common cellulosic material includes recycled newsprint, cardboard, cotton, or straw.

CEPAS (Comprehensive Environmental Performance Assessment System) One of two environmental building assessment systems used in Hong Kong.

CFCs (Chlorofluorocarbons) A compound containing chlorine, fluorine, and chlorine atoms that was used for decades as a chiller refrigerant until studies determined that its chlorine damaged the ozone layer.

CIFS (Common Internet File System) Protocol enabling file sharing over an IP network, typically used in a Microsoft Windows environment.

cloud computing The abstraction of computing services to the state where these are provided over an IP-enabled network, either an internal network or the Internet.

CNA (Converged Network Adapter) A single physical component inside a server host providing both network and storage connectivity over a Fibre Channel over Ethernet (FCoE)-enabled network. This replaces the network interface card (NIC) and the host bus adapter (HBA).

colocation Data Center space available for a customer's IT hardware. Colocation space typically consists of a large server environment that is physically divided into sections, each of which contains equipment owned by a different customer.

commissioning A systematic process to evaluate building equipment to ensure that all systems function according to specifications and interact correctly with other systems.

computational fluid dynamics A field of study that uses mathematical modeling to analyze problems involving fluid flows. Useful for studying thermal conditions within a Data Center.

consolidation The process of combining multiple smaller systems into one or a few larger systems. Consolidation applies to Data Centers, storage, servers, and applications.

cool roof A roofing system with high solar reflectance and thermal emittance.

CPE (Compute Power Efficiency) A Data Center efficiency metric calculated by multiplying IT equipment utilization by IT equipment power and dividing by total facility power.

CPU (central processing unit) The central processor in any computer responsible for computations and program execution. Newer server models combine multiple processors onto a single chip, also known as multicore design.

DAS (Directly Attached Storage) Storage hardware (typically one or more hard disks) directly attached to the server host. DAS cannot be shared with other hosts without intervention of the directly attached host.

DC (direct current) An electric current that always flows in the same direction. Using direct current power instead of conventional alternating current in a Data Center is considered intriguing because it avoids multiple conversions between DC and AC formats and the associated electrical losses.

DCE (Data Center Ethernet)   A Cisco Data Center network architecture delivering the unified fabric.

DCIE (Data Center Infrastructure Efficiency)   Data Center efficiency metric calculated by dividing IT equipment power by total facility power. The inverse of PUE (power usage effectiveness).

DCP (Data Center Productivity)   A collection of Data Center efficiency metrics calculated by determining the useful work produced by a Data Center and dividing it by the resource consumed producing the work.

DGNB (German Sustainable Building Certificate)   An environmental building assessment system used in Germany.

economizer   A mechanical device that uses cold outside temperatures to complement conventional Data Center cooling processes, thereby reducing energy consumption.

EEWH (Ecology, Energy Saving, Waste Reduction, and Health)   An environmental building assessment system used in Taiwan.

electrical mix   The mixture of energy sources from which electricity is produced for a given region, which ultimately defines its carbon emissions factor.

embodied emissions   The total quantity of carbon dioxide generated in creating an item, from obtaining raw materials to manufacturing to delivery to installation.

embodied energy   The total quantity of energy expended in creating an item, from obtaining raw materials to manufacturing to delivery to installation.

energy efficiency   In reference to power supply units, the amount of power that a power supply provides divided by how much energy is input into it. Expressed as a percentage.

energy intensity   In economic terms, the ratio of energy consumption to economic or physical output. Measured as a ratio of energy use per unit of gross domestic product. A country that has a lower energy intensity is considered more energy-efficient because it produces more items or services using fewer energy resources.

Energy Star   A labeling program, sponsored by the U.S. Environmental Protection Agency and U.S. Department of Energy, which highlights energy-efficient products. Separate Energy Star programs are being developed for Data Centers, servers, and storage devices.

FC (Fibre Channel)   A network transport protocol for storage area networks (SAN), connecting servers to storage over a lossless fabric.

FCIP (Fibre Channel over Internet Protocol)   Network transport mapping standard enabling transport of fibre channel traffic over an IP network. This reduces or eliminates the need for a standalone storage area network. Unlike FCoE, FCIP cannot ensure that no packets will be lost.

FCoE (Fibre Channel over Ethernet)   Network transport mapping standard enabling transport of fibre channel traffic over an Ethernet-based network. This reduces or eliminates the need for a stand-alone storage area network.

fly ash   A fine glass-like powder, created as a waste byproduct when coal is burned to produce electricity. Can be used as a substitute for cement in concrete.

Gbps (Gigabit per second)   A bandwidth metric unit, theoretically capable of forwarding one gigabit of data per second on a network link.

geothermal cooling   Using the Earth's temperature to cool a space. For Data Centers, this cooling effect can be tapped by installing cooling system piping underground and letting the underground temperature cool the water that flows through.

Grayfield   A property containing abandoned buildings.

green building   Designing a building so that it uses resources—energy, water, and materials—more efficiently and has less impact upon people and the environment.

green Data Center   A computing environment that uses resources—energy, water, and materials—in a more efficient manner and has less impact upon people and the environment.

Green Globes   An environmental building assessment system used in Canada and the United States.

Green Grid, The   An environmental consortium of Data Center hardware and software manufacturers focused upon Data Center energy efficiency.

Green Mark   An environmental building assessment system used in Singapore.

green roof   A roofing system that incorporates a top layer of live vegetation. Also known as a living roof.

Green Star   An environmental building assessment system used in Australia that focuses on design and management processes.

Greenfield   Pristine or undeveloped land.

greenhouse gases   Atmospheric gases that trap heat from the sun and warm the Earth.

Water vapor, carbon dioxide, methane, nitrous oxide, ozone, and chlorofluoro carbons are the most common greenhouse gases.

Greenwashing   Making exaggerated or false claims about a company's green practices or the environmental benefits of a product or service.

HBA (host bus adapter)   A physical component inside a server host providing connectivity to the storage area network.

HCFCs (hydrochlorofluorocarbons)   A compound containing hydrogen, chlorine, fluorine, and carbon used as a refrigerant in chillers in place of chlorofluorocarbons (CFCs) due to its reduced ozone depletion potential.

HFCs (hydrofluorocarbons)   A compound containing hydrogen, fluorine, and carbon used in chillers. Environmentally superior to chlorofluorocarbons (CFCs) and hydrochlorofluorocarbons (HCFCs) due to its lack of chlorine that damages the ozone layer.

heat island   An instance of an urban area having higher temperatures than a nearby rural area due to the reduced quantity of trees and foliage, airflow restrictions created by tall buildings, and exhaust heat from motor vehicles and buildings.

heat wheel   A mechanical system that transfers heat between two environments of different temperatures by slowly rotating panels. Also known as a rotary heat exchanger.

HK-BEAM (Hong Kong Building Environmental Assessment Method)   One of two environmental building assessment systems used in Hong Kong.

HQE (Haute Qualité Environmentale)   An environmental building assessment system used in France.

HSM (Hierarchical Storage Management)   A data storage technique enabling transparent movement of data between varying media based on data access requirements.

HVAC (heating, ventilation, and air conditioning)   Used generically to refer to all environmental controls in a building or Data Center.

Hypervisor   Computer hardware virtualization technology that enables multiple guest operating systems to run on a single host computer simultaneously.

Instance   One occurrence out of multiple occurrences that makes up the entire resource or service set.

IP (Internet Protocol)   Network protocol from the TCP/IP stack enabling data transport between hosts over the Internet or an internal network.

LAN (local-area network)   Within the context of the Data Center, the local network that enables hosts inside the Data Center to talk to each other over IP/Ethernet.

LEED (Leadership in Energy and Environmental Design)   An environmental building assessment system used in the United States and other countries including Canada, China, India, Korea, and Spain.

MAID (Massive Array of Idle Disks)   A disk grouping technology where only the actively used disks are spinning.

NABERS (National Australian Built Environment Rating System)   Environmental building assessment system that measures the operational performance of an existing building.

NAS (Network Attached Storage)   File-level data storage system, providing file access to heterogeneous clients over NFS or CIFS.

NFS (Network File System)   A protocol enabling file sharing over an IP network, typically used in a UNIX environment.

NIC (network interface card)   A physical component inside a server host providing IP network connectivity.

ODP (ozone depletion potential)   The amount of ozone depletion caused by a substance. ODP is expressed as a ratio of its impact upon ozone relative to a similar mass of trichlorofluoromethane (CFC-11).

Photovoltaics   The technology of converting sunlight into electricity.

Plenum   A separate space in a structure used for air distribution. In Data Centers, this term typically refers to the spaces below the raised floor, above a false ceiling, or both.

power factor   The ratio of active power to apparent power of an alternating current circuit. Expressed as a value between zero and one.

PUE (power usage effectiveness)   A Data Center efficiency metric calculated by dividing total facility power by IT equipment power. The inverse of DCIE (Data Center infrastructure efficiency).

QoS (Quality of Service)   The network capability to provide preferential treatment to predefined traffic types.

rack unit   A unit of measurement for the height of internal, installable space within a server cabinet or rack; 1 rack unit = 1.75 inches (4.45 centimeters). Abbreviated as U, as in 1U server or 42U server cabinet.

RAID (Redundant Array of Independent Disk)   A technology that enables multiple disks to be grouped and provide higher levels of redundancy than an individual disk can provide.

renewable energy   A type of energy that is replaceable by naturally occurring processes.

resiliency   The capability to provide an acceptable level of service outside of normal operation. The capability to recover quickly and effectively from adversity.

resource   The entity used to achieve an objective. Within the context of the Data Center, this typically applies to compute, storage, and network entities.

RoHS   European Union's Restriction of Hazardous Substances Directive banning placement on the EU market of new electronic equipment that contain more than certain levels of cadmium, hexavalent chromium, lead, mercury polybrominated biphenyl, or polybrominated diphenyl ether.

rotary UPS   An uninterruptible power source that uses flywheel technology to store kinetic energy. During a utility power outage, the stored energy can support a Data Center's electrical needs for several seconds while the load is transferred to a standby generator.

rubberized asphalt   A mixture of conventional asphalt and ground scrap tires, usable in traditional asphalt applications.

SaaS (Software as a Service)   A software delivery model where the software functionality is executed by the vendor and delivered as part of the consumption by the clients. Contrasts with the traditional packaged software delivery model, where software is delivered as a binary image as part of the contractual agreement and operated from the customer Data Center.

SAN (storage area network)   A dedicated network that enables servers to connect to networked storage resources.

SCSI (Small Computer Systems Interface)   A set of standards for physically connecting and transferring data between computer systems and peripheral devices such as storage.

Service   A function that is provided when requested. Within the context of the Data Center, this typically applies to applications and data repositories.

SOA (service-oriented architecture)   A software architectural method where functionality is packaged as a service to enable reuse of this functionality in a sustainable manner.

SODC (service-oriented Data Center)   A Data Center operating model where resources and IT infrastructure capabilities are treated as services to promote agility and reuse.

solar reflectance   A material's capability to reflect solar energy. Typically expressed as either a value between 0 and 1 or as a percentage.

sustainable development   Development that uses natural resources in such a way as to meet people's needs indefinitely.

sustainable wood   Wood taken from forests that are managed to ensure their sustainability.

synthetic gypsum   A substance created when sulfur dioxide is removed from the exhaust flue gas of a coal-burning power plant. Can be used in drywall as a substitute for natural gypsum.

TCE (Technology Carbon Efficiency) A Data Center efficiency metric calculated by multiplying power usage effectiveness by carbon emissions factor.

thermal emittance A material's capability to release absorbed heat. Typically expressed as either a value between 0 and 1 or as a percentage.

unified fabric An evolution of the traditional Data Center network. The combination of lossless forwarding and protocol mapping enables the unified fabric to transport both IP and FC over a single Ethernet-based network.

unified I/O Generic capability to treat all data input/output in a consistent manner. Within the Data Center context, this refers to the capability to transport all server network I/O (IP and storage) over a single network connection.

utilization A number between 0 and 1, usually expressed as a percentage, which expresses how much of a given installed resource is in use.

variable frequency drive A mechanism for controlling the rotational speed of a motor. Matching motor speed to system demand reduces energy consumption.

virtualization Abstraction layer enabling physical resources or services to be consumed as logical resources or services. This enables resources to be pooled and treated as a utility.

VLAN (virtual local-area network) Virtualization technology based on packet tagging that creates multiple logical LANs inside a single physical LAN.

VOC (volatile organic compound) An organic chemical compound that evaporates into the air. VOCs emit smog-forming particles and can cause health problems in people and animals.

VPN (virtual private network) A network based on encapsulation that enables private network connectivity over a public or semi-public network infrastructure.

VSAN (virtual storage-area network) Virtualization technology based on packet tagging that creates multiple logical SANs inside a single physical SAN.

WAAS (wide-area application services) Cisco technology that optimizes the performance of TCP-based traffic over a WAN environment.

WAN (wide-area network) Network providing connectivity between endpoints that are far away, typically remote cities, countries, or continents.

waste heat Heat, produced by machines, that has no useful application.

WEEE European Union's Waste Electrical and Electronic Equipment Directive requiring the manufacturers of electrical and electronic equipment to be responsible for financing, arranging take-back, and reusing or recycling of their products placed on the EU market.

XaaS (Anything as a Service) Extension of the SaaS model to services and goods that are not purely software. This might include communication, data, platform, and infrastructure.

Index

NUMBERS

7 x 24 Exchange website, 259

365 Main Data Center developer (San Francisco, California), 19

A

absorption chillers, 129

abstraction
  abstraction from heterogeneous assets, storage virtualization, 236
  abstraction layer, virtualization, 228
  service-oriented phase (paradigm shifts), 205

AC (alternating current) versus DC (direct current), 109-111

ACE3 (American Council for an Energy-Efficient Economy) website, 261

ADN (application distribution networks), 243

adsorption chillers, 129

AFCOM website, 259

affinity laws (cooling systems), 135-136

aging (skin), 169

Aguçadoura Wave Park, 107

AIA (American Institute of Architects) website, 256

air
  air handlers, coordinating, 148
  air-based cooling systems versus liquid-based cooling systems, 139-141
  airflow optimization (cooling systems)
    cabinet solutions, 146
    isolating hot/cold airflows, 141-143
    mapping hot spots, 146
    plenums, 143-145
    sealing gaps, 145
  outside air, cooling via, 130-131
  quality of, data center design/build strategies, 78-80

airline flight paths, evaluating data center locations, 72

airside economizers, 130-131

alternative energy sources
  biofuels, 102

automation (integrated)

data centers, 209

virtualization, 241

dynamic cooling, 242

follow-the-moon approach, 243

idling servers, 242

B

backward consolidation, 210

Bank of America Corporation, green businesses, 27

barrages, 106

batteries, 249

below-ground data centers, 133

Best Practices for Data Centers: Lessons Learned from Benchmarking 22 Data Centers, 6

bike storage lockers, 252-253

biofuels, 102

block-based virtualization, 235

blow-down, cooling tower water, 138

branch office consolidation, 225

Brazil

hydroelectric dams, 106

National Institute for Space Research, hydroelectric dams, 106

BRE (Building Research Establishment) Ltd. website, 256

breakpoint optimization, 212

BREEAM (Building Research Establishment Environmental Assessment Method), 19, 41-42

brick/stone (salvaged), data center design/build strategies, 73

brownfields, 75

budgets, hardware purchases, 194-195

build/design strategies (data centers)

air quality, 78-80

building commissioning, 90-91

building exteriors, 82-84

building materials, 73-74

construction sites, 89

embodied energy/emissions, 76-78

evaluating potential sites, 71-72

fixtures/appliances, 80-81

landscaping, 85-89

lighting, 80

office electronics, 81

power strips, 81

retrofitting existing data centers, 91

building codes, evaluating data center locations, 71

building commissioning

building management systems, 91

Cost-Effectiveness of Commercial-Buildings Commissioning study, The, 91

data center design/build strategies, 90-91

Building Green, Inc. website, 256

building materials

data center design/build strategies, 73-74

green building materials, criteria for, 74-75

building power management, power efficiency and, 250

BuildingGreen, LLC, 74-75

bus/train passes, subsidizing, 252

buying hardware

budget effects on hardware choices, 194-195

consolidating packaging, 193

C

E

F

M

Q - R

S

W

X - Y - Z

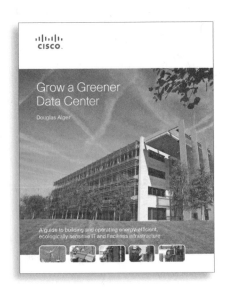

FREE Online Edition

Your purchase of Grow a Greener Data Center includes access to a free online edition for 45 days through the Safari Books Online subscription service. Nearly every Cisco Press book is available online through Safari Books Online, along with more than 5,000 other technical books and videos from publishers such as Addison-Wesley Professional, Exam Cram, IBM Press, O'Reilly, Prentice Hall, Que, and Sams.

SAFARI BOOKS ONLINE allows you to search for a specific answer, cut and paste code, download chapters, and stay current with emerging technologies.

Activate your FREE Online Edition at www.informit.com/safarifree

> **STEP 1:** Enter the coupon code: VHZJYFA.

> **STEP 2:** New Safari users, complete the brief registration form.
> Safari subscribers, just log in.

If you have difficulty registering on Safari or accessing the online edition, please e-mail customer-service@safaribooksonline.com